'Catherine has been involved in the cyberpsychology f brings a wealth of knowledge and experience to the fore: a fascinating and informative perspective and details the c but anyone can face when dealing with these issues. ' the relevant facts and explains the problems to the reader, so they can fully appreciate and understand this complex work. As an Online Safety Professional, I follow Catherine's work very closely, and utilise the cross overs from her work into my own work, which greatly assists in the online protection of minors in today's world.'

— **Andrew Briercliffe** – *"Online Safety Professional" – experience in Law Enforcement, Education and Social Media*

'Cath is versed in critical thinking and presents a clear path to categorise information, misinformation and disinformation in a sector where health and well-being are jam-packed with non-specialists.

'The resulting outcome of bad advice is that the developing child's body can be impacted by the skewed knowledge of online "gurus" giving out guidance that may well cause developmental and psychological harm.

'Movement, diet and body-based issues are rife amongst our young, with snake oil salespeople offering quick fixes. However, these pseudo-experts lack of awareness of our children's current technological landscape and our young people's social-media anxieties means the advice provided is ill-advised and, at worst, devastating.

'Our future generations deserve better and with my work looking to create more play opportunities for children that rely on less technology and sustainable real-world strategies to help with physical, emotional and mental well-being. It is excellent to collaborate with adults such as Cath, who labour to help adults understand the role they can play in creating safer online spaces for our kids.'

— **Darryl Edwards,** *Movement Coach, author of the best-selling books* Animal Moves *and* My First Animal Moves, *and a thought leader in creativity and innovation in fitness and health. Darryl developed the Primal Play Method® to inspire young and old to make physical activity fun. He blogs at PrimalPlay.com.*

'As someone who works on the frontlines with Catherine Knibbs on the war on young people, she has nailed the chaotic weight of things battling for kids' attention, likes, clicks, follows, and time – but mostly end up doing huge damage to them in the process. Smart phones, social media, many of the so-called "influencers" and less ethical brands have figured out there is huge profit in young people's low self-esteem, diminished well-being and faith that "they alone" can fix it – with the "they" often being bad advice, dodgy diets, dangerous exercise plan or a dependency on the filter and selfie culture that robs so much time and gives so much self-loathing in return. For all the parents, teachers, young people or just people who care about the future of young people, Catherine Knibbs' book is an essential read: it decodes all the modern mysteries and fads of the online world but also gives much needed tools to both protect your children – and you – from the many hostile forces they now have to contend with.'

— **Chloe Combi,** *Author, Speaker, Columnist, Futurist, Host of 'You Don't Know Me'*

Online Harms and Cybertrauma

This vital, sensitive guide explains the serious issues children face online and how they are impacted by them on a developmental, neurological, social, mental health and wellbeing level. Covering technologies used by children aged two through to adulthood, it offers parents and professionals clear, evidence-based information about online harms and their effects and what they can do to support their child should they see, hear or bear witness to these events online.

Catherine Knibbs, specialist advisor in the field, explains the issues involved when using online platforms and devices in family, social and educational settings. Examined in as non-traumatising a way as possible, the book covers key topics including cyberbullying; cyberstalking; pornography; online grooming; sexting; live streaming; vigilantism; suicide and self-harm; trolling and e-harassment; bantz, doxing and social media hacking; dares, trends and life-threatening activities; information and misinformation; and psychological games. It also explores the complex overlap of offline and online worlds in children and young people's lives. Offering guidance and proactive and reactive strategies based in neuroscience and child development, it reveals how e-safety is not one size fits all and must consider individual children's and families' vulnerabilities.

Online Harms and Cybertrauma will equip professionals and parents with the knowledge to support their work and direct conversations about the online harms that children and young people face. It is essential reading for those training and working with children in psychological, educational and social work contexts, as well as parents, policy makers and those involved in development of online technologies.

Catherine Knibbs is a Clinical and Academic Researcher, Consultant and Trainer in the fields of Cybertrauma and Online Harms, Director for Privacy4 Ltd and Online Safety UK, UKCP-Accredited Child and Adult Trauma Psychotherapist and TEDx speaker.

Understanding Children's Life Online
Books by Catherine Knibbs

Children, Technology and Healthy Development
How to Help Kids be Safe and Thrive Online
ISBN 9780367770150

Online Harms and Cybertrauma
Legal and Harmful Issues with Children and Young People
ISBN 9780367770112

Children and Sexual-Based Online Harms
A guide for professionals
ISBN 9781032427584

Online Harms and Cybertrauma

Legal and Harmful Issues with Children and Young People

Catherine Knibbs

Routledge
Taylor & Francis Group

LONDON AND NEW YORK

Designed cover image: Cavan Images/Cavan via Getty Images

First published 2023
by Routledge
4 Park Square, Milton Park, Abingdon, Oxon OX14 4RN

and by Routledge
605 Third Avenue, New York, NY 10158

Routledge is an imprint of the Taylor & Francis Group, an informa business

British Library Cataloguing-in-Publication Data
A catalogue record for this book is available from the British Library

ISBN: 978-1-032-26641-1 (hbk)
ISBN: 978-1-032-26642-8 (pbk)
ISBN: 978-1-003-28921-0 (ebk)

DOI: 10.4324/9781003289210

Typeset in Bembo
by Apex CoVantage, LLC

This book is dedicated to my 4-legged furry baby who stayed with me through almost 18 years of friendship, and was the best co-regulator through thick and thin. I miss you every day.

I want to thank my children for those lifelong moments of sanity, groundedness and humour. I love you both, I am so proud of you. You are amazing.

To my Flow For Writer Buddies: Heidi & Kathleen; I love you, ladies!

My writing mentor Maurice Irfan Coles, whom I miss so very much.

Gary and Sue, Adam, Helen and Sarah, who, as my real-world friends, allowed me to grow and spend time in the corporeal world, taking time with them and celebrating everything fun!

Thanks also go to the reviewers: Caroline Humer and Jean-Christophe le Toquin, Elizabeth Milovidov, Darryl Edwards, Chloe Combi and Andy Briercliffe.

To my Army buddies Bob, Dave and Robbo, and their partners Carol, Sarah and Dawn. Thanks for every silly moment, and here's to the life of Bob sadly taken from us. Let's keep the party going.

And a large thank you to the Flow for Writers at FRC – Steven Kotler, Michael Mannino, Brent Hogarth, Karen Darke, Ryan Wickes and Chris Bertram – for all the coaching. Every session made a difference.

To each and every one of you that makes a difference for children as practitioners, staff, moderators, managers and more, YOU ROCK and the children need you.

THANK YOU

Contents

Introduction

Now this book is about online harm(s) and so the caveat here is: I'm only going to write and talk about the negative and 'bad' things. The book is going to sound scary because of this and so it is important that we consider the BALANCE of positives that exist in the space of the Internet and digital technology, and boy are there plenty!

I love technology, I have so much of it in my life and I depend on it to carry out my professional life, using biofeedback and gaming with my clients; personally, it enables me to watch TV (streaming or films, or casting to it whilst I potter with housework or whatever), to listen to podcasts on the go and the other technologies I need such as my car, fridge, alarm clock and more gadgets than I can count. Where would I be without tech? I'd be a nomad living in the woods and probably less of a pain in the posterior to those whom I challenge here in this book or in the spaces of online harm and child protection.

This whole book is about the harms and their trauma impact, spanning each chapter and idea, and of course, here in this book, I can only address some and not all of the ills and issues. Please do not misunderstand this book as misery literature, clickbait or negativity-sell, as it will be heavy going at times for you, and in line with my training caveats, *you may put the book down at any time you wish and return to it when you are ready*. The book is not the easiest of reads, and because of this, I even took breaks writing it. I needed to for my health, well-being and ability to keep coming back to write more. I do not apologise for the depth of the conversations here and continuous page after page of 'stuff.'

This is to provide information and the necessary skills for practitioners to be able to work with this in clinical and outreach practice, youth work, policing, social work, adoption and fostering, residential settings and home settings – after all, many practitioners are parents too. If you are finding this stuff difficult to read and absorb, please consider how this feels for the children going through it. To walk in the waters of trauma, you will inevitably find yourself getting wet and perhaps needing to tread water at times. Please do this rather than drowning in the pain and suffering. Compassion and empathy can come from the sidelines *with* the lifeline rather than *in* the depths of the rising tides and waves. Compassion does not mean feeling everything the person does, and knowing which type of compassion will be helpful can also prevent this fatigue. These are learnable skills (Goleman, 1995; Goleman &

DOI: 10.4324/9781003289210-1

Davidson, 2017; Gilbert, 2011; Kirby, 2022). This set of books in parentheses is perhaps the best insight into reducing vicarious trauma that I can recommend, and these are just a few of them.

References versus the bibliography

A quick note here at this stage is I am going to use references where needed; these are likely to be books with a large volume of information pertaining to the subject being mentioned. I do not apologise for the lack of specific paragraphs or sentences from books, as the whole of the book provides a better understanding of the point I am making. Also as you progress through the volumes you will see the ethics, dilemmas and lack of robust research into many of the topic areas that involve young children, and so an overall understanding of a topic seems to be a good starting point for these books.

There will also be a bibliography and further-reading section at the end of the volumes, as there is a broader spectrum of knowledge that informs the contents of the book herein. These book recommendations are given as further reading, and some of the books I recommend I do not agree with entirely, or even some at all; however, they are books I have read to broaden my own knowledge. I read another person's perspective in order to gain the approach of the middle-lane driver mentioned shortly. No endorsements for these books are made unless otherwise stated at the time.

Middle-lane driver: not left or right, but balanced as much as can be

When I write to the subject matters around development in the child or adolescent years, and the influence of technology on this stage of a growing child, I am neither writing from a far-right or left perspective with all of the anger that often accompanies such views. Neither am I writing to say that the space we are in as a society for these young people is particularly great – or is this woke position so often cited? I will not be claiming that it is all about acceptance and that no one should be judged, as this liberal-freedom narrative is creating its own set of harms that will be discussed later in the book(s). We need balance and integral thinking, beyond what Ken Wilber calls the Mythical and rational. We need to go higher in terms of our critical, inclusive and broad thinking, and aim for integral thinking and life (Wilber, 2000), given we now have more technology and landscapes with which to integrate.

And so, one of the most important things I will write in this book is:

> The beliefs about the -isms and -ists we face today are rooted in a lack of knowledge and understanding *throughout history*, in *all* aspects, by *many* people who may not have completely comprehended, for example, it was not okay to burn someone at the stake, drown them, throw crow feathers at them or sacrifice them to the gods to remove the evil spirits once thought to inhabit

the corporeal body. We only know new knowledge as we progress, and learn, what seems to be in the reflective space of hindsight, what may be a bad idea.

Even so, some cultures around the world still have these kinds of beliefs, and when we can all collect together in a virtual space, our ideologies, deeply held in generations of unquestioning loyalty, are 'bound to surface,' and with them the venom, toxicity and abundance of the mythological monsters we all fear.

We may be intelligent human beings, but we are also slow to learn, respond and change over time. This is abundantly clear in the time it has taken us to reach the space we have today, where old ideologies and thoughts are now being 'double-clicked on,' are changing, being challenged by people and calling to witness the issues we face as evolving human beings, and this is happening in the spaces where children are growing and developing, and often are doing so without the reins of their parents holding them tight and without a generation of wise people to balance the scales of knowledge, because many of them are not in these spaces, frightened or delayed by the ubiquitous nature of integrated living 'in, with or through' technology.

And, but, moreover . . . we ain't there yet in terms of balance. We still stereotype, blame, judge, criticise and more, and whilst this is part of being a human, we cannot always recognise this is us, and so project outwards the 'them and us' groups. The groups however exist in multiple planes of time and space and occupy so many arenas that the children and young people who go there are subjected to aeons of history of 'them versus us', and you can be sure that divisions, polarisation and separation are rife today, and will continue to be so for some time as we jostle and settle into the digital space. Trauma-informed practice, living with and in, and communication in this space is far off in the distance, but I hold out hope for the light to shine through, one day. And if you read Stephen Pinker's work you will see we are heading into a less violent world when it comes to weapons and war (Pinker, 2012), however the digital space is only in the infancy stage of human development, so I don't know how that fares, or will fare, in the history books.

The new learning, thinking and knowledge that changes our thoughts, beliefs and practice only occurs once we have spent time, and quite a bit of it, learning and listening wholeheartedly. Terrible acts have been carried out in the past and people have been castigated, tortured, punished and killed in the process of progress. For example, we now no longer use phrenology (the study of bumps on the head) to assess and diagnose psychological or criminal issues, nor do we (I hope) still carry out operations on infants without anaesthesia because we believe them to be incapable of feeling pain. This practice was still carried out in the 80s, so we really are still rather slow in learning as discussed in the New York Times in 1987 (Boffey, 1987).

This means, in this book, that I am attempting to write from a balanced place, not blaming but explaining. I will not be arguing for issues per se. However, political, religious and cultural aspects will be discussed. Neither will I side with sociology-based arguments about patriarchy or radical feminism, or the conversations about sex and gender (though these are indeed discussed in this book) or diagnosis and pathology. But this is taken from the perspective of all I have learned from my clients over a decade, and how this marries up with theories about human behavior, because you as the reader have a history, filled to the brim with generations of religion, culture, race, sex and gender, and an approach to life that I could not possibly know unless I spend time with you and listen.

The information throughout the book is provided here for the practitioners and professionals to assess and make their own minds up on the matters. I do not claim to not have unconscious biases and blind spots and, of course, this is my caveat, that if these exist they do not remain unchallenged, and the process of being attacked is unlikely to produce the change we wish to see in the world. Challenge me, yes; straw man or attack me and it could produce a talionic response, so I'm told.

Some references may not appear on some of the subject matters, as they are speculative, lacking research or perhaps small in number, or just one article exists, new, undetermined and so on. Robust research takes time and, as you'll see in some of the chapters, some of the citations are even challenged. Cognitive and attributional biases are sometimes in play in the early exploratory processes of research, and some of these biases have made their way to the Internet and some books that tend to side with a hard-left or -right leaning, and hence these are often citations left out for this reason. I also use anecdotal evidence from my practice, for which there are no research-backed citations. The cases are anonymised in line with my ethical profession, and all cases have been discussed with the client, parents or carers as to the amount of information I am sharing. This means some of the things I wanted to share have not been added to this book. My training events have more exploratory cases and challenges in them to highlight the issues raised in this volume, as I can guarantee in these cases something I cannot with a written book, which is that I would be speaking to adult practitioners, and where this is under therapeutic training I am working with a code of ethics not present in the written format it is herein.

The sword of Damocles in writing this book

Dare I write and speak out? Cancel culture is a real phenomenon and one I have watched spill over into the real world with consequences that I personally have had to make choices about, even to the point of considering attending events (or not) and asking people not to photograph me or the people I am with, because I do not want confrontation if this appeared on social media. When did this become such a peer-pressured space that I cannot choose whom I can spend time with, even if they have extreme views to me? What a societal mess!

After all, as a therapist, I listen to people who do not share my views about the world, and it is my professional ethic to listen, lean in and learn. And so the first question for the practitioners reading this book is: where will your work take you into the pressures faced by young people and children, what are you aware of about what it is like to live in the 2020s and how that feels? Where does the virtual influence the corporeal, and how do you understand a young person and the harms they face if you cannot see the influence and overlap of the Venn diagram for their experience?

What they see, interact with and encounter is out of your awareness, and often even if you know the peripheral, you are not in the centre of the knowledge. What must it be like to work with a fraction of the issue, and why is it perhaps not a great idea to say we understand, when in reality we probably don't? Does this remind you of being a young person and hearing this line from the adults around you?

The deficiency of body knowledge, trauma-applied and embodied practice and the chasm of technological knowledge is present in so many adults today. What has been called the knowledge gap by the Center for Humane Technology has been increasing over the last 27 years or so, and we think we know what's at the bottom of the mountain these children are being asked to climb, when we might just be on a different mountain than the young people and their issues. So I'm going to throw you a rope with which to abseil down and meet the young people where they are. However, this is only one mountain and I cannot possibly know them all. Accepting this is part of our journey toward understanding the harms children and young people face in a world of technology. Get your climbing gear on so to speak, we have lots of work to do.

Polarisation

In the space of social media, there are far too many extreme, polarised spaces being built with which to demonise and slaughter those who disagree or oppose, and create an in-group-out-group society that results in opinionated information, based on human flaws and biases rather than balanced conversation, and it is this separation, interpersonal discord, intolerance, misguided loyalty to causes, people and things that is leading down the rabbit hole of mis-attunement and disconnections. This does not mean that technology is creating disconnections, but rather the intense desire to feel wanted and needed by your group and the unwillingness to listen and engage with those who do not share your views (Knibbs, 2019).

If *The Social Dilemma* taught us anything, it is that even creating a documentary about the social dilemma was fraught with the competition of making their documentary visible to many, and indeed could this have been driven by a desire for 'ours as the one to watch because ours is the truest form of truth' in comparison to the other films and documentaries that were being produced at the time? Ironically, the time this appeared in the media seems to have been using the same marketing tactics and online discussions that the documentary addresses in order to promote the film. When a company or people pour their heart into creating something they feel is important to share, this results in the desire to knock down the competitors, because that feeling of creating something that goes unnoticed is a terrible feeling. Some documentaries aired less, were talked about less and this must have felt terrible in comparison to the popular one (whether this knocking down of others is not actioned, it still exists). It can recreate the feelings tied into attachment styles that I so frequently mentioned in these books because we are hardwired to be seen (and noticed and revered, etc.).

The polarisation of professionals online and the 'truth'

Is there really such a thing? And given the current landscape of large organisations and governments arguing for the version of the truth that exists in their approach, you can see that social media and online spaces are filled with human behaviours. I watch many posts online about the virtue signalling of some people, whilst signalling themselves, and utter contempt against another's radical views in which theirs may be radical at the same time. A post appearing from professionals in the space laced with their own histories and narratives, which may be a trauma response, attachment-based reaction and response or virtue signalling of their own. Conflict and discord: it's what we *do*.

We don't come to the social media space (or indeed authoring books as I am here) without our own demons, desires and need to be seen in some way.

I, like many others who write or post online, am not here free of prejudice, judgment, biases and flaws. And of course, the passions I have are often driven by a frustration with the system that isn't in favour of trauma-applied knowledge, compassion and empathy towards our fellow humans, and we are not there as a society yet, and so my frustrations air at times, just like yours.

This book is primarily another push of my own to educate the next round of new practitioners, to inform those already in practice and hopefully to make a change to a percentage of children who are facing harm online by the space that will never be free of these harms. This is an attempt to reduce, mitigate and offset the harms, a book to provide new interventions and help direct children out of the depths of human depravity, abuse and ills that have always existed in the corporeal world and to bring a light to those dark spaces and times. You are the hope of becoming informed enough to do that for them.

Better than life: meta-sphere, metaverse and meta space . . . Red Dwarf already did it through a novel

Many moons ago Rob Grant and Doug Naylor wrote some books discussing 'The Game of Life' that the four members of *Red Dwarf* fame played (Grant & Naylor, 1990). It was an immersive game that became the backdrop for a brilliant comedy series on TV . . . making the parallel of where we are heading almost funny. Dwayne Dibley just got his second life. Second pun intended because that was another early version of a metaverse. We just got better at designing and integrating the new 'GAME OF LIFE'.

Just what is this universe that people and organisations keep telling us about, considering that some organisations are claiming it is theirs, or they own one, or 'it'?

So let's take the consideration of how this space is often described as being.

Web 3.0. But that's not 'it'.

Virtual reality then? This, it is not.

So augmented reality? Not that either, nope.

And so the seed of confusion is nothing new here because in tech we often give names that sound like they are nebulous, only to be understood by nerds, geeks or Silicon Valley entrepreneurs. So I will give the best explanation that I can:

'Life' is the moment we are born into a world outside of the womb, this space many of us refer to as IRL or *in real life*. However, so is the womb to the developing baby. We have a mind that begins to develop alongside thoughts, beliefs and attitudes and this space we tend to call consciousness. Even though consciousness is a term we cannot accurately measure or define, we accept it as a thing. When we use the Internet on a device, we call this 'online' or what is referred to as Web 2.0, and we understand that this 'online' space is made of many facets, arenas, pages of information and, of course, shopping and social media channels.

But when we talk to the metaverse, the many marketing videos and experts that have appeared on the Internet (for a space that hasn't been fully developed yet I may add, so I'm not entirely sure how they can be an expert of it, whatever it is.) often claim it, the metaverse, to be in 'there'. As in, virtual reality. And this conjures up an image and sense with which we can pull children 'out of it' or 'off it' and even 'ban them from it' and so on.

However, here is a thought experiment that can explain this metaverse: I want you to imagine looking into a fluffy cloud in the sky. At first, it seems to resemble cotton wool balls and looks light and fluffy. And as this descends you notice that it is made up of water droplets, and as it becomes level with the ground it looks more like fog than the white fluffy item up in the sky. It is a thing of beauty in the air against a backdrop of blue hues, can bring rain and when it descends is nothing more than droplets of water, mist and fog that float about, blurring our vision.

And so the metaverse is the cloud that we are all walking into, changing our vision and our sense of navigation, how we experience life, how we see the world and what may be the blurred boundaries of deep connection to the person next to us. And I've seen the film *The Fog*.

Ambient, it ain't.

Life is becoming the cloud that surrounds us and is no longer the space in which we send our photos and files *to*, it is becoming the space in which we inhabit. We are enveloped in digital technology, and life is now 'digital-us normal'.

How our cyber synapses are adding to the complexities of harm,
online spaces and the metaverse. How being human is changing tech
and how tech is changing being human

What was once a space in our heads for thoughts about ourselves and others is now a glass-head-style vortex of spaces in the cyber universe. See through and into those spaces that humans *really* go to in their heads.

To continuously outpour our stream of consciousness, we must say what we think, and in doing so, where we would once upon a time be able to walk down the street and wonder what people thought, we can now 'read their bubbles of thought' whether we want to or not. It's almost like being in a cartoon and being able to see neon signs above people's heads, where they are thinking, processing and emoting.

We can now find spaces online where, akin to being a toddler, we are surrounded by the narration of what everyone is doing. For example, if you watch an attuned mother with her small child she will be telling them what she is doing as she goes from task to task, educating the child in language, behaviour and contact. In parallel, with so many of us doing this online at every moment, well, the artificial intelligence (AI) and machine learning (ML) bots are also watching us, learning and developing a copycat knowledge of what it is to be human. The online space is littered with all the kinds of emotions we feel, activities we engage in and of course how we treat each other in order to relate, connect deeply, and where we are at war: psychologically, physically and as a species.

We are moving too fast for our own 'good' and in doing this we are not thinking ahead, because our own motivations for profit and progress overlook the principles of that golden thread. That thread suggests we treat others as we would like and expect to be treated ourselves, and if we can, *shifting from individualism and consumerism to service and collaboration* (Coles, 2015; Coles & Gent, 2022).

And so this book is about collaboration, service and change. This book is my step forward in doing this.

To my dearly missed friend Maurice Irfan Coles, thank you for your unwavering support and friendship. I miss you dearly and I take to heart the message you gave me: 'Be good in the world and create the change you want to see missy'.

This book is that step.

References

Boffey, P. (1987). Infants' sense of pain is recognized, finally. *The New York Times*. https://www.nytimes.com/1987/11/24/science/infants-sense-of-pain-is-recognized-finally.html.

Coles, M. (2015). *Towards the compassionate school: From golden rule to golden thread*. UCL: London.

Coles, M., & Gent, B. (Eds.). (2022). *Education for survival. The pedagogy of compassion*. UCL: London.

Gilbert, P. (2011). *The compassionate mind. A new approach to life's challenges* (revised edition). Constable: London.

Goleman, D. (1995). *Emotional intelligence*. Bloomsbury: London.

Goleman, D., & Davidson, R. (2017). *Altered traits. Science reveals how meditation changes your mind, brain and body*. Avery: London.

Grant, R., & Naylor, D. (1990). *Better than life*. Viking: London.

Kirby, J. (2022). *Choose Compassion. Why it matters and how it works*. University of Queensland Press: Queensland.

Knibbs, C. (2019). *Fit, fat or frumpy? The effects of social media (writ large)*, BACP Private Practitioners Conference, 28 September, BACP, London.

Pinker, S. (2012). *Better angels of our nature. The history of violence and humanity*. Penguin: London.

Wilber, K. (2000). *Integral psychology: Consciousness, spirit, psychology, therapy*. Shambala: London.

1 Psychological games

Every chapter, topic and section of this book can be seen through the lens of one or more of the other sections, chapters and topics

Psychological games, the weaponisation of vulnerability. How social media is and can be the weapon of choice in narcissism, personal attacks or virtue signaling.

Psychological games are a proposition created by Eric Berne, who is credited with being the founding father of transactional analysis. He described human behaviours as having needs that are innate, and comprising a requirement for contact, which he called strokes. These can be positive and negative and can be conditional or unconditional. These are rooted in our psychological, social and biological needs such as attachment, which I introduced you to in the first book (Knibbs, 2022). Berne suggested contact or strokes are essential to a person's life. 'Without them, the spinal cord will shrivel up'. This provides us with the reality of how important these behaviours and needs are and creates the theory of 'games' (Berne, 1964).

Berne suggested that we structure our time according to those needs and based on what we have 'grown up' with and can expect from the world. In contrast to Maslow's hierarchy of needs (which is often drawn in a pyramid shape, but if Scott Barry Kaufman's work (Kaufman, 2020) is integrated into society as much as Maslow's original work, you'll find he (Maslow, 1962) never drew a triangle or pyramid). Berne is suggested to have drawn a triangle for what he called time structure. Berne and Maslow were both in and around the world of humanistic approaches to psychology at the same time, and I wonder if sometimes concepts from one discipline got carried over into others, and this is perhaps why we ended up with triangles and circles being created in so many of these disciplines. I digress (perhaps my musings here are worthy of retention).

Basic needs in the family

If we grow up in a family where we never really have deep intimacy through attunement, attachment and, as we grow, conversations that are meaningful and compassionate, then we may never develop these skills to meet someone else in the same way. Our early experiences shape our adult capacities to be with others, and it is this process that feeds the playing of games as a way for us to try and recreate our

DOI: 10.4324/9781003289210-2

childhood and get those needs met. Freud called this a repetition compulsion (1920, originally in earlier writings too), and therefore we are often said to get into relationships that mirror our parents to try and 'work out those kinks' and feel whole. That is a much bigger topic than we can fit here, but safe to say that as a practitioner you will often work with people who recreate the same scenario (drama as in the triangle) time and time again.

Intimacy was placed at the highest point of the time-structure triangle, and this requires the deepest aspect of ourselves that we can show to another person. Given that this requires courage, vulnerability and risk, we often do not place ourselves here. I suspect therefore a triangle was used to reflect this concept, as the higher up the shape, the less volume there is (or I am geeking out again). In the work I do as a psychotherapist, this is often for my clients a feared place of 'being' and one that is reported to be a space of 'opening us up to being hurt by the person we are intimate with'. This is the most likely reason people do not do this as adults, as it's likely that during childhood this is exactly what happened to them. Or this is how they interpreted it (a conversation for another book). We develop resistance and protective measures, often called defences, against 'being hurt', and so we need to find another way in which to be and spend time with others that looks on the surface 'like' we are being intimate.

This means that we need to utilise another time-structuring method with which we can get our needs met, as a replacement for deep intimacy. Often it doesn't fill that need as deeply and so we meander through life looking to fill that void, so we can stake our place in where we feel we 'fit' on the OK Corral (Ernst, 1971), or in our life script. In other words, to paraphrase Brene Brown as she often says something like this when speaking publicly, '*if we go looking for the evidence that we don't fit in society and with others we will consistently find it*' (Brown, 2017).

We often find in the TA literature that time structure involves what Berne called psychological 'games', and to briefly describe these they are well-learned and practised processes that we repeat to try and get our needs met. Those needs are the intimacy needs, and the social and psychological needs that reflect Maslow's hierarchy (Maslow, 1943), and those mentioned (in Knibbs, 2022) when, quoting Dan Siegel (2010, 2016) of '*being seen, soothed safe and secure*'.

The 'end' result of a game, called the payoff, is preceded by the hope these needs will be met, and of course, the fact that we play these games repeatedly means that we are not achieving this hopeful outcome in the way we want (or really need). The payoff results in us often saying the same thing to ourselves, repeatedly. For example, do you ever find yourself saying 'why do they always do that', or 'why does this always happen to me'?

Games are usually played by more than one player, and all of us engage in these at some point during the day, week, month or year, and certainly, we play these many times during our lifetimes. Players can be an individual, organisations or society writ large. These games are played under differing degrees (three levels) with increasing determinate negative outcomes of rejections of social and psychological connection, and sadly life itself. It seems counterintuitive as I explain here that the games are played with people, called actors (not the Shakespearian kind) who recreate an outcome that feels bad, pointless, rejecting, angering and negative. Yet this outcome reaffirms the players in the game to repeat the game later (or at a higher level) in the hope that 'this time I can win', 'I will come out on top' or 'I'll get my revenge' (think Wile E. Coyote here!).

We can say these games are graded at levels one, two and three, and each one has an impact that gets more serious to those involved the higher the level. For example, one of the games Berne talks about is called cops and robbers. A level-one version is: childhood hide-and-seek where the 'robber' (the child hiding) gives away their position in order to be found, e.g., by laughing, moving the wardrobe door, or coughing. They can feel cheated, exasperated, relieved, angry and sad at being 'found' and this leads to wanting to play again to win against the 'cop'. Can you see the game the child wants to play is for the 'finder' to find them, when they give their position away so they can be justifiably angry? I am sure there are people you work with that play a similar game, and when you work with children and young people they may also be playing this and hoping you won't chastise, reprimand or punish them for which they can also be angry with you. For example, a young child stealing food who then lies to cover up the stealing and absolutely refuses to own up to stealing the food (to avoid feelings of shame) in the hope you will say it doesn't matter. They are looking to be punished to be justifiably angry (perhaps even at themselves reaffirming how 'bad' they are).

A level-three version of this game might be the adolescent who steals a car and drives past the police (knowing where they are) and then creates a chase that ends in the need for more police, helicopters and tyre spikes to end the chase, with the protest that they 'didn't do anything wrong'. Of course, they wail and cry out at being sentenced to incarceration for their crimes as this is unfair, unjust and they are innocent! You might also see the parallels of risk-taking behaviours here including underage drinking, drugs and sex of adolescents, and as always, I am leading you towards the conversations about digital space and the cohort of young people (and adults) who play games in digital spaces.

Games online

Berne's corporeal games just became complex, long lasting and can be reignited.

In order to look at what is happening online from this theory of psychological games, I would direct you to read *Games People Play*, if you wish to gain a deeper understanding of both TA and games. However, I'd like to give examples of a few that I see on social media/in gaming environments, and I will be changing some of the titles that Berne used so you can see where I am going with them.

Firstly, I will explain what games are, and then to illustrate I will provide you with a concept called the drama triangle (Karpman, 1968) as this is one of the most useful pieces of theory here that shows what a game is and how it's played out. I will describe the games by Berne, give a brief overview of the intended outcomes and then move towards my own interpretations and suggestions of the newer emerging online versions. This is an ongoing area of consideration, and I am lucky to have a colleague in the TA space (Stilman, 2022), who is also thinking about these issues in this way. Hopefully, this will become several us rather than a few. There is often a few cyberpsychology and psychoanalytical framings of our behaviour online, and often this is in the therapeutic and modalities space, and I would love to see more in other spaces.

Formulae?

A game has a formula according to Berne, and this in its most simple form is: one (or more) players invite another to 'play', this is taken up by the invitee (the *con* which is nonverbal and *gimmick* which is someone's 'soft spot'). The game continues (the *responses*) until something unexpected or confusing happens (the *switch* where someone changes what is happening, and the *cross up*, which is the feeling surrounding the sudden change in behaviour), and then the game ends (the *payoff*, though as you will see this is not unexpected at all). It is the end point where both players feel a negative outcome.

The formula goes Con + Gimmick = Response – Switch – Cross(up) = Payoff.

Or in simple terms, and ones used in online language because some of the nonverbal cues are missing, or as in the case of most games I see online, an interpretation is created in the mind of the player (they insert their own idea of what the person(s) are aiming to achieve):

'bait' – 'bite' – 'flame' – 'rekt' or 'burned' – and the **payoff** is as in the real world.

Getting rekt can include: ghosting, outing, deadnaming, stalking, trolling, being kicked, camping out, revenge posts and pretty much all of the issues discussed in the books so far.

The payoff

Often people will moan or complain about this to others after the game has finished, for example, 'why do I/he/she/they always . . .?' And the one you may have said to yourself if playing one of these games is, 'what did I do wrong?'

The drama triangle was proposed by Karpman, to visually show the three positions within a repeated psychological game. In short, these positions can be taken up by a player who initiates the game, by taking up a position on the triangle, and inviting the second (or more) player(s) into the game and onto the triangle. If a player accepts the game, the game of position switching continues until the outcome is 'dramatic' enough for it to end. The players can only occupy one position at any one time, and this is dependent upon the other player and the other players' interpretation. When it does all end the players feel the payoff . . .

So let's take an example of a game and see what occurs in the drama triangle. The positions are: Persecutor, Victim and Rescuer. It isn't rocket science as to what the positions require as characteristics, but let's go with an example.

Pots and pans

Mrs Smith is sad, tired, hungry and fed up, and when she comes home from a day filled with some terrible cases, she really wants a hug and to sob whilst being held. She enters the home and sees that dirty pots and pans are on the sideboard. She really wants to say to her husband that she would like a hug and to go to bed early as she is tired. She has feelings bubbling under the surface about having to stay up and do the dishes and wants to 'tell him off and call him lazy for not doing them', but she was brought up to 'look after those around her', and she despises this upbringing, but her script part is to play the dutiful wife. Mrs Smith does not say this to her husband but wishes that she could, and decides that tonight she will make a point of letting him know how she feels. She has a choice about how to do this but was brought up in a family where sad feelings were not discussed, and anger was how the family communicated. She walks into the kitchen thinking I'm going to tell him how I feel. Only Mrs Smith picks up the first pan and sighs heavily, whilst dropping it into the sink. All by mistake of course!

Mrs Smith has taken up the position of either Victim (the sigh) or Persecutor (the dropping of the pan on purpose, which was really not a drop but a forced 'bang') and it is only when Mr Smith 'reacts' that we will know where this game will play out.

Mr Smith hears the sigh, and he instantaneously reacts with 'What's wrong?' He rushes to reduce his wife from the anger and to calm things down, as he inherently knows the bang of the pan is her 'being angry'. He takes up the Rescuer position here. He was brought up to make sure no one ever felt anger and so he is quick to try and abate this feeling in others. He rushes to the kitchen and says 'Oh let me do them I was just going to, and was letting my food settle first'.

Now at this point, I am quite convinced a few readers will be familiar with the scenario, and so I would like to pause for a moment, and, in line with the other chapters, add that I have also played this game with family, friends and partners. I too am human, and this is the most reported game in my clinic (washing/housework/DIY, etc.) of families and couples. So let me continue with the explanation knowing that, yes it can feel like I'm describing something that you are familiar with, and I hope not to cause shame, embarrassment or any of that guilt, shame or pejorative feelings (I am only responsible for what I type, not for how it is read or interpreted).

Mrs Smith at this conjuncture of the game decides that she will go with 'anger' as her preferred method of communication and takes up the Persecutor position. She retorts back with sarcasm and says, 'Oh of course you were!'

And the couple moves into a well-rehearsed argument with the 'usual' back and forth about the washing of pots before Mrs Smith suddenly says, 'You do this because you don't care about me!' She has now taken the Victim position and Mr Smith is feeling confused. She rushes off to the bathroom crying.

The payoff? Mr Smith feels like he's 'always in the wrong, not allowed to take a break, a demon husband' and he now feels angry that Mrs Smith has accused him of not caring. He cares all right, there are the flowers he buys, the garden he tends and so on! He feels angry and betrayed that Mrs Smith feels this way about him! He is now in the Persecutor payoff position, the one he was trying to avoid. This position tends to have feelings of anger associated with it. Damn it! He does not want to rush upstairs and rescue her; she can cry all she wants as he is pi★★ed off!

Mrs Smith however is now crying and feels that she's always in relationships with men who do not care for her, she thinks her husband is going to leave her and that the dishes are his way of showing her that she is worth nothing and what did she do to deserve this? Doesn't he know how she cares for him? And of course, he's not coming up to tend to her sadness and so that only proves the point!

[This isn't really about washing pots, by the way, it just happened to be the vehicle with which many relationships fight over something more important. If only we could do intimacy we wouldn't have to fill time with these moments. The real needs under this were Mrs Smith's sadness and wanting to ask for a hug, to sit with her feelings and to be in connection with her husband. She recreates a situation in order to feel 'A' version of sadness, but it isn't the one that needed tender loving care.]

Escalating games because we know more?

Some of the games played online create situations that are almost predictable, with harm occurring to the original poster's family, friends and colleagues as a fallout of the payoff. I don't know that this was covered in any of the original psychology theories, as access to these people will have been limited by geography and lack of knowledge about how and who was related to whom. The connectivity of social media, forums and searches now means that game players can access many more people for recruitment into games and these can be played at higher degrees given this connectivity. This requires further research though and I am hoping this raises the curiosity of those researcher-type personalities.

Professionalism and game theory

For example, political landscapes, the polarisation regarding COVID-19 and of course personal issues that are put on full display in this public area can be understood as the longer versions of psychological games.

To give an example, I am often intrigued by watching professionals (from the fields of human behaviour online, e-safety, cybersecurity and therapy) put out posts that are personal, contain information about their family, their past and even where they will be on a certain day for training, etc. If they are burgled on their day of training for example, what game do you think they will play out?

Notwithstanding this, information posted online is worth its weight in gold for criminal activity and for the issues discussed in this book such as stalking, revenge, theft, cybercrime, shame, hoaxes, etc.

Pots and pans online

Using the game theory posited previously, let's pretend that Professional A (who works with children) is discussing their 'tricky' relationship with their parents online. We often call this being vulnerable, and there has been a trend to speak one's truth out in the open to help others so we don't feel alone (we will come back to the authenticity of these kinds of posts soon).

In the psychotherapy field, we are taught during our training that self-disclosure is a 'tricky topic' itself with an if, when and why question surrounding it. Some disciplines suggest that this is never useful, while others suggest that small aspects could be, when times are right and for the client's benefit.

So Professional A discusses their childhood abuse, narcissistic parents, learning difficulties and family dysfunction, their sexuality and of course where they stand politically and their views about the COVID vaccine, by using their profile picture to demonstrate this. For example, a tee shirt saying 'liberal, gay and vaccinated neurodiverse vegan and climate enthusiast who loves Ricky Gervais' (I'm not entirely convinced all of this would appear on one tee shirt but play along!).

Now whilst all of this falls under the rights to speak freely and express oneself, in a space that can be seen by all, would this be classed as professional behaviour or not? What is the issue with this kind of 'game'? Where you see the word therapist in the next paragraphs, please feel free to interchange this with your profession.

Let's take for example a very hurt, distressed individual looking to find a professional to help them. They scour the Internet, and wouldn't you know there is a practitioner with a similar story to theirs, who offers online work, excellent! The therapeutic intervention begins, after a short while the client is feeling distressed at the vaccine decision they need to make, and the therapist is 'not giving them the advice they want'. They don't believe in the vaccine and have been reading articles explaining why this is an issue for them and want the therapist to engage in a debate about it, *recreating a pots-and-pans situation*. The therapist says, 'I can't give you my opinions or advice on the vaccine', and the client knows full well where they sit because it's on their social media accounts.

They use the information they have accrued about the therapist and begin to create a situation in sessions inflaming the therapist, they want to become angry with the therapist (which they cannot really do, and the therapist does not spot), and so they leave therapy abruptly and file a complaint. They now begin to talk about the therapist online and join groups where the therapist is, using pseudonym accounts and flaming the conversations.

The client feels they know the therapist due to the information online that the therapist has freely given out over many years on social media profiles. The client may decide to utilise this in favour of attempting to make a connection with the therapist and themselves. Never before has the therapeutic alliance allowed a client to have this much information on the therapist and of course, to date (at the time of writing) there are no detailed protocols, policies or literature on what to do, how to handle this in a session or via email, text, voicemail or on social media. Games are complicated by this fact and an angry, hurt or revengeful client could take up many versions of the 'rekt' position at the end of the game, which technology will and does facilitate.

I'm the victim here!

Professional B is building their following on social media and has discussed their childhood trauma, sexual preferences, political leanings, hatred towards certain groups of people, approach to their work/life balance and their favourite music, TV shows, books and places to visit in all the hope of being real and creating a larger following of like-minded people. They often respond to the hate coming their way by returning this hate, with added 'burns' and 'takedowns'. This of course is often the advice given by social media planning platforms, training courses and influencers: to 'be real, authentic and connect with your audience'.

However, Professional B has children who are primary school-aged as they set out building their career online. Their estranged parents are also just getting used to social media apps and beginning to use these and join the same platforms as Professional B. Much information is given out about the children, parents and family in the process of the professional building their following because the professional feels it is good to 'tell *their* story'.

A few months later the parents of the professional begin to write about their child and reveal *their* account of what happened, giving away details that are highly personal and creating the space for the professional to be 'justified as a victim' when they find out this is happening. The professional passive-aggressively retorts to each post and creates a story of 'I'm telling the truth', and the followers begin to watch both accounts. It's like a free TV drama, playing out in front of them.

However, a few years later the children of Professional B are old enough to have a social media accounts, and so head to the online spaces to do what all other children and young people are doing. Suddenly all the people Professional B upset and angered over the years, who may be professionals themselves or have been waiting to see these children appear on these social media platforms, well they come whooshing at this child on their accounts, letting them know how their parent is X, or Y. They find themselves being harassed, stalked, bullied and all forms of vicarious hate that Professional B created in the social media space. They are attacked by accounts that are difficult to identify as real people. Professional B has an outcry about how toxic the social media space is and how awful it is to be the victim of such attacks.

There are several influencers with millions of followers who do this every day. They have children too young to be on social media and I wonder what will happen when they do. Our ability to share so much about ourselves in these spaces is leaving the next cohort of users a boggy pit in which they must find a way to not drown. By being related to people who do this, the connections that can be made by other social media users also leave this bog open to more toxicity over time and to use the game theory, thinking these games, like a wound, can be opened time and time again.

Let's get 'em!

Professional C holds a position of high regard in both their profession and in the social media space. They are active in posting their own opinions about the research they are involved with, and academically attack others that oppose their own field. Now in academic circles, this level of back-and-forth debating is often considered a part of the process, where one researcher, tutor or professor calls into question an opposing view, which is how science advances. This is not how these debates are appearing on social media with academics calling each other 'dicks', outing the fact they have been blocked by someone and creating a cyber mobbing attack on any articles or appearances that their rivals feature in. Often recruiting those who are 'with them' in their thinking.

What's interesting is, and I am sure the answer is no, would this behaviour be tolerated in an academic institution if these researchers, doctors, professors and the like were sitting at a table with each other in front of a crowd? And what would happen if they began to call each other 'dicks'? I reckon it would be quickly closed down and abandoned, as this is not helpful, or what debating is: polite, professional and professional modelling to students.

Now as games are played in social media spaces, many of us get to watch and many of us do, like voyeurs, and to be honest, this has fed much of my knowledge, by watching things 'play out' over time. I must have been in some games, and I know I have been in others because I have been aware of the interaction, the posting or the non-posting that I am doing too. I know you will also recognise your own patterns of behaviour here too. **We all do it** as I said – well, Berne said it, I am just reflecting it back.

The idea of 'let's get 'em' is called 'let's you and him fight' in Eric Berne's book, and the desired outcome is to recruit people onto 'our side' of the argument so that we elevate our position as the one with the highest IQ, reasoning and knowledge. Huzzah, aren't we clever!

Conversely, what could we learn from oppositional conversations and research? Most likely it is the feeling, recognition and acceptance that 'we could be wrong'. This evokes embarrassment, guilt and shame, and definitely taps into our childhood scripts. I am wondering if you can recall what this felt like as a child to be 'wrong' and why we avoid it so much!

Whom are the people watching online?

However, imagine that a student, client, colleague, child or family member is watching the professional 'savagely attack' someone on social media. Does this create respect? Does this create a willingness to learn new viewpoints or does this entrench the feeling that 'one cannot' produce an essay that is counter to the views of the tutor? Does this now become the echo chamber of research and progress? What about a client who sees the professional behave like this, can they trust us to offer a safe and warm space? What about the professional who is always playing 'wooden leg' and taking up a victim position, perhaps talking about their health, their experiences, and their family? Will this create that space in which people can again trust what is being discussed or is this a case of, as many of my adolescent clients tell me, 'mad people' on the Internet, or the fact that we the adults 'have lost it' and there is no way that they can trust politicians, doctors, researchers, teachers and anyone else who tries to educate such as parents?

They call us 'Boomers': the weaponisation of vulnerability

This was a term I heard Daniel Schmachtenberger use (about vulnerability, not boomers), and it is the epitome of some of the games discussed in this book. This is the 'plastic likes' scenario I discuss in book one (Knibbs, 2022) and young people are getting wise to this 'exposure' of our being seen to be real, sharing of information that according to some of my clients 'makes their skin crawl', and the younger generations are beginning to see through this authenticity and genuineness that 'isn't what it says on the tin' and is the slow and deliberate exploitation of their time and attention. Some of the younger people I work with are angry with us and believe that we have 'ruined' social media for them. They move to spaces where we are not, so they can congregate and socialise with people who know how to use the technology. They need their own spaces, they need to learn through their own mistakes and sadly some of them are rebelling against us and making mistakes that can result in death, hospitalisations, lifelong cybertrauma and irrevocable search histories that can impede their employment.

The diet of mistrust for the developing child

By our own demise of playing games, using the idea of free speech, and sharing information online in the way we do, attacking each other and fighting in a polarised way, which the algorithms love to feed to these children, and forgetting we are being watched continuously:

We the adults have created a generation of children who mistrust many of us.

References

Berne, E. (1964). *Games people play. The psychology of human relationships*. Penguin: London.
Brown, B. (2017). *Braving the wilderness: The quest for true belonging and the courage to stand alone*. Random House: New York.
Ernst, F. (1971). The OK corral: The grid or get-on-with. *TAJ*, 1(4).
Karpman, S. (1968). Drama triangle script drama analysis. *Transactional Analysis Bulletin*, 7(26), 39–43.

Kaufman, S. (2020). *Transcend. The new science of self-actualization.* Tarcherperigree: New York.

Knibbs, C. (2022). *Children, technology and healthy development.* Routledge: Abingdon.

Maslow, A. H. (1943). A theory of human motivation. *Psychological Review,* 50(4), 370–396.

Maslow, A. H. (1962). *Toward a psychology of being.* Princeton: D. Van Nostrand Company.

Siegel, D. (2010). *The mindful therapist. A clinician's guide to mindsight and neural integration.* W. W. Norton & Co: New York.

Siegel, D. (2016). *Mind: A journey to the heart of being human (Norton series on interpersonal neurobiology).* W. W. Norton & Co: New York.

Stilman, R. (2022). Attached to technology: Exploring identity and human relating in a virtual and corporeal world, *Transactional Analysis Journal,* 52(2), 93–105.

2 Trends, challenges and hoaxes

The war on drugs – as Nancy Regan said: just say no!

Every chapter, topic and section of this book can be seen through the lens of one or more of the other sections, chapters and topics.

What does this have to do with hoaxes and trends, challenges, dares, peer pressure?

Do you remember hearing, 'Chicken, buck buck buck bawwwhh', 'Yellow belly! Scaredy-cat! I dare you!' And of course, the converse of this, which many children hear as the taunt, 'Don't you dare!'

I remember hearing many of these phrases as a young person, taking some of them up as challenges, ignoring some and not others. This was all based on my ability to reason, or not, and my wanting to impress or wind up the adults who told me not to do said behaviour, considering the consequences and my age at the time. My thinking often looked like, 'What would be the likely penalty for carrying out the dare?' The punisher could be my parents, teachers or other adults, e.g., the police. Would I be considered a hero by the people egging me on, and what would be the social penalty of not carrying them out? Mostly the dares were jumping out of trees, climbing structures that were unsafe, holding my breath till I passed out, staring at mirrors looking for 'ghosts and demons', and as I entered the latter stages of schooling: playing hooky, underage drinking and smoking cigarettes. The usual stuff of the '70s, '80s and early '90s.

Now the thing about dares is they can range from fairly harmless behaviours to incredibly dangerous and threatening to life. Often, they can be described as 'dumb', 'stupid' and 'idiotic'. Yet these dares and 'stunts' are often what maketh the Guinness book of records in high-action sports and entertainment, which we revere! It can be a lifetime achievement and goal for some to hold a coveted certificate for a world record at or in something. Reading Kotler's work in *The Rise of Superman* (2014), the risks that Red Bull-style, action-based sports such as skydiving, snowboarding and surfing bring about from the biggest kinds of dares to life are considered to be 'awesome' and amazing (and bring some of the biggest macro experiences of flow).

Over the last decade or so I have watched (often through gritted teeth, no choice and/or boredom) TV *talent* programs giving a stage to some of these dares that range

DOI: 10.4324/9781003289210-3

from stunts, life-threatening magic tricks, eating competitions (e.g., marshmallows or Ferrero Rocher) and of course risks to animals and/or people's bones, self-esteem and self-worth as they perform on stage for the schadenfreude-like joy, shock and entertainment of those watching. We will get into that throughout the book, so note the parallel between these programs, talents and social media and how we often forget this link.

Many years ago, when entertainment consisted of lions and gladiators, court jesters and the congregated villagers watching the beheading of the local criminal or dejected queen, we likely developed a taste for other people's misery, pain and of course self-humiliation in front of others for entertainment. When you consider the crowds that could gather in public for these events, the oohing, ahhing and cajoling were likely to be the same as 'dares' today being egged on to perform and take more risks to receive some accolade, support and admiration from the crowds. Being seen by others, revered and talked about after the event are some of the driving factors of risk-taking and of course, as discussed in the first book, are underpinned by attachment processes and that stage of adolescence where this becomes the binding force of peer relationships (Siegel, 2014; Neufeld & Mate, 2019).

Pranks, stunts and abuse

And so, it's no wonder that with the invention of the television and the 'camcorder', we could begin to savour these moments repeatedly with the permanent record that video mediums offered. Why, we could even earn money for it by sending in our tapes (yes, cassette tapes) to TV shows and having them aired for all to see the mistakes, fails, falls, faux pas and fouls of the latest human, big or small, on the screen. We could send them to prospective producers to show talent, for an audition and of course to become the next popular icon or idol. We created Saturday-morning or -evening TV where we could air these highlights, keeping us indoors staring at a screen and laughing, wincing or bewildering at the latest human wonderment, and knowing we've likely had one or two of these close shaves ourselves at some point.

Conversations in houses may have emphasised how stupid, lucky, awesome, attention seeking and dramatic we are as humans. We very rarely watch TV with others without expressing our opinion on it in some way, shape or form. It's how we have a shared experience together. We create a narrative of (shared between us) values and humour, and children learn this by watching and listening to us. They can also pick up on some of these values through TV and radio and, importantly here, other forms of media.

Imagine, if you laugh at a scene on the screen and your partner, parent or friend does not, what internal message do you tell yourself about what they are now thinking? If they laugh, what do you learn about it, and them? And so, by inference, how children must be privy to the thinking of the adults (and others) watching screens, and by default, understanding, learning and internalising these values and opinions through the process called social learning theory (Bandura, 1977), which I will cover shortly.

For this particular topic, what adults and in turn the children consider as acceptable in the 'dares' space gets reinforced when others discuss it, making it part of the 'valued' conversation, and so children can find themselves watching things to know what others are talking about, or even watching to learn what parts of the conversation to agree with and to find other sources that mirror and support this viewpoint. This is often how the acronym FOMO (fear of missing out) gets utilized, without knowing why a child has the fear of missing out, and what the feelings may manifest as in behaviours. Too often FOMO is portrayed as a negative aspect of being online 'just because others are'. If you can see the patterns of attachment underneath this you can see that *to belong means to be in the group with all the knowledge others possess in that group*, for example, the 'in-jokes' and so on.

If, for example, stunts are considered worthy of all the pain that goes with 'self-inflicted' injuries, e.g., broken legs when trying out new skateboard tricks (or humour and laughs when injuries occur when drunk and falling down) then children may believe that this means they would receive empathy or care, *and the accolade* if they became injured if there was a 'great story' or tale to tell about how the injury occurred whilst taking a risk.

However, if injuries resulted in a distanced, 'Well it's all their own fault' narrative, what children may learn is that this behaviour would result in a 'Don't look to me for sympathy' response. Children may learn not to take risks that result in them being hurt.

Furthermore, hurting someone else in the process of a prank may be considered a noble thing to do in pursuit of a laugh, lols and lels. And so, this child may develop a 'prank on others are okay' framework. We will look at this in terms of trends, cyberbullying (happy slapping) and influencer content. For examples of this, there are devoted channels to 'pranks' where people are jump-scared, tricked and at times seriously hurt in the process of pranking. There are also videos of parents and guardians pranking their children in this space, which is emotional and psychological abuse dressed up as a joke. It includes some videos of adults and children pranking babies and animals.

For example, the trend of throwing cheese onto a dog or cat's face resulted in many people copying this, only for it then to be transferred to babies who exhibit a startled response and then a freeze response. The adults can be heard to be laughing at an infant who is clearly shocked, and in one video is left to 'deal with the incident' for up to five minutes. Watching these videos, I see the deficit of knowledge that we have as adults in today's world about events that are stressful to babies, and moreover, if we know this caused distress and still did it, would we say these adults are cruel?

I happen to use a video in my training (when discussing trauma responses) of a little baby whose mum blows her nose, and the baby reacts in varying ways throughout the few minutes. Once I have explained the process to the audience and we replay the video, what was once a funny video no longer seems this way and it becomes another video in a long line of not-funny moments.

For example, I have seen videos of parents giving their children hot sauces (Carolina Reaper hot, which is excruciatingly painful for adults), and videos of children thinking they have stained a carpet with ink, only for the parents to cry with laughter at the disappearing ink trick, and many videos of children whacking each other with planks, boards, face pies made out of irritating substances or ones that can cause allergic reactions and so many more, all in the name of humour, and when my children were little they created a video like this only for me to explain in no uncertain terms why this was not acceptable behavior; apparently I'm a bore. When they hit their mid-20s, we discussed this and realised I am still a bore, but I also had their mental health interests at heart. Adolescence is a great time and the maturity that comes with it is such a different lens.

Watching screens, watching you modelling, me copy

Many of the tiny children I work with in therapy have the beginnings of what we call script in the TA language. It is pure unfiltered learning of those they live with. For example, you can see the beginnings of what Freud called the superego, which is the internal critical voice we all have, the one that is our inner Jimney Cricket and steers us on the path of good rather than bad. Children will tell me who has been 'naughty' at school or home, and often their parent's voice and body language is present as they tell me this. I can also see the behaviours of the parents in the role-play of children who mimic their parents and siblings, and it is this I want to talk about for a moment.

Social learning theory; monkey see, monkey do?

In 1961 the idea that children might copy behaviour in terms of aggression resulted in a now-famous experiment using a Bobo doll, conducted by Bandura et al. (1961). In this study young children watched an adult on a TV screen punching, slapping and pushing over a weighted inflatable doll (Bobo doll) and as it rebounded, pushing it down again and shouting words like 'Sockeroo'. Children who were then placed into a room with a Bobo doll mimicked this behaviour and copied the words of the adult. This is known as vicarious learning and means that witnessing the behaviours of others can be internalised as acceptable, appropriate and expected. And so, this principle is also known as 'monkey see, monkey do'.

And it turns out this example is very aptly true! Quite by accident, when studies were being conducted on monkeys in a lab, one day a monkey who had electrodes in its brain was watching a lab technician eating some food. I've seen this transcribed and relayed in books as peanuts or ice cream, which doesn't really matter as the next sentence is the important bit. The monkey is watching or witnessing the technician eating and the technician notices that an area of the monkey's brain has 'lit up' in the same area as the motor functions needed to carry out the act of moving the hand towards the mouth when eating. Vicarious learning translates as *actual copycat behaviours in the brain* in the watcher, and so the term *mirror neurons* was born to reflect the parallel neuronal activity that has been discussed in many areas of psychology (Ferrari & Coudé, 2018).

Now to make this clear and simple, the mirror neurons would not necessarily have the same *level of activation*, otherwise the watcher is likely to do, to 'have to' engage in the same behaviour rather than thinking about it. If this wasn't the case, each time we saw someone carry out a behaviour we would be replicating it ourselves, and whilst that could look very funny, I'm not sure it would be helpful for our species, and we would likely end up in all sorts of dangerous, silly and repetitive situations.

However, the main point here is you have likely experienced this yourself or witnessed it when you are watching TV and become excited at a show. For example, you might be watching a runner about to cross the finish line and you move to the edge of your seat (think also football/boxing/rugby); this can also happen when a good psychological thriller, slasher or action movie is climaxing. The most well-known example of this for many of us is either *The Karate Kid*, *Rocky* or *Friday the 13th*. Your brain's ability to predict what it thinks is likely to happen, your empathic resonance (knowing what this might feel like) and your mirror neurons all combine in a beautiful synchronous dance and you 'feel' the excitement, anticipation and of course incoming disaster (where applicable).

Now imagine watching risk-taking behaviour in others, or trends that look fun, easy and have people smiling and looking like they are connected. Imagine seeing the comments underneath with lots of engagement and excitement and these posts are likely giving off the feeling of community, belonging and connection. Just what our brains and bodies love!

Some of the simple ones that got copied a few years ago, and I mean adults copying here, are in these examples: # wakeupcall (celebs taking a picture of themselves upon waking), resulting in adults taking 'authentic' images of themselves in bed, just to show how real and woke they are (like literally). Which is now an app for young people called Be Real.

There have been #theicebucketchallenge and #nomakeupforcancer, #harlemshake (including military, emergency-services and white-collar workers), #InMyFeelings, #plank and #thefloorislava (turning into a TV program and game) to name a few. Young people and some children also got involved in these and this is more than likely due to vicarious learning and wanting to be viral, important and seen (by their family, as in an attachment need not seen on the Internet).

There have also been dangerous trends that adults 'started', and which made their way down to children rather quickly, and as I discuss in my book in 2016, a viral video can take approximately seven minutes to become a trending topic on social media (Knibbs, 2016). Now if you don't have a knowledge of something – for example, the trends that have included eating a teaspoon of cinnamon, Carolina Reaper peppers or toxic substances – you can be fooled into thinking they look like things that you could 'easily' accomplish, as the coughing and spluttering, eye-watering squeals and nonfatal immediate injuries on show on short clips make it easy to make an assumption that 'everything turned out okay' because that's what TV, film and cartoons have been showing us for many years. Children do not make an assumption that this is going to end badly, because these videos are on popular platforms, and so why would it turn out badly? And here you have to try and remember back to your childhood when your thinking and understanding of the world is placed in the trust of media, fairy tales and happily-ever-after endings.

The more dangerous trends have also followed the rarely shown life-ending catastrophic clips, opting for the moment of the trend, ending before the person being filmed is carted away in an ambulance, foams at the mouth or something as obvious, and even when this does happen the children tell me 'it's fake', it's for attention and 'isn't really that bad' or 'it was even funnier with that bit'. We have for a long time placed warnings on bottles of bleach and hazardous substances, and adults are required in the workplace to understand the health and safety legislation. We know that medicines should be 'out of reach of children' and we protect our babies from plugs, table corners and whatever the latest thing that could hurt them is.

However, when a child sees another child partaking in challenges and trends like: push someone backwards over a kneeling 'stooge', self-strangulation, masturbation until you faint, cough syrup into the anus, drinking hand sanitiser (it contains alcohol), necking a full bottle of Jack Daniels (or other spirits) and #necknomination (which was similar to the ice bucket challenge but involved a pint of mixed alcoholic spirit, toxic and 'out there' substances like bleach, urine, vomit, spices, laundry liquid and whatever they can find under the sink or in the cupboards), then you can see that many of these children would not even know about the consequences of mixing bleach with certain substances for a number of reasons. a) They are not biochemists, b) they do not have the knowledge about what substances can do to internal organs and c) they are children.

It was fascinating to see how quickly these challenges and trends move, and I warned a local school of this #necknomination when it was occurring, as I had seen a year-11 and -10 child (aged 16 and 14 in that school's uniform) on social media, drinking various substances and quoting, 'Do it before she gets in' (meaning mum). Sadly, the school took no action, believing this to be something other children do, and of course, there is no bullying in this school either. But less than four days later I saw a year 7 (aged 11) doing the #necknomination. I wonder how many of these children have damaged gut linings, ended up in a hospital, sick for some time or worse. This trend did not make it to the mainstream media, possibly because no child died as a direct result. And some of the trends mentioned were not entirely UK-based.

These trends become understandable in terms of young people engaging in them, because many of their empathy circuits cannot possibly understand the immense heat of a pepper, alcohol intoxication, asphyxiation, cold exposure and other tortuous experiences. These trends, which you can read more about in the health chapter too, are being carried out by adults and on the 'bro podcast circuit' where many of the current viral podcasters are pushing the limits of the fully matured body, and younger males are copying.

> If we, the adults, chose to eat hot foods, drink/inhale poisons and experience extreme events like ice baths, blood-restricted training, fasting and 'psychedelic trips', we do so from a place of maturational choice because we can weigh up the pros and cons and know our bodies can tolerate much more than a child can.

Time travel as an adult brain process

We have dedicated areas of our brains that can time travel to the future and look at the what if's of the event and experience, and decide if we want to engage and partake. We can rationalise consequences and calculate the likelihood of outcomes. We can think about the risks involved and make a considered decision. We can use our prefrontal cortex dedicated to this task. Children do not have this circuitry fully online and, during adolescence, even if they did, they might ignore it in favour of peers and hyperrational thinking (Knibbs, 2022). They only see the intention behind, 'If I do this Billy said he would be my friend'. You can literally tell a child till you are blue in the face, but if the prefrontal cortex is not hearing you, you can end up looking like a Smurf. So, we need to think about this and how we discuss peers, belonging, autonomy, choice and friendships.

Tribalism and community

We circle back to the attachment process of wanting to be seen and liked by others. Sometimes this is quite obvious, and children can reflect on why they do the 'stunt' or dare and can explain in words that Timmy and Lucy only wanted to be their friend if they ate the chewing gum off the floor. In other spaces, the child who feels so remote from their peers is going to have much more of a drive to want to be in the group.

Practitioner pause for reflection

Time for another memory experiment; can you remember wanting to be part of a group in your primary school? Can you remember the yearning to 'not be picked last' for the team in PE, or perhaps you were already a popular child and never experienced this but watched it in others, or perhaps you were the one to challenge and taunt the other children?

Those who wore glasses, wore clothing from the poor-parents' shop, the ones who ace the tests, the misfits, outliers and outcasts. Do you know how powerful that feeling of wanting to be part of a group is? How the family dynamics of trauma and attachment can exacerbate this yearning to be in the group and can drive children to carry out behaviours they know are going to hurt, get them in trouble or even hurt someone else, and yet they still do it anyway? How shame compounds this and why these children rarely step into that shame and own it (neither do many adults to be fair). So, thinking about your place of employment, place in the family and desire to belong to a community, are there things you would do or have done to be accepted?

Attention needer, not 'seeker'

These are the children who are often referred to as 'attention seeking' when carrying out trends, challenges or even telling stories (hoaxes), which is really attention-needing behaviour. These children do not know how to ask for their needs to be met, nor may they even know what their real needs are, and so they engage in behaviour that creates interest, ridicule, shame, attention, sanctions, exclusion, rejection and more in the hope that this will quell the feeling of exile and disconnection. Though these children would never call it that using these words, perhaps they might say they are lonely, doing it for a laugh, don't know why they are doing it, it's only a dare, can't see the reason why people are losing their mind and it's really no big deal.

These are the red-lane (of fluctuating red and blue lanes) inhabitants discussed in book one. They are seemingly satisfied to have negative attention rather than none at all, and in respect of this may be the ones who engage in the most dangerous, outlandish and negative kinds of dares, stunts and trends. These are likely to be the children excluded from lessons or school, placed in isolation or already in the criminal justice system. These are children from families where pain, abuse and trauma are a daily aspect of living, and these are the children many of you as practitioners are already working with.

They do not have 'time' to critically analyse trends, stunts and dares because they are hot-wired for risk and their bodies and brains are in fight and flight most of the time. They cannot think and appraise these trends for levels of risk, even if they wanted to.

Advice from the Department for Education and the online safety space

But the good news is we are moving in the right direction talking about these issues. I am seeing a rise in schools now attempting to inform parents in a helpful way about trends and hoaxes (covered in a moment) after the Department for Education (UK) brought out some guidance about informing parents about online challenges and hoaxes (DfE, 2021). It was also very nice to see one of the resources, The Education People (2021), which quoted my blog about the human algorithm.

But the advice on the governmental page seems to tail off, leaving the responsibility with the school. The safeguarding leads to doing their own diligence on whether a trend or hoax is true, and may need naming directly (though generic advice is it does not need to be, and this is dependent upon the country you're in), and I am sure that many of these roles in education are too busy, or perhaps not versed in knowing where and what to trace to establish the credibility of a trend, hoax or challenge. They want their parents to care for and to keep their children safe and often believe they are doing the right thing by letting them know where the danger is. 'Look out!' is the feeling behind this, and to be honest this has been successful in keeping our species alive for some time.

Moreover, the source of many of these informational posts has actually occurred through well-meaning police forces and safeguarding professionals, who are not privy to the DfE advice exactly, and are selling the shock-and-awe framing as an attempt to stop this behaviour. This is the 'don't be a victim of this crime' approach, and we know this is sadly not the way that this message works. Or, these organisations and individuals, I am sad to say, are looking for virality and hits on their posts. Especially if you can have an image or video link attached, and some scary-looking stats or numbers. It is often a race by organisations to be the one to put information out about these kinds of issues, creating panic, worry and more virality of the issue. This is the human algorithm and it's fed by ego as well as fear.

> Clickbait through scary informatics and awareness raising of online issues are the adult version of both trends and hoaxes, and this may well be misinformation or disinformation too.

Hans Christian Anderson, fairy tales and the monster under the bed

Let's veer off into the direction of hoaxes for a moment, which follow the same pattern as previously mentioned, yet have a particular spin of falsehood, as well as scary and bogeyman stories. This overlaps into the world of misinformation and disinformation and is also the main aspect of the cyber scam attacks called phishing, smishing and vishing.

Urban Myths, spooky stories and scares are a part of our tribalistic ways of passing down important parts of our ancestry, warnings about all kinds of behaviour and expectations and how we attempt to prevent children from wandering off into the dark where wolves, lions or other prey lurk and wait to pick off the little ones. Around the campfire, tales would be told of the evils that exist out there and why staying close to us here is the safest option. Noises in the dark are given spooky, scary and frightening elements so that our bodies naturally become wary of those noises in the forest and so we don't venture far without light and company. These stories are still told to date in the form of TV, films and comics. Fantasy and fiction are also best-selling novel genres and bring in the biggest turnovers in cinema takings. We love stories of things that are not true, but we also need the help of others at times to help us work out whether this really is a falsehood.

The Bogeyman, Father Christmas and Creepypasta Killer Clowns

Pennywise, Freddy Kreuger, Norman Bates, Michael Myers and Dracula.

The Exorcist, The Omen, The Birds, Frankenstein, Psycho, Hostel, Saw (1–99), *Hellraiser, Creature from the Black Lagoon, Bodysnatchers, Alien(s)*, the 21st-century prevalence of zombies in all kinds of films and more recently the prevalence of wizards, vampires and werewolves all taking their spot in the space of *fantasy, falsehoods and 'hoaxes'.*

The idea of a hoax is to elicit fear and confusion and, as the payoff, to point out the gullibility of the believer. In many hoaxes, this has a monetary gain, such as the cyber scams of con artists, or perhaps even for people to part with money to see 'the bearded lady' or 'the man with two heads'. There is even a worldwide museum dedicated to the weird and wonderful, and some of the artefacts and stories may well be falsehoods. Nevertheless, our curiosity is willing to pay the entrance fee! Where the story is shared of horror-based myths, we are looking at the 'creepypasta' phenomenon of myth and legend, which might just be true. Killer clowns, Slenderman or Teletubbies on the streets? Could it be?

The hoaxer attempts to trick us, akin to the con artist and akin to the game of now I've got you son of a bitch (NIGYSOB), the outcome of which Eric Berne (1964) describes is, 'Ha, got you!'

Alchemy and mysticism, myths to neuroscience

But what if the hoax is about a message or scientific enquiry and the struggle to find the truth? Could it be misinformation or disinformation, and what is the intent behind the story? For example, going back to the most famous story told to children as a way to get them to 'tell the truth' is 'The Boy Who Cried Wolf'. One of the most feared, confusing and perhaps even hated types of people for little children is the clown (with little reasoning as to why, apart from the make-up looking scary, not 'funny'). The idea of the snake oil salesman selling the 'elixir of life' has long existed parallel to the alchemists and magicians explaining chemistry, biology and science using methods that we now know to be ludicrous. It has existed even more recently, with the art of phrenology and a 'profiler' claiming to be able to discern paedophiles by the shape of their hand (though I cannot now find the post from LinkedIn, but felt I wanted to share this here). What we can now do with science and through the positivist approaches of experiments, hypotheses, the art of rationalising and the inferential process produces evidence to 'debunk' these myths, often called 'proving'.

The skill of being able to compute, rationalise and consider probabilities comes with age and maturity, but also what Ken Wilber (2000) calls transcending and including, away from the mythical and magical phase so often attributed to the childlike state of world knowledge. This has been covered in the introduction, and within the chapter on information, misinformation and disinformation. And, here is the same paradox of the thinking process that our limbic systems in fight or flight suffer with, and why we so often rush to continue the hoax story.

But what is most fascinating is when the truth airs, how many folks now state 'they always knew this was a falsehood' and they insert a cognitively dissonant 'excuse' as to why they engaged in the behaviour, sharing and contributing to the hoax. This is the space of, 'I always knew Father Christmas, the Easter Bunny and tooth fairy were not real, I was just playing along' – hope shattered, dreams shattered and disappointments abound. Often though, it's a relief when we find out the bogeyman isn't real!

Witches, wizards, werewolves, vampires and vikings merch?

With the advent of being able to access many of these stories and mythical ideologies, the rise of anime cartoons and connections to the roots of evolution, one thing is certainly noticeable, and this is the popularity of dressing like a wizard – perhaps the use of a cane for everyday outings by the younger people who are identifying with these characters. You may have noticed the rise in viking haircuts, tattoos, clothing and the many different forms of 'kitty' or unicorn-style apparel for people streaming online. You may have also noticed the larger, longer coats for the 'alternative' and dark souls wandering among us, and often I hear the adults saying it's a trend. Is this a positive one? Is this harmful and is this how online trends become the next best thing in 'merch'? and what about Adidas, Nike and other large brands (given they are already 'trending' in Web 3.0)?

Practitioner pause for reflection

Consider the stories you have been exposed to as a child and how you came to know the truth and what kinds of research you did to work out whether you were 'being played'. Were these stories shared at school, by your family or on the TV, for example?

I'm going to use a famous hoax to elaborate on the process here, taken from the idea of copypasta (an idea taken from copy/pasting and is based on text, transitioning into creepypasta, which are creepy-type cartoons such as Salad Fingers and is the anime-based image of Momo and the most recent Huggy Wuggy monster). How can a five-year-old who is hearing news of, for example, 'Momo' or 'Huggy Wuggy' know how to discriminate, and how can you appease the fear of a child of this age? What about the eight-to-ten-year-old cohort who have that next level of thinking that Piaget talks about where they can now understand more of the abstract, and consider that the hoax of the Momo character might just be real? And what about the older children who are in the adolescence phase of 'knowing it all', risk-taking and have been alerted to the Halloween killer clown and are spooking themselves even more by the conversations, taunting and teasing they engage in as part of the group-cohesion process?

And if you want to know what feeling I am talking about, how many times in your life have you climbed or descended the stairs rushing and holding your breath and leaping as far as you could, zoomed down a corridor that's dark or gotten into your car quickly and locked the doors before sighing with relief? I thought so.

Hoaxes are part of our community, it's almost in our DNA you could say. The bad actors who wish to profit, steal and create discord exist in all tribes, communities and societies. Where we are with technology means that this newer form of chain letter 'death threat', this information, misinformation, disinformation, hoax, untruth, scary story and whatever label we want to put on it makes it so that we can fire up the speed of that transmission and tap into the death-threat feeling, exponentially. We can create unwarranted fear and we have exacerbated the trustworthiness of our peers above and beyond the stage of rational and cognizant thinking. We are, in the words of *The Social Dilemma*, in a race to the bottom of the limbic system. And false news, propaganda, hoaxes, mis/disinformation and scary and negatively balanced stories are driving the cyber synapses, firing and wiring.

The human algorithm is fast becoming the new hivemind of superhighway synapse connections built around false neurotransmission and, in the paraphrased words of Hebb, '*Neurons that fire together wire together*' (Hebb, 1966*). Like tree roots that have been entangled underground, the synapses of cyberspace are interwoven, and they are growing stronger bonds of what can only be a version of regressive thinking into the limbic highways of fear and what some may call human stupidity.

[★I own an original copy of this book, which is very rare, but do not have an earlier version, which I am still searching for if anyone has one?]

From drill videos to information that can radicalise

A point to note as this chapter ends, as I have not covered this in depth here, are the gang-related hoaxes, challenges and misdirection by use of mis/disinformation. There is a space in which gang members will create content, usually music videos, which have the 'challenge' to others contained within the rap lyrics, which are then often combatted with a return acceptance to the challenge or perhaps a further antagonist challenge and refute to them. These videos have in many ways circulated from the streets with tags and graffiti into a space where they look, on the surface, to be like other rap videos with the intent hidden in the vocals. It has been reported that London Metropolitan Police were following and removing many of these videos with their post on the site now removed, and so I am citing the Vice article that discussed this earlier this year of writing (Pritchard, 2022).

These videos can, as with all other types of media, be hosted on platforms other than YouTube and can remain active until the challenge is accepted and then they disappear. Platforms that allow for the short duration and deletion of videos like this are commonly utilised for this kind of provocation challenge. However, I am limiting the conversation around this topic in this chapter as this is covered more in the literature around PREVENT. This is also how some school fights are 'set up'.

Moreover, challenges set in online games and the hoxes shared there can leave children googling for information and finding content that relates to this kind of hoax, for example, the Huggy Wuggy hoax was shared in gaming spaces (the most common one reported to me was Roblox, followed by Minecraft) and this led children onto the Internet to look for material relating to this, often signposted to YouTube where the algorithm would offer other material.

This indirect route from gaming, music and videos can on one hand lead children into the world of hoaxes, challenges and disinformation, but this is also the route cited for children who are radicalised into gangs, extremist groups and more, and at the time of writing, this is being researched as a major concern by colleagues I know in this field.

References

Bandura, A., Ross, D., & Ross, S. A. (1961). Transmission of aggression through imitation of aggressive models. *The Journal of Abnormal and Social Psychology*, 63(3), 575.

Bandura, A., & Walters, R. H. (1977). *Social learning theory* (Vol. 1). Prentice Hall: Englewood Cliffs.

Berne, E. (1964). *Games people play. The psychology of human relationships*. Penguin: London.

Department for Education. (2021). *Harmful online challenges and hoxes*. www.gov.uk/government/publications/harmful-online-challenges-and-online-hoaxes/harmful-online-challenges-and-online-hoaxes.

The Education People. (2021). *Online safety alerts. Think before you scare*. www.theeducationpeople.org/blog/online-safety-alerts-think-before-you-scare/

Ferrari, P. F., & Coudé, G. (2018). Chapter 6 – mirror neurons, embodied emotions, and empathy. In K. Meyzer & E. Knapska (Eds.), *Neuronal correlates of empathy* (pp. 67–77). Elsevier Inc.: London.

Hebb, D. (1966). *The organization of behavior: A neuropsychological theory*. Wiley and Sons: New York.

Knibbs, C. (2016). *Cybertrauma; The darker side of the internet*. Self-published and available on Amazon Kindle and Blurb Books.

Knibbs, C. (2022). *Children, technology and healthy development*. Routledge: Abingdon.

Kotler, S. (2014). *The rise of superman: Decoding the science of ultimate human performance*. Quercus Publishing: London.

Neufeld, G., & Mate, G. (2019). *Hold onto your kids. Why parents need to matter more than peers*. Vermillion: London.

Pritchard, W. (2022). *YouTube is working with met police to take down rap and drill videos*. Accessed March 02, 2022. https://www.vice.com/en/article/bvnp8v/met-police-youtube-drill-music-removal.

Siegel, D. (2014). *Brainstorm. The power and purpose of the teenage brain*. Jeremy P. Tarcher: New York.

Wilber, K. (2000). *Integral psychology: Consciousness, spirit, psychology, therapy*. Shambala: London.

Further links about trends, challenges and hoaxes

www.samaritans.org/about-samaritans/media-guidelines/.

https://swgfl.org.uk/magazine/digital-ghost-stories/.

www.theguardian.com/uk-news/2022/jun/03/met-police-project-alpha-profiling-children-documents-show.

3 Information, misinformation and disinformation

Every chapter, topic and section of this book can be seen through the lens of one or more of the other sections, chapters and topics.

Whisper, whisper, whipser, whippit, wicked?

Have you ever played the game as a child, (usually in schools) where you line up several people and the first in the line tells someone a 'secret', and by the time it gets to the end of the line the message is completely skewed and may not even represent the original spoken word? What was it called? You probably named the game based on a foreign language, which of course is no longer politically correct to do so, and hence my non-naming of the game here in that manner (it was called '★★★ whispers' in my day).

Gossip. The modern-day way we keep each other free of fleas?

No really, it is said that as human beings we don't need to sit and groom each other's fur daily in an attempt to bond, to keep the fleas, ticks and mites away as our near ancestors would have done, and as the chimpanzees still do to this day. The new bonding process is one that has developed with language, and so we keep each other abreast of the dangers, concerns and threats we face (Dunbar, 1998). Remember the Neanderthal example I gave earlier about needing to know how to attack and kill what could be our next meal? Well, it seems that we have gone one step further, and for our species to evolve and keep the other groups away from us, the ones who might steal our food and clothing, or attack us during the night, we can with the use of language inform our group as to the dangers that exist out there.

Stories by campfire

From the assumptions we make about paintings on the wall in caves or on Egyptian tombs, to Greek myths, to books such as the Bible and other texts passed down through the years, the way we communicate the information that could be important, the dangers we need to be aware of and the installation of the morals

DOI: 10.4324/9781003289210-4

and values that hold our societies is strung together in the stories we write and tell. Many of these stories have lessons and metaphors, many of the stories are made up and could not possibly happen, some are shrouded in magical ways, godlike scripts and mystical aspects and some are placed at the heart of indigenous communities and the way that world is perceived.

Symbols, words and language convey what we want others to know and understand and this has (apparently) been the way of our species since we could draw, speak and write. For an excellent book to read here, see *Sand Talk* by Tyson Yunkaporta (2019); what a delightful book this was and one that shaped my thinking about what it is we think we know.

As we move throughout the centuries, this knowledge has been questioned, changed and updated, and in line with Piaget's model of how children mature their thinking, this can also be said to apply to our levels of knowledge and understanding. When you consider how we make sense of the world and what we encounter, we are constantly assimilating and updating our schema, unless of course we do not read, converse or go outside of our comfort zones in the space of information. This is what is often called the echo chamber when you see this in relation to online spaces.

I would like to first challenge your thinking about the *information and its truthfulness* by quickly bringing up the following topics and then quickly moving on (as the topics that follow can spark emotive feelings in many people). So **briefly**:

1. We have been through two World Wars to date, and because of this, many, many people lost their lives for a cause that they were not fully informed about. Hitler asked the German people to burn books because they contained lies and untruths, or perhaps these went against what he wanted to push as a political agenda (please do your own critical analysis of this). And to date, when you read a piece of historical writing about this period, that has been written from the perspective of the country writing it, you will find conflicting information about these times when you read other countries' perspectives.
2. In 2020, many countries were placed into lockdown during the COVID-19 pandemic. At the **early stage** (the first couple of days to just over a week), it may have been unclear about the level of accurate information the public received, with some people suggesting (online and in conversations at the local supermarkets) that this was a political ruse and no such virus existed.
3. As we moved into the lockdown, the information about the COVID-19 virus was that it would cause uncontrollable 'voiding of the bowels', and so there was a fanatical rush to get as much 'loo roll' as possible, leading to a shortage in many places.
4. God made the world in seven days, but actually, this was six as he took Sunday off.
5. The holes in the ozone have been mended.
6. Santa Claus is real.
7. There is a way to 'fact check' everything written on the Internet, and these are unbiased ways of knowing the truth, so when you see this tag on a post you can trust it entirely with 100% certainty.

Some of those facts and statements are fibs. Well, they are not if you are a young child perhaps and believe in the obese man who *visits children during the night to bring them gifts for being good boys and girls* (this sounds like an illegal activity known as grooming?).

If you are religious and a Christian, you may believe the fourth but know that it means 'god' time and not man-made time such as hours and minutes.

And the statements relating to soldiers, members of the public and users of the Internet is *how can you know for sure?*

Knowing and sense-making

This is a philosophical concept and means, in short for this chapter, the way in which we see the world, and make sense of it, based on our way of knowing what we know and how we know. This is not going to be a chapter on metaphysics, but we do need to have a short lesson on what this means if you have never encountered this idea before. It will be simple, and I will keep it brief! To do so I want to explain three concepts, and then we can move along like the droids because these are not the issues you were looking for in this chapter.

Ontology is the way in which we come to know the truth or knowledge of the world. In short, do we see that knowledge is objective or subjective? Do we interpret what we see in either of these ways? For example, you may have learned in school that rocks are solid (objective) and from our parents, that hunger is something we feel (subjective).

Epistemology is how we came to know this way of seeing this truth. It is our environmental influence. For example, education in the UK often teaches an objective view of the world in science, as in you can measure how many particles are in a substance, how hot the temperature is and how fast a car is going.

Phenomenology means our own interpretation by us, the viewpoint of the world. This is a very subjective look at the world and, of course, is the 'filter' we use: for example, religion or science. It is the meaning that I place on my experiences, and my experience of the colour red is going to be qualitatively different to yours and we can never know for sure what this difference is.

> (Do check out the meaning-making lecturers, scientists, philosophers and educators mentioned in the introduction, because this topic is fascinating and underpins the essence of this chapter)

Keep it simple!

Our way of seeing the world is why we have so many viewpoints, so many versions of the truth (I'll come to that word in a moment), what our beliefs and ideas are made up of, what we learn, what we are told, what we do not believe, what we think, what we feel and what we know we know, and most of these are difficult to explain to someone else.

In our minds, through the topic of cognitive psychology works by Baddeley (2007), Eysenk & Keane (2000), Miller (1956) and many other greats in this field, and through the support of neuroscience, we have been able to ascertain that people have different types of memories and knowledge, and therefore it can be difficult to use words to explain some of this. For example, we have declarative memory such as knowing the capital city of England is London. We can tell you where the cups are in the kitchen, and we can explain the recipe for how to make a cake. But we also have procedural memory, which is our knowing how to do something, for example, catch a ball, ride a bike and how to check the cake we are baking and know that it is perfect right here, right now.

We also have this kind of memory for our own experiences (autobiographical) such as being able to declare which school we went to aged seven, and where this school is. And yet we would struggle to explain how we learned to catch a ball unless we broke it into steps like a recipe, based on our knowledge of how a child learns to catch a ball. We might not be able to tell you at what age we learned to catch the ball, but we will know we did it because we can catch a ball.

Memory, our filters and how we analyse incoming information

In transactional analysis we have a way of seeing the world that is often based on our perception of our right to exist and who we are (also known as the OK corral; Ernst, 1971). This window to the world (Hay, 2015) is considered that which we bring to our daily life. It is, simply put, how we perceive our autonomy and why we might struggle with information, sense and meaning making. I will endeavour to explain why this is important.

If you think of a quadrant: each of these is the way a person sees themselves in comparison to others. One quadrant holds the idea of, 'I am okay and you are okay'. The next is, 'I am okay and you are not okay'. The next, 'I am not okay, and you are okay', and lastly, 'I am not okay and you are not okay'.

So let's take each of these and think about the home in which a child is raised and how they come to learn about the world. I will give some short conversational examples to highlight these from mum's perspective so you can see how this is conveyed to the child.

I'm okay, you're okay

Child: 'Mum, I got told today that Santa isn't real!'

Mum: 'What do you think sweetie? I know that you saw your uncle dressed up at the fair and you know he was pretending for the other children, but what do you think?'

Child: 'Well, I know it's a nice surprise for my sister and she thinks he's real, but I did see dad bringing in the presents from the car last year. Don't worry, I won't tell Suzie though'.

Mum: 'That's great that you can see the idea behind keeping it magical for Suzie, and I hope you don't feel too disappointed about knowing it's us that do this?'

I'm okay, you're not okay

Child: 'Mum, I got told today that Santa isn't real!'

Mum: 'Well, I'm telling you he is!!'

Child: 'But I saw dad bring in the presents from the car last year'.

Mum: 'No you didn't, don't be silly, that was for something else. Santa is real, now do you think I'd lie to you, well do you?'

Child: 'Errr no' [now thinks that she really didn't see dad with the presents, and they must be for someone else. She now cannot trust herself and what she knows because others are telling her she is wrong, so she must be].

I'm not okay, you're okay

Child: 'Mum, I got told today that Santa isn't real!'

Mum: 'Oh god I knew this would happen, I really didn't mean for you to find out, and that must mean that I am going to get a right telling off by your dad when he finds out. Oh god I'm so stupid. Can you do me a favour, could you play along with daddy and tell him you believe? You're such a good girl, and you can make him believe you. He will think I'm such an idiot, oh damn it'.

Child: 'Of course mummy!' [child now knows she has information about the world that places her in a knowledgeable position above or on a level with her parent. She won't challenge people unless she wants to take the 'high ground' and make it known to them that she is clever or knows for sure. She also knows this results in others feeling bad when she does this]

I'm not okay, you're not okay

Child: 'Mum, I got told today that Santa isn't real!'

Mum: 'Oh shit really, by whom? Well, that's just grand because now you've spoiled it for us all. Have you told your sister? How did you find out?'

Child: 'Well I did see daddy bring in the presents from the car last year and when Billy told me I kinda knew he was telling the truth'.

Mum: 'Well it's spoiled now, your dad is going to be angry with both of us, and if you don't play along he will know. He will think it's me too so we had better just smile and pretend, you got me?'

Child: 'Erm okay mummy' [child now believes what she knows and saw is a terrible thing to know and this can result in others feeling bad, so don't tell the truth, ask questions or rock the boat].

The child goes to school

In the science lesson, she is told that puberty begins at 11 and the body is fully developed by the age of 18, and this includes the brain. Now this child happens to be the daughter of a neuroscientist father and adolescent health worker. She knows from conversations at home that this teacher hasn't given out the full truth, or perhaps she doesn't know about brain science and what we know about maturity, adolescence and neuroplasticity, just like you the reader who has this knowledge now. Does she speak up? Does she challenge the teacher, or does she tell her friends this is not true or is a lie? Does she now, in the age of the Internet, go home and make a post about this, send someone a WA critiquing the child, or does she ask Mum or Dad to contact the school or do they put a post on social media about this 'lesson'?

Well, these answers depend upon those beliefs she has about herself and her right to speak up or out. If she challenges the teacher and is reprimanded, will she learn to stay silent or will it become a way of passive-aggressively posting about these issues in online forums and calling people idiots?

Maybe this child also believes in her teacher because she likes her and takes in the education without questions because teachers know what they are talking about, and she had the handouts and the book there to 'prove it'. Teachers are not allowed to educate about things that aren't true, are they? Well, this also depends on her upbringing in this community, social circle and time in history. As spoken about in book one, until the '80s we thought infants couldn't feel pain and in the past, we drowned women to see if they were witches #schemaupdated. We now know *gravity exists* thanks to Einstein, *evolution is as it is* thanks to Charles Darwin and *sand is great* thanks to Brian Cox.

So why do we need to know about worldviews, ways of knowing, self-interpretations, meaning making and of course the family script dynamics of what *should* be believed? Well, in short, each of these predisposes us to what we think we know about the world, what we are prepared to listen to, what we can allow our minds to 'open up to' (a personality trait too) and what we are prepared to make sense of should this information make it into our awareness. The capacity to utilise this. The traits, cognitive approaches and ways of seeing the world of the people you work with matters as much as the issue. For example, how can you expect changes, and create an open dialogue if you force *your worldview* upon the ones you are helping?

Online truths, untruths, misdirection and smoke and mirrors

And so we move to gossip, well-intended advice, misinterpretations, opinions, fears, amygdala hijacks, interpretations, subjectivity, half-untruths, sort-of truths, half-truths, lies and THE truth. For an exceptional read on this topic, have a read of Terry Pratchett's book *The Truth* (2000). You may find a recurrent theme in the books whereby we recognise that humans are often the common denominator in many of the issues discussed, and not technology. So let me use a metaphor and concept that you are likely very familiar with if you have chosen to read this book: the algorithm.

Many people have heard of the algorithm, but do not necessarily know what it is or how it works. Yet you understand guessing, estimating and probabilities because you do this all the time in your waking hours. An algorithm, simply put, is a process that is created to 'work out' what the most likely outcome will be. It is the things that feed themselves, and now I feel I'm writing a horror novel.

For the geeks: an algorithm is a mathematical set of (computational) propositions, instructions and decisions, often depicted by images of flowcharts and logic gates in order to solve a problem. However, the understanding many people in my therapy room present with is that it is a computer code intended to create a behavioural response. This, it would seem, is down to the language used by the corporate companies in the public domain as they try to emphasise and explain how their technology works. Unfortunately on a number of occasions, I have witnessed politicians and people in high-power roles attempt to use this language, whilst not fully understanding it and further compounding the confusion that the layperson has when they are looking at technology (or in my experience when I am trying to teach and the listeners misinterpret what is being said, as many of us are not #nerds, #geeks and computer programmers). The language of technology can be confusing, talks about 'end users', not people, and discusses complex equations and processes that the average person doesn't really care about, so, aligned with teaching e-safety, road safety and health and safety, it often results in complacency, boredom and half listening.

All of which can be problematic or not? I mean if I asked you to explain an algorithm now would you even care, what does it matter, Cath, I am trying to learn what to do with and say to young people about online harms and cybertrauma. The truth is, it probably doesn't matter that much, but if I can gently provoke your reticular activation system, then my work is done by giving you this information. And you will never know if that is the truth of the matter because we can't measure what I just said (see what I did there?).

Are you going to trust anything I say in this book from now on?

Best I use supporting evidence for my claims then (is a wink emoticon appropriate here?).

You see, brains are lazy, but not in the negative sense of choosing not to do something due to lack of motivation or giving a hoot, but lazy in so far as efficient and great at creating shortcuts to save processing overload. Simply put, there is too much 'stuff' and information to attend to at any one minute, and so the brain likes to have this background noise *in the background* until it becomes necessary to pay attention. For example, you may remember in the first book I talked about the orienting response, which is a primal reflex that turns our attention to something that moves just in case it is a threat. We have this internal threat detector in our nervous systems – neuroception (Porges, 2011) – and we have the visual, auditory and olfactory systems that also threat detect, and this is why we turn toward movement, smell and sound (van der Kolk, 1994). Taste and touch also work in this way.

To highlight this, another thought experiment for you: have you ever tried to not look at the driver or passengers in the car that you are overtaking or is overtaking you? What about that person that walks past the meeting window or the birds or the leaf that just whooshed past? It's akin to 'not being able to help it'. We want to know what that was, or what they look like, or what they are doing and where they are going. We want to know if they look like a threat, e.g., are they angry because we just cut them up on the road? Or we can choose to look at them in a threatening manner if they cut us up! Our eyes are drawn to this movement, and we cannot help ourselves in the judgement and thinking process that accompanies it either.

Brains like to create plans, maps and predictions about the world to save us time and effort so we can dedicate our time to the important stuff. In doing so we make errors of judgment, errors based on our past experiences, errors in what we think we have seen or heard (think visual illusions here too) and we are likely to see the world in our framework or what is often called our way of seeing things. Kahneman (2012) talks about our brains and thinking as processes, having one system for fast in-the-moment judgements (often with errors) and one dedicated to working out analytical (also with errors) judgements due to implicit biases of the slower process. Our brains are constantly keeping us alive by decisions they make, and even if they are wrong that good old Amy R can tell us, 'See I saved your life so who cares if it wasn't *the truth*, you're alive aren't you, I did my job!'

And so brains and bodies are created to ensure that this negativity bias is always on hand (Hanson, 2018).

The algorithms we use in our head are based on those phenomenological meanings, those epistemic and ontological computations based on our age, time and space, and what we are subjected to in the world, and the online spaces are adding to the complexity of this informational overload and it's making us, well, *stupider* (not a real word but one that gets used by children in my clinic, I like it)? Are we taking the time to critically analyse what we read, or do we swallow it whole and take up arms based on a few tweets, posts and comments? It would seem that way. Jonathan Haidt (2012) has discussed this in depth in his book *The Righteous Mind*, with the *Social Dilemma* documentary created by the Centre for Humane Technology (CHT, 2020) highlights about the limbic hijack of why we behave like this. Especially when the feed on social media taps into these biases and uses misinformation and disinformation to drive the polarisations and uprisings we have been seeing in the last few years.

What about the lexicon of information, misinformation and disinformation?

As with the rest of the book, I will give a brief explanation of these terms, however, please note that we would be well versed to think critically about some of the issues by saying that people consciously know what they are doing all of the time (if you have been paying attention to the impact of trauma and attachment you will know why this is true here). Furthermore, intent, as discussed in other chapters, is perhaps one of the most difficult concepts to 'prove' unless and until we go down the *Minority Report* route and have brain implants that can predict, with accuracy, what and why someone is doing something. These terms that follow are a broad spectrum of how these terms classify this type of sharing of information. For many of you readers, the next idea isn't going to be a surprise, that these actions can be used as a part of the issues associated with cyberbullying, trolling, flaming, trends and hoaxes, abuse, grooming and all of the other harms that are within these volumes.

The metaphysics of how we understand the following means that we can look to language and semantics, computer and information technology or philosophy. One of the earliest articles I could find that approached all of these terms was in the computing space (Fetzer, 2004), however much of the recent scholarly, governmental and regulatory aspects has been focused on either COVID-19 and the vaccine versus anti-vaccine communities or about elections and the sway of fake articles and hacking. So looking at the recent book by Culloty and Suiter (2021), we can see this as a perspective that is approaching what we encounter via electronic technologies and not 'some bloke at the pub' or 'what Aunt Vera said last Sunday'. For example, Culloty and Suiter quote that the COVID-19 pandemic resulted in:

> The World Health Organisation (WHO, 2021) called it an 'infodemic': an overabundance of accurate and inaccurate claims that left many people confused about what to believe. In this context, it is unsurprising that a sense of crisis has become entrenched among policymakers, scholars, technologists, and others.
>
> (Page 8)

But, please bear in mind children often hear information, misinformation and disinformation in family settings, and in the community in which they live. Especially those under the age of ten, who are often not reading the news articles, but maybe seeing news headlines, memes or short posts online. This can also be TV, radio and, as said in the chapter on health, podcasts.

Consumption, access and maturity

If children have an abundance of devices, and access to many sites and platforms that they are not old enough to sign up for under the children's code, or data protection regulation legislation, which is currently 13 years of age, then this could mean children are exposed to information that is beyond their level of maturity, and as such discerning the wheat from the chaff is going to be even more difficult given the cognitive capacity of children younger than 12 (see Knibbs, 2016, 2022, for an in-depth examination of this). So whilst the following is a definition of what information is, please bear in mind this may be fantasy and fiction for children under the age of 12, or perhaps 10, or they may not even understand it at all and that therefore does not meet the semantics of what information is for this age group.

Information

Collins English Dictionary has two variants of this word:

a) Information about someone or something consists of facts about them.
b) Information consists of the facts and figures that are stored and used by a computer program.

So the parallel aspect here in both of these variants is the *idea of a fact*. A fact, going back to that earlier aspect of metaphysics is both objective and subjective and can be the phenomenology of a person's experience, because a feeling is a fact, for example, hunger. Now what becomes opaque with this kind of epistemological thinking is how we know what hunger is and how we measure it, if we even could. And so, being that squeaky wheel that is always asking why, how do we know a fact is a fact or does this mean a scientific fact, undisputable until someone falsifies it, which is the rationale of science, and of course what we do personally with our assimilation of new 'facts' and updated schema? Ah, that timeless ontological mess of do we really know anything at all?

I am aware I muddled and played with words there, but if I was seven and I heard on the news that coronavirus was going to kill 80% of old people, I wouldn't necessarily know if that was a fact, and I probably couldn't work out what 80% was, I would just know that Granpappy was old and he was over 80 (I know, I saw the birthday cards) and I would make an assumption this fact was true. True. Granpappy is going to die of coronavirus.

This truthful information is based on statistics known by healthcare and epidemiologists, but this seven-year-old just hears fear conveyed as a truth.

Misinformation

The *Collins English Dictionary* defines this term as: *wrong* information, which is given to someone, often in a deliberate attempt to make them believe something which is not true.

This is portrayed as the misleading use of information, and if you notice the italics, it denotes it is incorrect or wrong in the factual aspect attributed to the definition of information earlier in the chapter. However, what I would like to poke the bear with here is: who decides the information is 'wrong' rather than misunderstood or a mistake that someone may make? Again, the route of science is when the hypothesis is refuted, we can say something is no longer true. So when the fact finders and attribution of a tag or mark on a piece of information is labelled as 'misleading', is this based on critical thinking, research and evidence or using the evidence we have to date (meaning it still may be possible to refute the hypothesis)? For example, I have in the past seen information portrayed as being true, only to find out later that the evidence produced was skewed and in one case a significant result found due to an input error on the calculations. I am sure that you have seen the information about superfoods and carcinogenic food groups being flip-flopped about, such as the claims made about coffee, tomatoes, goji berries and more.

Given we had the 'infodemic' of facts being shared online about COVID-19, and there was the playground-type process of throwing research at each other online, how is the public not versed in research supposed to know what is correct or true, let alone untrue, misleading or lies? Using cherry-picked facts to argue skewed results, manipulated research, strawman and steelman arguments, and the academic vigour of counter-research arguments and debate, it is no wonder that there was the 'infodemic' of confusion and what on earth type feelings I am sure many of us felt. And as the practitioner reading this, I wonder how many young people asked you, the expert (as they often see us as), what your thoughts were, and I wonder in which direction you were skewed, biased or believed. Well, that may depend on what platforms censored and when, and that is a whole chapter in itself. Safe to say you will have been exposed to information that was fact-checked and the 'stuff' that platforms censored may not have been in your awareness unless you know the darker streets of the Internet where those conversations took place (keeping up with tech is a full-time job, and knowing the forums and spaces that emerge as direct results of and in opposition to censorship has been tiring to keep up with).

UK Parliament (2022) has also produced guidelines and reports on the spread of misinformation and disinformation around the COVID-19 pandemic, suggesting that:

> The world also faced an 'infodemic' of information – both accurate and false. The Government takes the issue of disinformation and misinformation very seriously. . . . The Government recognises the threat presented by disinformation and misinformation online and is taking action to address this. The Government is aiming to publish the Online Harms full Government Response later this year.

The London School of Economics (Edwards et al., 2021) and Ofcom (2022) also looked at this, and in a report from Edwards et al. suggesting:

> Misinformation can result in the public not taking public health advice as in the case of Covid-19 and the vaccine uptake rates with much of this information being shared online as to why they should not. And in the case of climate change, there can be a denial of this even being genuine information.

> In short, misinformation results in questioning, denial and delay in following advice, mistrust of politicians and journalists and conspiracy theories appearing about all sorts of issues. There are claims of mass psychosis, from podcasters and influencers using this term (for example Joe Rogan), and articles suggesting that there is a mass-delusion, epistemic crisis and maladies of mistrust (Pierre, 2022) and what the Centre for Humane Technology refers to as 'The Knowledge Gap' (https://humanetech.org).

The seven-year-old

Zoe is sitting at home listening to Newsround, which states that the vaccine is going to be given to children soon; she hears Dad in the kitchen say, 'Not on my life is she getting that poison injected into her, I heard it can cause autism'. Now Dad is not deliberately telling Zoe that the injection is going to cause autism, but he heard it on a podcast about the vaccines given to pregnant women in the past, when the presenter was making a comparative statement about this type of misunderstanding some years ago (this debate is worthy of reading around in Ben Goldacre's *Bad*

Science, 2008). Dad has misunderstood, and now Zoe is 'in receipt' of misinformation. What do you think she will think, feel and do? Is it within your role to correct her, and what do you think Dad's response might be to that?

Disinformation

Again, starting with the Collins definition: 'If you accuse someone of spreading disinformation, you are accusing them of spreading false information in order to deceive people'.

> 'They spread disinformation in order to discredit politicians'.
> '. . . a disinformation campaign, deliberately misleading citizens'.

A great example here of how this can be seen to be the deliberate act of sharing false information, often referred to as fake news, as well as disinformation (and deepfakes, covered shortly) is what small children would refer to as lies or fibs. And the intent behind the sharing of this false information is to create a change in behaviour and entrench mistrust in those they spread the false information about. It sort of sounds like how politics was once described to me, and yet if you look at this particular aspect, this is exactly what governments, politicians and leaders have been accusing each other of for some time, way before the Internet existed, and is how fights and wars can begin, based on propaganda, rumours and falsities. Looking at the disinformation process in the book by Culloty and Suiter (2021), they refer to three elements: *bad actors*, who are the people creating, spreading and pushing this content, and this occurs on *platforms* whereby they can also be a part of the problem by allowing this, supporting this either through non-removal or hosting it, and allowing the further distribution – and the *audiences* who further this through meaning and interactions. A final reflection in their book is the actions that are taken to counter this, which they detail in a chapter on countermeasures.

This three-part process would suggest that people have a motivated interest to cause panic, fear, uproar, mistrust, divisions, polarisation, civil unrest and perhaps even war.

These bad actors can be humans or bots and could be:

A jilted lover or employee who shares inaccurate information or lies about an ex-partner or boss, for example.

A political agenda at the local or national level that is pushing for the narrative of their group, and causes mistrust using false information about their 'opponents'.

The creation of doctored text, images and video deepfakes.

Groups who have religious or ideological views.

Angry parents whose child was hurt, abused, assaulted or even reprimanded by adults, staff, school, police or the justice system.

Scared parents who think that certain actions will harm their children and who take up arms, so to speak.

Vigilantes aiming to get justice for a non-guilty verdict, or case that has been dropped.

Or anyone with a vested interest in creating a false narrative about someone else for many reasons, which include revenge, hatred or disgust. For example, homophobic family members, biological parents who have had their child taken into care or family members who are now estranged.

Or someone who shares this information after reading it and believing it (mis or dis?).

The audiences who engage with this material are often making decisions about the (dis)information they see based on emotions, scripts, beliefs and their level of intelligence in being able to critically analyse the statements, facts and figures. See Kahneman (2012), as this 'system one and two thinking' is also a term now used in the conversations appearing in the domain of media literacy. The countermeasures proffered by Culloty and Suiter (2021), Digital, Culture, Media and Sport Committee (2021) and Ofcom (2021) all suggest media literacy is the key to being able to discern whether the information is from a credible source, with Ofcom showing in research in 2022 that 30% of adults fail to question misinformation (this research looked at respondents aged 12 plus).

What has been interesting to see over the last few years has been the introduction of roles in digital platforms for disinformation officers, experts and journalistic fact-checking units, departments and more. Given the large media focus on the issue of the 'interference' of the US elections that appeared in 2016, the knowledge of this issue has at one point been a conversation that many people have engaged in (Bradshaw & Howard, 2019; Pierre, 2022). However, as with the pain-forgetting process, many people have forgotten that disinformation is still being carried out, and so have returned to their default setting, in so far as they would only see this as a thing if it were outrageously in contrast to something they believed already.

And this is not a new phenomenon; for example, take the people who believe the moon landing was faked, the Earth is flat and a certain president won the election even though his competitor took the role (I am aware I might just be pushing certain buttons here in some readers and I have no idea if you believe any of these things, I am using them as largely argued points).

Practitioner pause for reflection

Lastly, the point I would like to end with, in this chapter, is: the children and young people exposed to online sources and content are not intelligence agents, they are not super sleuths or special services. They are working their way through the world and are exposed to opinions, facts and fibs, and their job as a child is often 'not to question', nor would they be able to if they didn't ask the 'why' question. However, we rapidly close this down in the early years because it would require us to think and give answers when we are busy or, perhaps, we don't know the answers. It is okay for us to say this and to use these moments to become mini journalists ourselves, looking for what Steven Kolter said (2020, personal communication) was his minimum in journalism of five credible sources, and looking for the outlier of the person who said something different than the other four! We are looking for the piece of information that debunks, or questions, a number that can verify and support, and keeping in our awareness that marginalised people and groups often have a point to make and can be prepared to 'fight dirty' to keep their views.

> Learn what cognitive dissonance is and remember that all aspects of our lives are now under threat by false information at any time in the online space. This includes propaganda, lies and conspiracies fed by algorithms and those algorithms are often the '*human algorithm*'.

(Knibbs, 2019)

References

Baddeley, A. (2007). *Working memory thought and action*. Oxford University Press: Oxford.

Bradshaw, S., & Howard, P. (2019). *The global disinformation order: 2019 Global inventory of organised social media manipulation*. Oxford Internet Collins Dictionary: Oxford. Information, Misinformation and Disinformation. www.collinsdictionary.com/dictionary/english/information.

Centre for Humane Technology (CHT). (2020). The Social Dilemma (2021). *Centre for Humane Technology*. https://www.humanetech.com/ Aired on Netflix 2021.

Culloty, E., & Suiter, J. (2021). *Disinformation and manipulation in digital media: Information pathologies*. Routledge: Abingdon.

Digital, Culture, Media and Sport Committee. (2021). *Second report of session 2019–21*. Misinformation in the COVID-19 Infodemic (HC 234). House of Commons: London.

Dunbar, R. (1998). *Grooming gossip and the evolution of language*. Harvard University Press: Harvard.

Edwards, L., Stoilova, M., Anstead, N., Fry, A., El-Halaby, G., & Smith, M. (2021). *LSE Consulting. Rapid evidence assessment on online misinformation and media literacy*. https://www.lse.ac.uk/business/consulting/reports/rapid-evidence-assessment-on-online-misinformation-and-media-literacy.

Ernst, F. (1971). The OK corral: The grid or get-on-with. *TAJ*, 1(4).

Eysenk, M., & Keane, M. (2000). *Cognitive psychology: A student's handbook* (4th ed.). Psychology Press: London.

Fetzer, J. (2004). Information, misinformation, and disinformation. *Minds and Machines*, 14(2), 223–229.

Goldacre, B. (2008). *Bad science*. Fourth Estate: London.

Haidt, J. (2012). *The righteous mind. Why good people are divided by politics and religion*. Penguin: London.

Hanson, R. (2018). *Resilient. Find your inner strength*. Rider: London.

Hay, J. (2015). *Windows to the world*. United Kingdom Association Transactional Analysis Conference: Blackpool.

Kahneman, D. (2012). *Thinking fast and slow*. Penguin: London.

Kotler, S. (2020). *Flow for writers*. Personal Communication, May 2020.

Knibbs, C. (2016). *Cybertrauma; The darker side of the internet*. Self-published and available on Amazon Kindle and Blurb Books.

Knibbs, C. (2019). *The human algorithm*. https://childrenandtech.co.uk/2021/05/21/the-human-algorithm-that-schools-and-parents-feed-through-fear-concerning-social-media-trends/.

Knibbs, C. (2022). *Children, technology and healthy development*. Routledge: Abingdon.

Miller, G. (1956). The magical number seven, plus or minus two: Some limits on our capacity for processing information. *Psychological Review*, 63, 81–89.

Ofcom. (2021). *Life online podcast: The genuine article: Tackling misinformation*. South West Grid for Learning. Accessed August 23, 2022.

Pierre, J. (2022). Mistrust and the possibility of civil war. *Psychology Today*. www.psychology today.com/us/blog/psych-unseen/202209/mistrust-misinformation-and-the-possibility-civil-war-in-america.

Porges, S. (2011). *The polyvagal theory. Neurophysiological foundations of emotions, attachment, communication and self-regulation*. W. W. Norton & Co: New York.

Pratchett, T. (2000). *The truth*. (25th Discworld Novel). Doubleday: London.

UK Parliament. (2022). *Online harms and disinformation*. House of Commons: London. https://committees.parliament.uk/committee/438/digital-culture-media-and-sport-subcommittee-on-online-harms-and-disinformation/.

Van der Kolk, B. (1994). The body keeps the score: Memory and the evolving psychobiology of post-traumatic stress. *Harvard Review of Psychiatry*, 1(5), 253–265.

World Health Organisation. WHO. (2021). *Infodemic*. www.who.int/health-topics/infodemic.

Yunkaporta, T. (2019). *Sand talk. How indigenous thinking can save the world*. Text Publishing: Melbourne.

4 Cyberbullying

Every chapter, topic and section of this book can be seen through the lens of one or more of the other sections, chapters and topics.

Cyberbullying: no such thing?

> What is 'cyber' 'bullying'? The complexities of typology, definitions, intent and omission of power from standard theories and phenomena create a space as big as life itself, and what do we do about those darn bots?

Starting with hackers?

Once upon a time when the Internet began, I suspect we hoped we would be able to label and categorise events according to 'where' they occurred, or indeed how. For example, having your data, server or computer intruded upon, without your permission, invite or knowledge, became known as *hacking*. And in today's world, if you ask someone to break into your system to test it, they are often called ethical hackers or penetration testers. If anyone reading this is thinking they know what a hacker looks like, or what kind of person is a hacker then you only need to go back to the movies of the '80s (too many to list here) and you'll often find that the stereotype is of a lonely young adolescent, versed in programming and 'code'. This person was typified as the geek, nerd or weird, usually portrayed as a young male who would be furiously typing at the keyboard and 'hacking' the FBI or some large bank.

This stereotype has been discussed (as recently as 2020) by senior officers from the police, cybercrime professionals and other colleagues in cybercrime and advisory-related spaces, conferences and meetings that I have attended over the last decade or so (alongside the stereotype of that male being on the neurodiversity spectrum). However, the facts are generally skewed in the direction of hackers being young males, as they are the ones who have mostly been arrested and charged over the years (Nissenbaum, 2004; Steinmetz, 2015).

And so, early in the computing space, criminal behaviours could be typologised and became about what, where, when and how. This approach of being able to study behaviours online (often criminal or deviant in nature), led to

DOI: 10.4324/9781003289210-5

a branch of psychology called cyberpsychology that would reveal the intents, modus operandi and explanations of the personality types and motivations of cyber criminals' behaviours; it even resulted in spin-off TV series about cyber-crime such as *Cyber CSI*, where a well-known cyberpsychologist called Mary Aitkin (2015) advised the makers of this program see www.maryaiken.com/. We have also seen the rhetoric and explosion of psychological theories presenting themselves to explain activities online, as well as the human behind these behaviours; this paradigm, discipline and section of the British Psychological Society (BPS) is expanding all the time, which is incredibly exciting. www.bps.org.uk/member-networks/cyberpsychology-section.

This leads me to the overlap of cyberbullying into this theoretical space, and where we began to where we are now. So as with most of the subjects I write about, let's go back to the start, which always starts with babies and toddlers. But first let's see what bullying is so we can employ this learning from a child-development perspective to the online space.

Bully, troll or lolz?

Bullying in the corporeal world (the real world), has been defined over the years and contains some elements that make this identifiable, and in discourse, we use this definition to explain behaviour that contains these elements. The most common definition of bullying is the one used by the Anti-Bullying Alliance (https://anti-bullyingalliance.org.uk/), which reads:

> Bullying is the repetitive, intentional hurting of one person or group by another person or group, where the relationship involves an imbalance of power. It can happen face-to-face or online.

This definition, according to ABA, is grounded in 30 years of research. And their website includes terms like 'baiting':

> To 'bait' someone is to intentionally make a person angry by saying or doing things to annoy them.
> Baiting is a provocative act used to solicit an angry, aggressive or emotional response from another individual.

Also, they include advice on this issue, with tips like:

> What NOT to do [capitalised on the website and so emphasised here]:
> **Don't** take the bait!
> **Don't** argue with a person or appeal to their sense of reason or logic while they are baiting you. They want you to rise to it!
> **Don't** retaliate and fall into a trap.
> (I will talk about the injunctions here in just a moment)

And finally, there is a page discussing banter, which the dictionary defines as follows:

> Banter is the playful and friendly exchange of teasing remarks.
> With a tip for professionals about:
> Understanding the four elements of bullying is vital to knowing whether something is bullying: intentional, hurtful, repetitive, involves a power imbalance.
> And:
> All offensive, threatening, violent and abusive language and behaviour is always unacceptable, whatever your role.
> (ABA, 2022, accessed online)

Bully babies, toddlers and aggression like no other?

We teach babies and toddlers to be kind and, in return, these young children can understand the concept of being mean, nasty and 'no hurting!' For example, the young toddler or one-year-old that just bit their sibling or hit the pet rabbit. We often use these words to educate and discipline (hopefully not punish; although I know some parents who bite their children back).

These little humans can and do use the term bully, without comprehending the reasons why a person is carrying out this behavior, and they don't need to. It's all about the impact the child feels. Sometimes the child will say the parent is a bully for saying no, not letting them have their way or for teasing them, which many parents do (according to the previous definition, this is not banter). These tiny humans are correct here when it's teasing and they feel inadequate, hurt, powerless, humiliated, angry, confused, shamed, ridiculed and so on and so on. But that's not how many parents report this. Not in my clinic anyway.

Toddlers are aggressive. Not just as a behaviour that we can see, but necessary as a transitional process to becoming someone who can empathise, socialise and relate. Toddlers are unable, and I repeat unable, to emotionally regulate their behaviours, which include outward forms of aggression, frustration and anger towards another person (or animal). They need the adult to help them regulate their body and brain emotions, in what we call co-regulation, until they can do it themselves (Delahooke, 2020, 2022). They learn this through cause-effect processes such as: I hit x and y happens. This might be seeing the other person or animal cry out in pain, the stern adult reprimanding them for their behaviour or the victim reciprocally hitting them back and causing them pain. It's all a learning curve. And often the process of learning socialising norms, e.g., not hitting others, results from a fear of being reprimanded. Children learn quickly through fear and shame, and this is the punitive measure most parents sadly make, because if you ask them what is going on when their toddler strikes out, they may tell you 'they assume other people will think of them as being bad parents', and so they shut this behaviour down rapidly to ensure that the toddler 'plays nice' with other children. Other parents punish because they were bullied and they say 'they cannot tolerate bullies and won't have their child being or becoming one'.

Shame. It underpins so much of our behaviour and it's how we often educate children and others. So, let's look to the development of morals and how this shows up in children, so we can see another layer to the behaviours we see online.

Kohlberg and moral development

Using some theories from moral development, in this case, the most well-known of Kohlberg's writing (1971), we can see that a small child aged three to seven begins to understand the world through the eyes of intent and impact, and of course this often goes hand in hand with the development of the theory of mind proposed by Piaget (1926), or what is called mentalising by Fonagy (2001; Fonagy et al., 2004), and empathy in the work of Goleman (1995), and Hanson (2018). This is the next level of comprehension to follow after the toddler rage, moving the small child into the world of what behaviours are acceptable and why.

In Kohlberg's theory, children develop a sense of right and wrong, usually as is instructed to them by adults (through religious and societal messages), and through this, they are able to see that they have an impact on the world through their behaviour. This moral development requires that a child can think in those 'me, my and self, other, them and you' relationships. What a person may feel when, what a person might do when and what a person might think when an event occurs. This requires cognition and the development of that 'front end of the house with the critical thinking residents' I mentioned in my book (Knibbs, 2022). It requires imagination, perspective, empathy, compassion and interpersonal relationship values, and this is where the morals really begin to lay down what is considered 'right'.

Transactional analysis

This section is going to explain the concept of the little professor or little scientist (called the little adult in TA) which is the early, experimental hypothesis-testing agent that lives inside all of us. This is the toddler who pushes the cat off the sofa to see what happens, the toddler who jumps from the chair after being told not to and so on. It is a part of our personal and ego development, which says 'I wonder what will happen if?' and sometimes it likes to test those moments of 'don't you . . .' You know, just to see what happens. Some children test this repeatedly and some only ever carry this out once.

I mentioned earlier 'injunctions' (highlighted in bold on the don't messages) and to develop that thinking here a little I need to explain what these are in terms that are easy to understand. We will begin with a memory exercise. Can you remember back to your childhood, carrying a cup of liquid (tea, pop, etc.) and you would be walking with it when your parents exclaimed, 'Don't spill the drink!' Can you remember what this felt like, or what likely happened; where the idea of spilling it now was front and centre in your mind and so became the thing that happened? Shortly followed by some sort of 'I knew it' remark?

These don't message can be so potent that a child hears them and believes there to be something about them that requires this to be said. In TA it's often said the child swallows the don't message and it becomes internalised with a lifelong fight to alleviate the distress that it creates. Now, these early childhood injunctions are about the person, not a 'don't spill the drink' message.

However, the internalisation of this 'don't' prefix becomes a feeling that goes something like this:

> 'I got told not to spill the drink and it happened . . . therefore . . . it's me, there's something wrong with me . . .' and this becomes the feeling, word and behaviour associated with the shameful feeling of 'I am bad'.

Now imagine a child is relating to another online and says something that falls under the banner of bullying, non-banter or baiting, because half an hour ago at the end of school one of the other children said something that evoked a feeling of shame. Or perhaps they are gaming, and they fail at a particular task and respond from a nonregulated state. Someone teases them about their skills, and they respond to that teasing.

> Oh no!!! I rose to the bait, I fell for the trap and that must mean I really am bad, I said something mean, nasty, racist and I am a terrible person.

For some children: cue terrible feelings about the self, which could possibly result in self-harming behaviours, self-critical talk, lowering of self-esteem, self-hatred, depression, anxiety and so on and so on.

Victim–blaming language, don'ts and do people really have a conscious 'choice'?

This is one reason why victim-blaming language has the impact it does on the adults in society, never mind the children – for example, 'oh it's my fault I got mugged because clearly, it was my fault as I got told how not to become a victim, and I must have not followed the advice properly', or, 'it's me' or 'I became a victim of burglary because I am bad, I got told by that poster "don't become a victim" and I did! If I followed the advice but it still happened, then there must be something wrong with me', and to think of volume one's issues here: 'I got groomed because I did something I was told not to and that's definitely my fault'.

Victims don't have a choice, it is exercised upon them, done unto them and is about the behavioural choices of the other person (it can be said that there is a reason why they carry out that behaviour and that requires deeper thought, more human-behaviour theory and more trauma theory than I have time to go into in this book, but for this chapter think that most of the cyberbullying behaviours discussed here are about relationships for these children and not heinous crimes like murder).

Practitioner pause for reflection

How easy is it as the practitioner working with the child if we only follow do and don't messages? What would you do or say to the child in the previous examples, if you explained that they took the bait and therefore they were now at fault? Would you be able to identify whether this was bullying, retaliation to baiting, a moment of dysregulation, frustration or was linked to other corporeal issues that overlap into the online space? What do you think about don't messages and how do you feel when you hear them?

How does it feel for you to get advice from another person only to forget it in the heat of the moment, and what do you say to yourself afterwards?

> This is really all about neuroscience and attachment, and if we understand the brain's processing in the moment of dysregulation, trauma histories and threat (perceived or real), we can understand why these processes occur. Therefore, my first book (Knibbs, 2016), was comprehensive in covering this as the foundation for the books on online harm and cybertrauma named herein.

If you haven't read the sections on gaming and social media in my first book, please do, because section number one describes the relational process that underpins bullying in those spaces, and it's more complicated than I can describe here, but safe to say that human behaviour is always rooted in interpersonal connections, processes and attachment. If our early experiences are filled with punitive measures, not compassion, rage, disappointment, shame, disconnect, relational poverty and neurodivergence away from social and emotional intelligence, then you are going to repeatedly see these issues, and no amount of telling the *cortical thinking brain in isolation* is going to result in changed behaviours. If that were the case, my job as a therapist would be as easy as the Bob Newhart video (2010): 'Stop It' see www.youtube.com/watch?v=Ow0lr63y4Mw.

Stop it, don't and never! If this is no good, what is?

At this point, I need to confess that I have potentially riled up and baited a few readers, so let's bring this back to the theory and what we know works in the world of co-regulation. I have not said we should not teach children not to behave in deliberately intended ways to hurt others, though it may have been read that way by some. The way we develop morals and values is to think through behaviours and empathise with the feelings of others so we learn not to engage in those behaviours, when we are in a regulated state. Please do notice that last reflection, we can only ever make conscious, deliberate choices in a well-regulated state. Conscious choices require a prefrontal cortex 'online', and being able to think forward in time, with language at the helm helping us decide what to do that fits with our understanding of morality, compassion, empathy and consequential behaviours. In the words of Dan Siegel: '*when we are safe, with a mind that is coherent, differentiated and linked (2016) and we are in the driver's seat!*'

Thinking back to the little-professor approach in TA, we can see that children experiment in the world to see 'what will happen', and in doing so test these theories often and with different people in different contexts, in order that they can create an updated set of rules about relationships, build values and fit into the society they live in, and how they can build and maintain those friendships. Children are very quick to learn how to do this in the world of gaming for example, where they visit on a regular basis and 'listen in' to the others in that space. Often these are adults, and yes we know they really ought not to be in these places, but if it isn't here it could be the local town centre where they hear some of this language and watch people to learn by example. They really are little scientists and professors! So when they are watching the adults, they are building their new 'book of rules', called the schema in cognitive psychology a term used by Vygotsky (1933) which is discussed at length by Rieber and Carton (1993) in the book about Vygotsky where he first looked at learning difficulties and special education needs.

Piaget and the schema, and how a child thinks

Piaget proposed that this schema is updated through the process of assimilation of new evidence and experiences, and of course this is what we may think of as learning. If you also consider the process of survival as learning to adapt, you can substitute this for the idea of intelligence. It is likely that you are thinking of intelligence as those good old measurements of IQ and scores on tests. So, let's update your schema to the idea of intelligence being multifactorial and consisting of many facets such as emotions, language, social skills, self-regulation, creativity, mindset, passion and more. It includes domains often called the humanities such as music, art, and relationships as well as those that are quantifiable, such as logical tests and language skills. For a wonderful reflection of intelligence and how it is more nuanced than the paradigm in which scholars are still seemingly fighting over the best measure of this, do read the work of Scott Barry Kaufman (2013) as well as those who follow in Piaget's footsteps in this space.

Piaget and the process of thinking and reasoning describe to us via a stages model of how a child assimilates and integrates the information we pass to them (alongside their own experiential learning) and how this develops into those morals, values and ideals. How they can take the messages of the world they live in and understand it and make sense of it. Cue the world of modelling online by adults and how this becomes aligned with the levels of thinking.

Piaget suggested that children evolve their thinking through complexities as they age. These stages are: sensorimotor, preoperational, concrete operational and formal operational. In the early stages given here, they are how we see the under-six-or-seven-years-of-age cohorts. These stages are not to be dismissed, as part of this thinking process involves that thinking as being held within the child as feelings associated with events, behaviours and rules of the world (remember the injunctions?). However, when we get to the latter two stages of concrete and formal, we are looking at children who begin to use rational-thinking processes and utilise critical thinking with abstract concepts and ideas, and this forms the mature adult brain at the later stages of adolescence. It is in this latter stage, post 21 years of age for most children, that a child can question the motivation of behaviour in order to be able to 'spot the signs' of the bait, comprehend the intention behind those moments that might be banter and its possible misdirection and of course understand the meanings behind the behaviours, language and threats perceived and felt as bullying.

The president or queen of the Internet?

However, when it comes to the morals of the world, children are often 'given' these rules by their parents as to what is considered acceptable or not *in this* family, and here in the extended family and beyond. Now going back to the idea of alloparenting (Wilson, 1975) that I approached in the first book, you can see that morals and ethics are also societal messages that we get from others. This then means that the rules here in this society in this time and space are created by the elders of our tribe and, of course, lawmakers. What is interesting about this idea is children are being exposed to other cultures, elders and rules of the world online that have no 'one' person directing these rules; for example, there is no president or queen of the Internet, or online gaming spaces. There is the proposed 'netiquette' and social rules created on each platform, app, game or forum, but there are also spaces that have no rules as the rule. It seems that each platform can create, enforce and censor those who don't follow their rules and they can write such rules as part of their platform rules. But they don't own the space, it isn't regulated (yet) and even if it were there are spaces that will never follow suit.

In short, I would like to invite you to update your schema, assimilate the following and create a generalised approach to online well-being and safety and help the adults regulate this space. I would like to invite you to make sense of these morals, values and norms and make sense of the online space, so you can explain to the younger generations about what is morally acceptable and why, and on what platforms, in which countries and with whom.

It's nigh on impossible, isn't it?

So please consider if you, the adult with a mature (full house of residents in your) brain and cognitive, critical-thinking ability are struggling with this, then how do we explain it to young people entering into this space about banter, bullying, exclusion, hate speech, free speech, jostling, lolz, lelz and the most important part that I define with cybertrauma: this omission of power, intention to harm and at times lack of repeating occurrences, which is given in a corporeal definition of bullying and is not always present in the online spaces?

Omissions of power, intent, repetition

Now, why is this important here? Well, if you take the definition of bullying, this is not just the one that appears on the ABA site. You can explore the elements in this way:

> *A power dynamic.* In the real world, this is quite easy to establish when looking at physical attributes such as size or perhaps sex, weight or weapons. The power dynamic may be about the attributes of intelligence, class, language

capabilities, the hierarchy of position (in a school, company or organisation) and position in the family or village. The power dynamic can be about the intent behind languages, such as threat, coercion and consequences. The power dynamic can be about state and country, law, religion and other factors, such as policies in place, like those at school. What is often very clear to see, logically and pragmatically, is the power dynamic, because it involves the comparison to another human being whom we can speak to, or in the case of law-breaking, arrest and question. There is an identifiable A N other in this dynamic.

Power dynamic that can be untrue in the digital space: an eight-year-old child on *Fortnite* tells another player repeatedly they are shit at the game and should just go kill themselves. The other player is 56 years of age. Power or 'naughty child'?

A reply message on Twitter reads: What do you know you piece of shit?

Moments later another reply to your message: You are so fat, you would float in a boat of gravy.

Not five minutes after this, another message: You have a face for radio, keep it that way and stay out of public.

These are bot replies I saw to a professional.

Who has the power in these situations, and would we say this was bullying? Would you tell someone you were being bullied by an eight-year-old or would you say you were being trolled, lol'ed and harassed? What about the bots, if you felt hurt and upset at the comments?

Repetition of Offence. In the definition, repeated incidences allow us to measure, objectively, a pattern of behaviour that we can count in some way. What is fascinating about this definition and the real-world application is that, when we speak to young children, we often scold them on the first 'event' as being bullying behaviour, even though it doesn't meet the criteria for repetition used in the definition. For example, a toddler bites another in the nursery and is told, 'Hey we don't do that (it's not nice), and you are a bully' (I hear this often from adults in public and I sit with the question that this may not have been a one-off event, hence their use of the word).

Also, do we count repeat offences by the same 'person' or number of accounts, as in the case of cyber mobbing? What about the issue of 'text-bombing' where one person creates a program to continuously hassle someone else, but they only typed out the code once and pressed go?

Repetition of Offence that may not be true in the digital space. In my (Knibbs, 2016) book, I discuss the child who had her profile picture doctored by her peers to make her look like a cartoon pig. This event only happened once, however, the fact that the image could be seen by multiple people was the trauma she faced, with her using the word bullying in my practice. This happened once, the image was removed and this group of peers (we think it was a group) did not carry out this offence or others after this, however, my client was as distressed as other children in those repeated situations, and my job is 'never to grade, scale or compare whether a repetition denotes a feeling of being bullied'. This would be like saying, 'Oh it doesn't meet the criteria or threshold for that,' and that is massively dismissive on my part as a practitioner to do this to a child and their emotions.

Intention. In the definition, this word is placed with significant importance, as this denotes that when repetition occurs, it is intentional behaviour that is being carried out. And this is very true, given a onetime event may not be intentional, but the second, third and fourth must be by definition. Now, not to geek out too much, but I'm going to use logic that is within the realm of computing using a proposition called *the And gate*. This means that, to assume and confirm intentions as being hurtful (spiteful and intentional) and carried out by the bully, then there *must have been a previous interaction, with the impact witnessed* by the victim as to the impact of that behaviour. Therefore, as the logic goes, it's intentional when it meets the two criteria of *repeated behaviour **AND** with prior knowledge that this would cause harm, hurt or pain.* Otherwise, the pretext of 'I didn't mean to' can be used.

Intention and proving it so? Now, I'm not a court barrister, but one thing I know for sure is that intention is often what is being pursued in the cases brought in front of juries and judges. It is the 'without a doubt' process that the prosecution aims to prove. It is the idea that we can show with evidence, beyond reasonable doubt, that this behaviour was carried out with the intent to, for example, end a life. And unless the defendant 'fesses up' and says, 'Yep I chose to do that of my own volition', then it's up to many people to make that decision in a courtroom.

Many times, I see adults' decisions on whether a behaviour was bullying or not, whether it was retaliation, and when I sit with my clients in therapy I sometimes sit with children who have autism, neurodivergent thinking, trauma and other emotional dysregulation difficulties who cannot tell me whether their behaviour is intentional or reactional. They are often taking the bait, wound up over several weeks or months, irritated because they are frustrated, don't understand the rules of a game, tired, lashing out because they were abused the night before, terrified, having a flashback and more.

Case-by-case basis

Practitioner pause for reflection

As with all the issues I bring to this book, my intended dissection of all of the issues is to provoke critical thinking in you, the practitioner. How would you suppose to understand the online space and the bullying that occurs there if you don't take into account the myriad of ways that this event can occur and the omission of some of the corporeal-definition aspects? What would you do with photoshop issues versus the backdoor bullying I discussed in the first book, or being kicked from games where it may even look like there is a fault with the server? Can computer systems be bullies? These issues all require critical thinking and conversations about the context and history of an event. Pretty much like you would do in the real world.

The impact on the victim is often the 'gauge' in which we action bullying

Imagine a familiar sight and sound in houses of every kind, everywhere: the noise often heard from siblings that results in sharp attention from parents is along the lines of (crying out), 'Mum, they just hit me!' The standard reaction of parents is to rush to the site of the children, quickly assessing who the instigator was, who has the power, who now perhaps has the toy, and as fast as lightning make a decision about the event and carry out their preferred interventions of parenting the squabbling toddlers, children or adolescents.

Usually, this is accompanied by the rhetoric of *x* has hurt *y*, *x* has been *insert adjective* about the behaviour and *x* now needs to *insert actionable behaviour* such as an apology because of *x* causing *y* to feel *z*. The parent is the judge, jury and executioner in one fell swoop here.

And so children learn the formulae of bullying as: *this* behaviour carried out upon another causes *this* emotion or behaviour and causes me to be *labelled as* nasty, unfair, mean, horrible, bigger than, cleverer than, angry, shallow and the *action required* at the end of this is to *say sorry* (and promise never to do this again).

This sorry-ness is often a way to (in my client's words) make them give the item back that was punitively taken away, unground me, get off the hook, go to the cinema, see my friends, watch TV, play on the console, have my sweets and so on and so on . . .

Now, this is not to say all children who say sorry are not remorseful or are looking to get off the punishment. But I am thinking of the number of times I've worked with a client who, for example, in one instance is sitting down with the head teacher after retaliating and promising never to do or say said behaviour again. Or in some cases is the instigator of the bullying behaviour. And what we know about child development, emotional regulation and trauma schemas are that they are using their rational-thinking brain when engaging in these conversations with the head. They mean what they say and some of these children will be feeling shame and terrible about the pain they caused to another, especially if they have a religious upbringing, or may face a secondary process of confessions and shame after school. So let's think about this child being beaten by the adults when they get home after this incident.

Trauma as a motivator

And yet, with this child in the face of threat, whether this be perceived or real, if the power dynamic is thought to be, or assumed to be, in the other person, they will 'default' into their stress response. For some of these children, this is the fight response and goes something like 'hit first before they hit you', or 'say something terrible' to the other person. Now the victim, in this scenario, is possibly the one with the power in terms of height, weight, strength, what they can and will do to this child, or perhaps the child who is hitting out has been told by another peer this will happen and is taking the 'low road' option. Upon lashing out, this is picked up by the staff as bullying behaviour and this child is reprimanded in the head's office.

In the words of computer programming: **goto start**

> If this child is a victim of trauma, or abuse or in constant threat-detection mode, the intention is to stay safe, stay alive and for others to stay back. It **is** intentional in its manifestation, but not motivated thinking. This appears as bullying behaviour in line with the definitions.

Neurodiversity and bullying

If we go back to the child with neurodiversity as a way of seeing the world, what is often accompanied by this diagnosis is the social difficulty of theory of mind, which allows the person to imagine, empathise and to 'step into their shoes' in an exercise of understanding about 'my actions upon them'. This is often why children with autistic traits and diagnoses struggle with friendships. For example, some of the children I work with in therapy who are neurodiverse will behave in ways that cause them distress in their friendships. For example, one young male, aged eight, used to say how he enjoyed teasing the other children by stealing their toys and pens until they cried, and he would reflect back to me in therapy that it was funny when they cried, because he understood crying to be a good thing after a recent lesson that explained people can cry for both good and bad news, and people can cry when happy; therefore in his thinking, 'this was a good thing'. He also took joy in seeing the other children cry, and the teacher called this 'evil' without understanding his thinking process.

Kohlberg's moral-development theory helps us understand why bullying can take place, it can help us understand that guilt and shame are the inner forces that prevent certain bullying behaviours for *some* children as the consequences for hurting another person. They also can consider that it means they will likely get into trouble if they do it 'on purpose', or as is written in the definition: with intent. For those children who do not understand this moral rule, or overrule this for reasons that may be complicated by trauma, internalised morals from the family that do not match society, not caring because guilt and/ or shame are not driving forces of change in them (e.g., autistic spectrum disorder), we must explore the context, through discourse, and critically analyse what is going on.

Regardless of the intent, misdirection or reactive behaviours of some children upon others, it is necessary to hold conversations and educate about the impact of bullying, and here the organisations such as ABA, Diana Award and Kidscape are suited to providing that education. However, for you as the practitioner working with both bully and bullied, context is important, as well as all of the previous critical analysis to help you work with whichever child it is that is on your caseload.

The dark triad

Some children may exhibit behaviours that look like the dark triad (Paulhus & Williams, 2002) that is often seen in personality-psychology theories. This is where narcissism, machiavellianism and psychopathy are in a triad and are often expressed as contempt for others. If you were to ask a question of the public about a troll online, a cyberbully or a flamer, it's likely they would describe a person as this. Now, children do not have personality disorders (you need to be 18 in the UK to 'possess' one), and some children are labelled as psychopaths, non-empaths, evil, dangerous and expletive-based adjectives by professionals and family members, who are often frustrated, shocked by or don't understand the behaviour they have just witnessed. And this is adults talking about children in the corporeal world!

From corporeal to virtual. 'Cyber'-bullying

Understanding real-world processes of bullying allows us to broaden this thinking into the world of cyber-based spaces, and for those who are ahead of me here in thinking: you may have noticed the element of proximity in the corporeal versions of bullying, i.e., being with or near a person in the real world in order to carry out the activities, behaviours and aggressions upon another person in order to be classified as bullying (aside from shouting at another person who is not that near, for example, football referees!).

And so proximity is also an omission from this type of bullying, as one person could quite literally be on the other side of the world. This is an important point to note about the neurobiology of this event. The bully does not have to be in physical proximity because the false zone of safety sees to that (see Knibbs (2022), for an in-depth explanation of this and why the proximity of the device is more than adequate for the impact of this issue).

Examples from therapy

I'm going to start with some examples from therapy, and I would like you as the reader to consider the following conversations and identify whether you would call this cyberbullying, or not.

Client aged 14: 'Well I mean it was just a picture, but they used Photoshop and made my nose look like Miss Piggy because I had the pink tee shirt, and that's when they created the fake account'.

'And so what was that like for you, when you found this out?'

'It made me so mad, I wanted to punch the girl who did it, cos that's what she thought was bantz and it proper made me cry cos everyone could see it, I mean who'd do that, like, right?'

'It sounds like it really hurt'.

'Yeah and now I've got this picture associated with my name so of course, anyone is gonna see it and then it'll become like the nickname I get and what am I supposed to do about it? Like they don't get it, I've been to do something about my weight and this proper sets me back and I don't know why I bother'.

'So you feel this is impacting your choices about your fitness goals?'

'Yeah cos like I said last week that this was gonna be about my weight and gettin back into classes cos I'm sick of being in the other room with Miss ★★★★ when they are doing sports and I know I haven't been able to do it like them, but how can I when they take the piss like this? I might as well not bother with any of it. And I *know* she did it but like what am I supposed to do? Cos like the teachers can't do owt, or even Facebook cos we tried that and they said they'd look at it, but like nowts happened and it's still up'.

'Yeah well, they put it on Twitter and didn't name me directly though so I haven't got a leg to stand on'.

'And what are you thinking and feeling about this third-personing?'

'Hmm, well its a case of saying "did you see what *she* did (emphasis on she) in class or school", and of course it's their accounts talking to each other, and they are talking about what I said, which really wasn't that bad, it was just a stupid answer and now they are all piling on to create a drama, for which I know it's about me but they haven't named me so what can I do?'

Later in the session: 'This is so crap though as it will stay on Twitter forever, and anyone could go back and check, so like when we are all 50 or something and you check Twitter they can see oh, that was about so and so (me) and of course, it just brings it back up again. It's there forever and I can't do anything about it. Ever.'

This girl went on to describe, as per my article (Knibbs, 2014), in the BACP magazine, that the representation of her distress in the sand tray could not take place because my sand tray had finite edges, and of course time does not, and so, there is not a sand tray big enough to place her figure in so that we could represent the impact this would have.

This one moment in my therapy room in 2012 was so profound on my thinking about this space. *I know* that digital spaces last forever (my cognitive knowledge and IT experience), and I had also experienced the rubber-banding back to my school days with some images shared by class peers, and knew this feeling somewhat, but I had never until this point had the 'whoosh', *the smack in the face of the reality of this issue* like this. This young 14-year-old had taught me one of my biggest moments relating to this space.

And it's not just 'kids'

Once upon a time, there was a 40-something-year-old, not a client of mine but yours truly. The complete irony of this story is this behaviour was carried out by a person who is cited as a cyberbullying professional.

To keep this as free from identification as possible, I will leave out the year that this happened and finer details of the issue, hence my age being somewhat vague to limit historic back filtering. This issue cannot be happening to just me and was so bizarre to experience, that as it progressed, I actually found myself laughing at the behaviour because I was trying to 'wrap my head around the process', so to speak. I was taken aback that adults also behaved like this, yet, of course, knew that they did. What is reaffirming, disconcerting and at the same time utterly unbelievable is that when this happens to you, you recognise the impact could be terrible for some other people. However, as the day unfolded, I found myself saying, 'Is this for real?' is this person really carrying out this behaviour and what would happen if I pointed it out? Would we then descend into the depths of rage, denial and further anger, resulting in behaviours that we call trolling?

This was one of those such occasions where, in the moment, I was, at first, offended by the actions of this individual and was looking to see what I did to provoke such a response, as most people who feel attacked usually do to defend themselves. In a short story format: I asked on a social media platform if I could have the evidence pointing to some claims made by this individual, about the number of children who are bullied (as per the post) as I am a researcher, critical thinker and don't believe all that I read. Claims made on social media, in presentations and on slides without accurate references to research irk me. Because, as the saying goes, six out of seven dwarves are not happy (not a dig at disability here but a reference from comedic paradigms).

I wanted to know what studies these were in relation to, and so I asked in the comments where these numbers had come from. Cue the mistake of assuming. Rather than receiving what I thought might have been a citation in the reply, I found myself receiving a direct message with some interesting 'thoughts and opinions' about me as a person and my question. As I sat there thinking that maybe I had been off in the way I asked, or the context had been misunderstood, I went to 'update' the question to make it clear that I was asking for research and not to attack the person, only to find my comment removed from their post and a remark about them being an expert in this domain.

'Oh wow!' I thought. 'Wonder what I said that pissed them off?' And so, like a wounded sulky child, I thought, okay, I'll head onto another platform and do my socialising there where my friends are (this is what we do in relationships when rejection, abandonment and attachment patterns are provoked). This replicated the walking away I would have carried out in the real world. As I opened the other social media platform, I was met with the list of 'things you could have missed since your last visit here' (good ol' algorithms!) and this included posts from the last hour and day. Also, the most recent posts are usually at the top of the feed. I was met with a post on this platform that said something like, 'Isn't social media great when you can delete posts from idiots', by said individual that had recently 'backdoor DM'd' me on the other platform (a way to describe the hidden bullying, trolling and harassment that occurs).

Cue attachment pattern: the need to tell someone to a) verify this was a real thing, b) narrate the trauma, abuse or event, c) get someone else's take on it to ensure I hadn't gone down the paranoia-thinking route. And so, I picked up the phone and dialled a friend's number. I laughed as they picked up the phone as I was in disbelief that I was encountering this behaviour from this professional. Of course, my friend delightfully let me know that I could well have 'poked the bear' so to speak and that I shouldn't let this bother me. . . . 'Oh and maybe stop asking for citations and actual evidence from professionals, as some may not like to be challenged, eh, Cath?'

This is not going to happen, I'm afraid, as I can't write books, or educate my clients based on hearsay.

'Just' walk away, close the lid, turn it off and why this advice is moot

Now my story is like many other people's on social media and in today's world; the messages we receive are ladled with emotions that we often put into them due to the missing cues of nonverbal communication, tone and prosody. Emoticons can, and are, used as an attempt to change the dynamic of the conversation. But alas, we have this inner voice system where we can and do read text in the voice of someone else, especially if we have heard it before. Again, another little thought experiment: imagine you are seeing a yellow cartoon figure that says 'Doh!' or 'Ay caramba!' and you might just have heard (internally) the voices of Homer and Bart Simpson. So when we receive a text from someone we know, we tend to 'read in their voice' and add in whatever feelings we think are pertinent to the text. For example, when I ask warring parents about their communication, I am often met with them reading texts out to me 'in the voice' of the other, with the sentence 'so I knew he/she/they were feeling x with me'.

Subjective interpretations inferred from the text are possibly the worst way to resolve a disagreement (I love the meme that is based on this). If this is the case for a text from someone we know, imagine what we infer if the text from a cyberbully is full of aggressive language, swearing, telling us to end our lives, telling us what they think of us, our families, our history and so on. We can add our own meaning to it, and for a person with low self-esteem, this can be disastrous. And this is where this section of the chapter can be seen to overlap with self-harm and suicide, eating disorders and more.

The irony: 'don't let it bother you' and 'close the lid' is the advice often given to young people who encounter this kind of behaviour online. The issue is: of course it bothers them, friendships in childhood and adolescence are needed as a way to survive and develop. It's not a case of find other friends, because to a child 'these' are my friends. The idea of 'starting again' is akin to moving school often, and the research shows that children who are from families that move a lot, for example, military or other professions that require postings around the country or countries, struggle with deeper friendships than other children. I wonder if this will be abated somehow with the advent of virtual spaces, and the longevity of being in these spaces with others helping these children develop deeper friendships, albeit in virtual settings.

Cyberbullying research

For many years, I was intrigued about how other therapists were dealing with this situation, as I was hearing in my training the previously mentioned advice given as the one-size-fits-all solution, and was troubled by the lack of knowledge about the types and motivations of cyberbullies being misunderstood by counsellors in schools or school staff at the time (the 'it's not on our premises so it doesn't count' narrative that I can still happen upon). So I asked questions as part of my research during my MSc, with counsellors, about their understanding of this issue, alongside how they received supervision (Knibbs et al., 2017). The journal is paywalled so I shall expand the findings in the next section.

Findings

Cyberbullying as a concept is understood to be an event that always has some element of corporeal overlap. The bullying involves electronic devices and is bullying that occurs through this medium. Clients would bring 'evidence' to sessions in an attempt to be believed by the counsellors, some with screenshots, or printouts. Supervisors at the time did not understand how the Internet worked and would suggest to the counsellors to advise their clients to turn it off, close the tabs or laptop or phone, switch it off and ignore it.

However, the bullying impact itself was described by the counsellors as: being toxic down to the bones, pernicious, deeply hurtful and distressing (to hear/watch), and their knowledge about the platforms was varied, with some being excellently e-safety-aware as well as counselling, and some with very little knowledge about the space where they could and should report, block, screengrab and so on.

Typology and why cyberbullying may be difficult to define and action

Cyberbullying is one of the cyber-based issues with quite a lot of posts, advice and handouts, training events and media-driven conversations. But what exactly *is it*?
   Here are some types and styles of being bullied online:

Flaming, Trolling, Outing, Photoshop Rendering, Reposting, Liking, Deadnaming, Backdoor DM's, Hacking (many types), Fake Accounts, Strawmanning, Cancel Culture, Deplatforming, Memetics, Session hacking, Multi-Platform Attacks, CopyPasting, Hoaxes, Twitchhoarding, Kicking, Camping Out, Friendly Fire, Text Bombing, DDOS, Revenge Porn, Upskirting, Sextortion, Blackmail, Gender Deniers, Gender Conformists, LGBQTIA++ Attacks, MRA Versus RADfems, Mobbing, Fudding, Rugging, Vigilantism, Hoaxes, Misinformation, Activism, Polarisation, Spamming, Video Sends, Filesharing, VR stalking, VR/AR Abuse and Assault, Haptic Feedback Assault or Abuse, Village/World Stomping, Raids, ID Fraud, Game Records and Shares on VOD, Replays of n00b Youtubers and Fraping. And this list is not exhaustive.

Practitioner pause for reflection

You do not need to know what each one of these is in detail! It is likely that the young person you are working with will use one of these words to describe what's going on or will detail to you what's happening (and may have a name associated with it or maybe a newly emerging issue). What is required is to listen out for the facilitation of abuse by and with the technology and how the child feels about this. This is how we support a child in the real world, and online is no different, whether it is solely online or overlaps with the real world.

All of the issues named previously are carried out online, on social media, on a device and to a person, their website, their business or friends, family and spaces inhabited by us or others. How do we decide what cyberbullying actually is, especially when these issues can and do overlap into the real world? For example:

> Billy is playing a game when his mum shouts in a sing song voice for him, 'Billybubba come down for your dinner, I made your favourite; spaghetti whetty bolly wholly with sosssys'.

And, like the rest of the players, Billy had his mic on with 20 of his school friends.

The replay of what mum sang transitions into the school the next day, and he is teased about his spaghetti whetty, and each time Billy goes online for the next few days there is a new meme and he is called spaghetti boy by his gamer friends. It begins to take its toll.

Billy is not 5, he is not 8 but 15 years of age. Mum was teasing him about his tea because today was his birthday, and she was having some fun with her son in a playful way, forgetting he was using his headset and with no idea of the consequences of her actions outside of the home. And this is one of those issues that was socially awkward for Billy given his age, peer group and sadly the girl he wanted to ask out who was online when she heard this too. Billy was mortified about each and all of these outcomes.

Question: would Billy's mum have called out like this if he was on the football field with his friends? Does Mum know his friends are listening in this way? Does Mum know that the game could have been recorded and this moment uploaded onto YouTube for many others to also hear and see Billy's gamertag, which now results in a plethora of uninvited DMs and contact on social media and gaming spaces?

Maybe not, as she can't see the friends (or forgot) and does not understand the gaming space? And, when this becomes the topic with which Billy is repeatedly teased, is it bullying, cyberbullying or both?

From corporeal playing fields to virtual

What really mattered for Billy in therapy was the fact that these moments of playfulness by parents are common in some houses, and many parents or carers have pet names for their children or there is an in-joke private to that family. There may even be a way of talking to each other that is silly, childlike and involves baby talk (especially if we have pets to talk to, and yes, guilty of that!). We spent quite a bit of time discussing that his peers had heard something that 20–25 years ago would never have happened (unless friends had visited a house unbeknown to the parents) and so we decided his mum's education in this matter needed to come from him rather than me in this case. I also needed to explain to Mum that her home and safe space was now 'technically invaded' by a house party every day. Imagine saying that to all of the parents and carers you work with and you might just be grasping what our homes are now like. Privacy is by default moot unless we never allow the house parties into the house.

Mum, during our conversations, felt justified in saying that her home, and her behaviour with her son (and other family members) was no longer what she thought of as her ordinary life at home with her family. She was now feeling under scrutiny, and she needed to think about this 'horde of boys' in her house and was not happy about this. A question I reflected to her, and one for you the practitioners reading this book is: when did our houses become infiltrated with strangers, when did we allow this and why should we have to adapt our behaviour to accommodate this fact?

The impact

The definition of cyberbullying I used in my research is a shortened version of my cybertrauma definition, because over the years I have come to believe that we are looking at the online space in the same way we are now slowly but surely looking at life and the word trauma. There are many definitions of the word trauma, and I give some of these in the first book (Knibbs, 2022). What I firmly believe is that we are creating an ever-expanding lexicon of issues, some of which have legal definitions in order that the Online Safety Bill, criminal justice system or lawful service can action them. It makes sense to do this; however, if we take the word trauma for one moment, we can see that a terrible event happening to a person can also be defined in this way, e.g., mugging, but **the impact** is what matters for us as practitioners.

From earthquakes to mugging

In both of these scenarios a person may feel like their life is in danger, and so we can see that they will be affected by this event and potentially suffer trauma post the event. One of these events is natural and the other is against the law. And in the world of online harm, terms like legal and illegal may be the way we define these types of issues. The earthquake, let's say for pretend's sake here, is a **legal AND harmful** event. I am using a different version of the terminology from the Online Safety Bill (at this current time at the second reading in parliament) because the word **but** takes a passive and discounting framing and I feel professionally this is harmful in itself (that's a professional opinion by the way).

Once the earthquake is over, we would not as professionals say (I hope), 'Oh that's just how it is, move on, pull up your bootstraps and get over it'. We would work with the person who may now be having nightmares, sweats and feeling terrified about going outside or family members being killed. We would see the impact of an event, whether it could be classified as illegal or not.

> And so the reflection here for you as practitioners is not to see the label of cyber-bullying, in whatever format that emerges, or is 'classified', but to see the person and the impact.

Cyberbullying as a phenomenon

From my research (and akin to the definition of cybertrauma) I posited the following definition:

> Cyberbullying is a phenomenon that occurs through the medium of electronic devices and involves either direct or indirect aggression, harassment or vitriolic prose, images or videos or other uses of digital media intended to cause psychological and/or emotional harm. These events can be singular, repetitive and can happen immediately, retrospectively or be delayed.

There really isn't a clear distinction between online and offline anymore, and this overlap is going to become more blurred as we head into augmented, virtual and holographic spaces. If we take bullying, we can see earlier in the chapter that even in the real world, this involves words or physical injury to a person. The same is true to some degree of the online, virtual, electronic, internet and digital spaces. What a person experiences in the face of this event is subjective, personal and we as the practitioners do not get to 'grade' it based on our knowledge of the experience or issue.

Bullying **is** traumatic (think back to your childhood when this happened to you and how easily that memory appears in your mind right now). Cyberbullying is also traumatic.

New thinking?

In the paradigm of trauma, there used to be a way to speak of events that are now slowly being removed from this narrative, as there are professionals who grade traumas as being BIG T and Little T. We know that repetition of emotional and psychological trauma is *as damaging as a singular event*. Again, I refer you to the idea that cyberbullying *does not need to be repeated* as a person can have a singular event and be traumatised, and we don't get to decide whether it is grand enough to meet the Big T typology.

Additionally, these events are often in the public domain and seen by a large crowd, and so this type of trauma is indeed new and one that is going to take clear robust research to explore. Many of us as adults have never experienced this in our childhoods (because it didn't exist) and so we really need to listen to lived experiences about this phenomenon, rather than overlaying our lens of what we think or know bullying to be.

We could also drop the element of 'power' in some cases, if we follow a new line of thought here. How does this count if: we consider the online disinhibition theory, which suggests that disinhibition is not knowing who the other person is?

So how do we measure the power dynamic?

Also, if we cannot see the impact on the recipient, or they do not see the post, event or meme, for example, how can we measure it as intentional? For example, I was not hugely impacted by the event I shared earlier and so I was not traumatised, nor did I feel victimised, and so does this count? For example, had I not seen the second post, then I would only have the first to go on, and this may have been an example of miscommunication. An email that was sent by a CEO to an employee may be construed as bullying if the communication lines were not clear or unambiguous. It was only due to the second post that I could have been impacted like the 14-year-old I discussed earlier.

Do we need to rethink the way we describe cyberbullying by use of the victim's perspective? For example, cyberbullying is: an event that results in a recipient feeling traumatised, abused, offended, hurt, ridiculed stupid, rejected, outed or punished. Events may include . . .

And yet, if we do this when we look at victim impact rather than the perpetrator behavior, it becomes quite clear, quite quickly, that we could assess any behaviour as cyberbullying, if the issue involves an Internet-ready device that could be the definitive aspect needed in order to classify this. Whether it involves corporeal aspects or not, it is cyber by the inclusion of the Internet-ready device.

Or do we change the language to technologically facilitated abuse and bullying? Or are we set in stone about the language we currently have?

And what about microaggressions?

I am not going to detail these as the chapter is moving on to the next subject and these may be a part of cyberbullying but could be another form of abuse that we classify, however, this is going to be difficult to assess if we cannot pin down exactly what microaggressions are exactly (Taffel, 2020). However, there is a new, emerging passive-aggressive way of responding to people in the digital space that involves implicit processes such as racism, sexism and more, and is being seen as a privilege-based stance whereby people will suggest, accuse or even go to extreme lengths to point out microaggressions. This term was initially associated with racism, but now is subjective and can be seen to be that which oppresses a minority group (or not). The microforms of aggression are not new; however, the online space is making this an unacceptable way to respond to people, with the antagonists often saying that a person who has put up a post is 'doing it on purpose'.

Thus, even those benign posts that could be a person's musings, a reply to someone else or a nonresponse is now at the mercy of those who wish to point the finger and call this a microaggression. The world of witch-hunting that took place hundreds of years ago just got the equivalent of a facelift, and levelled up to become a new way to hunt down those of us who are so unaware of our microaggressions that it takes the 'call out culture' (those who are often championed as the woke brigade) to let us know about our faults here.

And I wonder if that last sentence was an unconscious aggression on my part?

References

Aitkin, M. (2015). *Cyberpsychologist*. See www.maryaitkin.com.
Anti-Bullying Alliance. (2022). *Cyberbullying definition.* https://anti-bullyingalliance.org.uk/.
British Psychological Society Cyberpsychology Section. www.bps.org.uk/member-networks/cyberpsychology-section.

Delahooke, M. (2020). *Beyond behaviours: Using brain science and compassion to understand and solve children's behavioural challenges.* John Murray learning: London.

Delahooke, M. (2022). *Brain-body parenting: How to stop managing behavior and start raising joyful, resilient kids.* Harper Wave: New York.

Fonagy, P. (2001). *Attachment theory and psychoanalysis.* Routledge: London.

Fonagy, P., Gergely, G., Jurist, E., & Target, M. (2004). *Affect regulation, mentalization and the development of the self.* Routledge: London.

Goleman, D. (1995). *Emotional intelligence.* Bloomsbury: London.

Hanson, R. (2018). *Resilient. Find your inner strength.* Rider: London.

Kaufman, S. B. (2013). *Ungifted. The truth about talent, practice, creativity, and many paths to greatness.* Basic Books: New York.

Knibbs, C. (2014). Cybertrauma. *BACP CYP Journal*, December. www.bacp.co.uk/bacp-journals/bacp-children-young-people-and-families-journal/december-2014/cyber trauma/.

Knibbs, C. (2016). *Cybertrauma; the darker side of the internet.* Self-published and available on Amazon Kindle and Blurb Books.

Knibbs, C. (2022). *Children, technology, and healthy development.* Routledge: Abingdon.

Knibbs, C., Goss, S., & Anthony, K. (2017). Counsellors' phenomenological experiences of working with children or young people who have been cyberbullied: Using thematic analysis of semi structured interviews. *International Journal of Technoethics*, 8, 68–86.

Kohlberg, L., & Turiel, E. (1971). Moral development and moral education. In L. Kohlberg (Ed.), *Collected papers on moral development and moral education* (pp. 410–465). Scott, Foresman & Company: Glenview, IL.

Newhart, B. (2010). *Stop it.* www.youtube.com/watch?v=Ow0lr63y4Mw.

Nissenbaum, H. (2004). Hackers and the contested ontology of cyberspace. *New Media & Society*, 6(2), 195–217.

Paulhus, D., & Williams, K. (2002). The dark triad of personality: Narcissism, machiavellianism, and psychopathy. *Journal of Research in Personality*, 36(6), 556–563.

Piaget, J. (1926). Cited in (2002), Piaget, J. *The language and thought of the child.* Routledge: London.

Rieber, R., & Carton, A. (1993). *The collected works of Vygotsky. The fundamentals of defectology (abnormal psychology and learning disabilities).* Springer: New York.

Siegel, D. (2016). *Mind: A journey to the heart of being human (Norton series on interpersonal neurobiology).* W. W. Norton & Co: New York.

Steinmetz, K. (2015). Becoming a hacker: Demographic characteristics and developmental factors. *Journal of Qualitative Criminal Justice & Criminology*, 3(1), 31–60.

Taffel, R. (2020). The myth of micro-aggression. *Contemporary Psychoanalysis*, 56(2–3), 375–393.

Vygotsky, L. (1933). *Play and its role in the mental development of the child.* IN: Vygotsky, L. S. (1967). Play and its role in the mental development of the child. *Soviet Psychology*, 5(3), 6–18.

Wilson, E. O. (1975). *Sociobiology: The new synthesis.* Belknap Press of Harvard University Press: Cambridge, MA.

5   Cyberstalking

Every chapter, topic and section of this book can be seen through the lens of one or more of the other sections, chapters and topics.

Stalking: known or unknown and who is doing the watching?

How strong our secret desire to know what the Joneses or Robertsons are up to is, and how we can peer through our neighbour's windows like never before. Covertly watching in secret?

We can harass, monitor and create fear at the click of a button or two. And so can big tech. Overtly letting the victim know we are there, watching and letting them 'see us'.

As with all other chapters and this 'cyberspace', this is not as easily defined as we once thought.

Covert and/or overt

To begin, I hope to explore how this issue differs from the real-world stalking that we often see in films or TV shows. How this is pernicious and can be a lifelong issue for those who were exploited as children, are exes of all types and those who seemingly have that superfan, 'weirdo' or 'creepy friend' that always seems to know what we are doing and where we are. I am sure that many readers may have experienced something like this, and the children in my therapy office regularly discuss this type of behaviour and have never considered or had someone ask how they feel about it. When they do, the words used are those in the previous sentence, because it feels weird, and creepy and comes with a feeling of 'being watched'. Our threat detection systems are continuously aware that this is happening, could be happening, might happen and we cannot see the watcher. It's like the one superhero power that we would all enjoy for a while, yet it's the one we despise the most. Well, it would be if we knew for certain it was happening?

Public places and the Big Brother town-centre CCTV

From public-shopping-centre cameras to social media profiles. From CCTV on houses to emails and more. This issue is complex and multifaceted. We often wander

DOI: 10.4324/9781003289210-6

around the real world with a background awareness that we are being watched, hardly noting the signs telling us so. We are likely faced with our mugshot as we shop at the human-less counter in the supermarket, are captured by the dashcam of a passing car, and for some of us, captured on Google Earth in this way. We are in constant observation by the thing we call 'Big Brother'. And in today's world, it is said, facial-recognition software is making this much more about surveillance than recognition. This is not to hate upon this technology, as I'm sure that a parent whose child is lost in a crowd would be so thankful for this technology if it found their child. And in part, this technology is able to help us in this way, but there are some who find this intrusive and against human rights to privacy: for example, someone's professional wanting to enter into the local Ann Summers shop and buy a 'gift' for themselves, or the alcoholic entering into a public house, the young offender out past curfew or the gambler going into the bookies, the celeb wearing a baseball hat in the hope they won't be spotted by cameras or the public.

But what if technology allowed someone to watch us for sinister reasons (and maybe some of you consider the previously mentioned in this way)?

Sinister and illegal

Mostly the misuse of technology for sinister observational processes and outcomes is discussed in criminal cases of an ex or current romantic partner called 'romantic terrorism,' though there is nothing romantic about this aspect (Haye & Jeffries, 2015): domestic-abuse and sexual-exploitation cases. Stalking is an issue that is gaining concern for many in terms of its association with coercive relationships, sextortion and domestic abuse.

Sinister and legal

This issue is one that often brings a sense of discomfort when I explain to people that there is the possibility for this process to occur without your knowledge when you put your life out on social media. Take for example my client (an adult), who was estranged from her family, with a family friend on both hers and the family's social media accounts on a number of platforms. In the earlier days of social media, when she was tagged or her friend commented on her posts, her family could see what she was doing and for many months; this wasn't even on her radar until she went to visit another estranged family member. Upon sharing this event on her social media, and her friend commenting, she was met with a number of phone calls and letters (postal types, not emails) picking up the family feud from years ago and reigniting the need for yet another court order.

Sinister or not sinister and who knows what for?

If you watch *The Social Dilemma*, released in 2020, you will see that the documentary points out the large number of data points that social media profiles hold on you, so who else has this 'big data', what are they observing about you, what are they holding onto and for what purposes? It is often thought that this is about advertising and selling up and selling on and for a comprehensive look at this read the book by Shushona Zuboff (2019).

Stalking, not 'just' observing

Let's take, for example, the overt type of stalking mentioned at the start of this chapter. You can see the criminality found in these cases, and they often have a traceability to them that puts the puzzle pieces together, so to speak. The problematic side of the issue can be identified, and there is often a story of how this came to be a symptom of the issue. For example, 'jilted' lovers, as they are referred to in the media (films, TV and news), are in a roundabout type of way trying to connect with the separated partner after a breakup. They are desperate to keep the relationship and are doing whatever they can, whether unhealthy or dysfunctional, to maintain that connection. This is based on attachment needs.

And to maintain their 'presence in the other person's psyche' (i.e., to let them know they still exist), they are continuously wanting the other person to know they are still there by whatever means. In real-world examples, this is the ex-partner who just happens to be at the same shop, café or sports facility, for example, that used to be frequented by them when they were a couple. Many of my clients whom this happens to (and it is a large number) will say it is creepy, overbearing or that they feel really uncomfortable with it. And in the real world, we call this stalking – though the ex-partner would say they have a right to be at said location for said reason, making this a difficult process to work with at times. Taking a brief look at the statistics that are currently available via domestic-abuse charities, and research carried out by Black et al. (2011) you can quickly see how large a problem this is when you read 60.8% of female stalking victims and 43.5% of men reported being stalked by a current or former intimate partner (this research is cited from 2011, several years ago).

So, as a good researcher I have been trying to identify for you, the reader, how we define and measure this crime within the UK. I felt myself going on a bit of a goose chase with this and finding the following on the Office for National Statistics website (ONS, 2022), where crime is calculated by type each year, and tables, graphs and reports are produced for the public and researchers to use. You can find reports and user guides and, through this, I tried to find a good, robust definition of stalking. I failed . . . here is what I gleaned:

> Stalking is defined as two or more offences reported. www.ons.gov.uk/peo plepopulationandcommunity/crimeandjustice/methodologies/userguidetocr imestatisticsforenglandandwales#offence-types

When I looked to the tables about stalking, I found this reporting (only up to 2017) cyberstalking, which includes unwanted messages that were considered obscene, threatening or harmful to people aged 16–24, totalled 3.3%.

In reports of national statistics of crime in 2020, the results pertaining to stalking statistics (not defined as cyber) is 14.8%, with domestic stalking as 2.5% men, 4.6% women, within the last year.

Other definitions and crimes?

Intimate violence includes stalking, however, if there are weapons, physical violence, burglary and all of the other crimes that have labels and typology, these may well be included there and not 'here'. Also, what about intimate-image abuse, which is frequently called 'revenge porn' for those 18+ (see volume 1 for details on this) and what about whether we call this violence against women and girls online, and classify cyberstalking under this behavior, as I have seen written in some places – 'pestering', and interpersonal terrorism. www.endviolencea gainstwomen.org.uk/wp-content/uploads/Online-Safety-Bill-Full-Brief-final.pdf. A meta-analysis of this crime also resulted in confusion about definitions, scholarly disagreement and what is called operationalization, meaning how to measure something (Kaur et al., 2021).

To date, this is one of the biggest issues with crimes that are complex, include cyber typology and are reported and subjectively interpreted by the police. If there is bodily damage following an incident, preceded by stalking, what do you think the crime will be seen to be and logged as? The stalking element would need to be reported by the victim each and every time they see, hear or felt the intimidation. And I can tell you from my client base they don't have the time to do this given the long waits on telephones and dismissive officers they speak to, and often they don't have 'the evidence' of cyberstalking if the person uses sock puppet accounts, comments in a group (see the example shortly) and is frequenting the same spaces online but not directly interacting?

If you are aware of the statistics about ex-partners in domestic-abuse situations, Women's Aid reported (2020), there is a *huge rise in the likelihood of violence after separation. 41% (37 of 91) of women killed by a male partner/former partner in England, Wales and Northern Ireland in 2018 had separated or taken steps to separate from them.* Cited from www.womensaid.org.uk/information-support/what-is-domestic-abuse/ women-leave/.

And at the time of writing, the case of Sarah Everard was front and centre in the media, with many feminist posts regarding rates of stalking and homicides. I mostly found feminist and radical feminist posts and articles, as was significant and warranted, and wanted to highlight this as the prerequisite to my sharing of those links in this chapter. This certainly highlights the need for clarification of typology, reporting and research that is required here (as with all of the other issues in the books).

Why keep showing up?

This behaviour can be understood in terms of attachment, and this behaviour is readily observable in children who have, for example, recently been scolded by their parents when they suddenly become clingy and 'whiny', with the parents looking for respite from the child who is now desperate to hang on with more strength than a limpet on a rock. And so it is with the online space. People are looking to get their needs met, they need to be seen, and still want to 'hold onto' the relationship, can be called besotted, which may mean still in love with, or obsessional or devoted to or fearful of abandonment, and this latter phrase is really what is being 'tapped into' when someone says 'go away and don't bother me', and as described here, you only need to look at how a toddler behaves when given this message. The ones who walk away defiant generally don't engage in overt stalking, they perhaps are like the toddler who looks and then 'shuns' you but keeps an eye on you out of the corner of their eye. I am not surprised to hear time and time again in my clinic the number of people who are covertly 'monitoring and watching' their exes, their families and friends. And social media allows for this to happen, minute by minute. Your daily life windows are 'see-through' if you are present online and sharing your life online.

Overt and online

Then there are those watchers, on-and-off engagers and stalkers who have no romantic relationship with you. There are those who see what you do online, almost every post, and there are the 'haters' ready and waiting to let you know they are there. You are being watched.

Alice through the looking glass

Have you ever noticed that on your social media feeds, there is that person who goes from ignoring your posts to liking every post? Maybe your current partner, friend or relative is always quick to react and 'see' when you post. What does this feel like, knowing that they have your back, like what you share or are always watching you? Are they really doing that or is there another reason? How does it feel to know that the moment you switch on your social media in the morning or later in the day, that 'somehow' they know to text or call you? Weird, isn't it . . . Or is it?

I once had a friend who had notifications set up to let them know when I and other close friends (set up in a list) posted online, and of course, I didn't know this and why would I? Once, we were out to dinner when I took an image of the meal, as I was impressed with the presentation of the dish, and off it went to the image-based platform. Like the whole world, I was 'doing what everyone else did'. Anyway, my friend's phone lit up with the message 'Cath posted on XX platform' not seconds after I posted it.

I wonder what your gut feeling is right now? Did I think, 'Ahh, that's nice I'm in their circle of important people', or perhaps I had an internal meltdown and said nothing but felt confused or weirded out? The question here is: does this feel like stalker behaviour as you read this? I'll let you decide.

This 'follower' behaviour, not called *social media stalking* but your 'friends list', facilitated by tech companies, is the norm, and most of us bought into this because being followed is something that we like to know about our friends and families on social media. Some social media platforms allowed for a normal part of your daily life to have notifications for 'keeping up with' your 'friends'. It was like being able to look into your friends and families' homes and see what TV program they watched, what foods they ate and when, who cooked, washed up and of course what they read, thought, said and did at every moment of the social media day. *And this is considered okay?* I find human behaviour fascinating in this regard.

> I wonder how you feel about this when you see it written down like this? Are we encouraging nosey-neighbour behaviours through the medium of the looking glass into someone's life, and what about the fact they put the information 'up' for us to peruse, judge and watch? And why would you want to? What's in it for you?

Heck, you could even compare one person's house against another's, or any space you visit to that of your own personal space, garden or wherever. Do you have the same furniture as the Joneses or the Robertsons? Is your TV as good as theirs, is the garden as big and are the decorations on the Christmas tree better or worse? The idea of being what Harry Enfield and Paul Whitehouse created in 2007, 'Michael Kane the Nosey Neighbour' www.youtube.com/watch?v=oRivqpinXRM, becomes less about those twitching net curtains and more about stalker-type behaviours. Oops, I mean 'following' others?

Moreover, if you were busy, the posts are there for you to revisit, you could time travel back to a specific day and time and look through their social media windows and scroll through the posts almost without being noticed.

'Comparison is the thief of joy' is a statement often uttered by tutors, gurus, therapists and coaches worldwide. Yet, this is exactly what we spend our days doing and I find it really fascinating that we are so reliant on being able to see the inside of everyone else's 'house' without questioning this as a change in society's behaviour to the accepted norms.

For those of you reading who are over 35(ish), do you ever remember as a child going round to relatives, or local group or clubs with your parents and hearing the phrase, 'the best room', or being served a good old cup of tea in teacups and saucers and having sandwiches served with crusts cut off like an afternoon tea? Did you grow up in a house where this was an everyday occurrence, but there was always the best china, the best sunroom or space? Did you ever look around at the adults doing this and think it was strange in any way? The reason I ask this is this was how the adults around us engaged in socialising and having time with their friends. Visiting like this is less common nowadays, and of course, was absent for almost two years due to the pandemic. Nonetheless, this is why the older generations struggle with the behaviours of always 'seeing' what their friends and families are up to on a moment-by-moment basis in online spaces such as social media. They quite honestly do not get it, and I'm sure this is a common response outside of my office and with the older people I talk to, too. They would take in all they needed to when visiting Auntie Margaret and see whether she was still using doilies (if you know what these are).

Harmful, illegal, cyberbullying or being a BFF?

As we are talking about overt stalking here, let's begin with the previous examples to think about what this is and when this starts to become illegal or harmful. As a young person posting on Instagram, if there is a certain 'friend' who likes every post, it can become disconcerting, annoying or indeed a sign of loyalty and being a best friend for life (BFF). It can also be 'detected' as a form of cyberbullying when the likes are disingenuous (see plastic likes in book one).

Having your social media posts reacted to, in a way you can measure, gives the basis for acknowledgement, and for some, the reassurance of self-esteem: some research has suggested that young people have a designated number of likes as a baseline and this forms a way of measuring self-esteem for young people based on those likes (Burrow & Rainone, 2017; Besharat Mann & Blumberg, 2022).

Other people may use a post to see how important they are, revisiting the post on numerous occasions to keep track of the post and its reach, likes and engagements, and of course social media obliges this process by displaying these as a physical reminder of just how important you really are, or not. Even if, as happens on some platforms now, the removal of these likes is the new change, young people will look for comments and interactions with the post as the new marker of importance and who is there. Where this does not happen, this can also affect self-esteem. This is a no-win situation really and, unfortunately, where this is deemed as the 'dopamine' hit for a like, it's also the bullet-train speed express to the lowering of self-esteem when it doesn't happen, and this is tied into the dopamine-expectation theory (Lieberman & Long, 2019; Lembke, 2021). Young people do this in the real world, let alone where this is exacerbated: online.

Mental health, as we defined earlier, is an impossible vector to measure, given the issues we have with the word and concept of health. So perhaps mental self-worth might be a better term? This is affected by many of these 'am I being watched and seen' detection systems, and this takes us back to those 4 S's of Dan Siegel's: seen, soothed, safe and secure (2010). However, it is our sense of interpersonal importance, validation and attachment style that drive these checking behaviours, or the interpretations we make on the back of them. 'Self'-esteem, worth, value, importance, confidence, hatred and depreciation are all connected with this. Likes, or the lack thereof, are the metrics here, and having the followers follow is how we know – how many subscribers, followers, friends and so on. But knowing they follow, well, that must be determined as a thing we want, and the issue with this is we do not get to decide what, whom, how and which posts we want to follow. That is decided by the follower, and that is where the feeling of the 'Peeping Tom' often gets compared to here by my clients. It can be difficult to explain this aspect when we only want people to like the posts we want them to like, and explaining this to a young person can feel like painting fog.

Fan or not?

But what about if that person is anonymous, via a pseudonym or even a 'sock puppet' account (false or fake account) and could be a family member, friend, customer, client, patient, ex-partner, colleague, ex-friend, current partner or any of the above? What about if, every time you do something online, they are 'there' present in the training or meetings? They are often with a 'broken camera', watching your live streams, a follower on other types of platforms and is like that bad penny that keeps showing up. You know it's them, but they are using an alias or they are using their own. And isn't turning up to your events supportive? So when does it move into being stalker behaviour?

Block, ban, report the visible and overt stalker?

This is the advice often given to children when educating them about those who hassle, harass, 'pester', annoy, won't leave alone, etc. But the advice given to adults who experience this with a 'stalker' is to report, collect evidence, change your phone number and so on. So why do we approach the same behaviour with a slightly different language and advice for young people? For example, how do we teach the recipient of this behaviour what trolling, bullying, flaming, stalking or harassment is when they are all overlapping in their typology? And when does follower behaviour move from reassuring, to annoying and harassing, and how? Do the young people collect evidence and where do they store it, if their device does not allow them to hide the files (from themselves)? What happens if they keep revisiting the post, comments or text? How does this help with their mental health and well-being?

Practitioner pause for reflection

How would you approach this issue of a follower following and interacting with every post, would you call it stalking? What about the child, and how they feel about the person who is in their social media feed all of the time if, for example it is reported to you that *x* person is stalking *y* person and *y* person tells you this is their boy/girlfriend, as happens in sexual exploitation and coercive relationships so often? What about the young person who is contacted repeatedly by a member of their family of origin if they are in care settings? And what about that random person, can you identify them, or realistically do anything about it other than advising to block and report. What happens if they use different names or identities?

Camping out as stalking, or is it bullying?

When you are working with a young person and they say, 'Oh so and so was doing my head in last night camping out, and does it all that time on *X* game', would you be sitting thinking that you needed to talk to them about stalking, or would you be advising about blocking and reporting someone in a game as a different type of behaviour? I mean let's get silly with this example so you can understand the parallel.

If little Billy goes to the football pitch to play, and every day when he gets there Tommy is ready and waiting to pinch the ball or run off with the jumpers thrown on the floor, we would be looking at an abusive set of behaviours from Tommy and label this as bullying or harassment. It would be unlikely that we would say Tommy was stalking Billy, wouldn't it? So now we can think of Laura, who goes to the local Tesco only to see Mick loitering again on the corner of the street, and waving to her as she gets into her car. What would we call this?

Does it only become stalking when that behaviour transitions into multiple locations and times? If so, did you ask the child who talked about the camping player if this player is on other games with them? Or perhaps knows of them being in online spaces that they visit? Is it stalking or is it perhaps a team that is placed on multiple games or online locations? Surely being invited into a party on multiple games is okay, so what about the gamer that requests this, as being seen 'online' means they can reach out to you repeatedly in this space? Is it game requests, spamming or stalking? Game requests and messages can even be sent when you are not there, for that moment you sign in. And are we going back to the blue-tick distress phenomenon mentioned in my first book, when you know someone is waiting and watching for the blue ticks (or read receipts) to be shown when you read the message (Knibbs, 2022)?

Have you ever considered that someone sending messages on WhatsApp-type platforms could be stalking you to see when you are online and have read their message, and if so what do you find yourself doing to avoid this? Sadly, if you use certain platforms that are tied together, then it can alert a person watching to your presence. This takes the idea of being watched and knowing you are there to the moment some people open their eyes and their smartphone. This feels really intrusive or akin to a small child standing at their parent's bedside waiting for the eyes of the parent to open before launching into today's important conversation and questions. Can I have breakfast now?

Knock knock: who's there?

And for covert stalking, maybe you will never know until you are notified, that you are being watched. It's like the world of data breaches in so far as you only know there has been one if you have the systems in place to let you know it has happened. If you are in the public domain, and online in any way, then in the words of the Jacksons, 'Somebody's watching me'. Yes, someone *is* always watching.

We need to expand our thinking about real-world laws and definitions to online spaces, because the psychological impact of being stalked online is often the same (Short et al., 2015). However, you can change the direction and time you travel to school in the real world if you needed to; you could also move house, move job or change your phone number.

The identity you have online is connected to so many spaces that this may be difficult to do in the same way as the corporeal world. Therefore this is why this is such an issue for children who are exploited online. The thinking required here means changing our thinking to match the online space. Blocking, banning and reporting may not work if Tommy can become Laura or Billybob, or a dog, at the drop of a hat. You cannot always know who is who online, so tracking the follower or stalker can be difficult. The impact may be the same as in the real world, however; the presence of a bodily figure, a car or some form of physical connection to a real-world stalker is enough for us to say that the person is real and the crime is occurring. But what about the online stalker, what does a person do when the stalker changes their identity, uses a VPN and continuously changes the goalposts, so to speak? How do we catch the bogeyman, and what is the advice offered about this kind of cruel taunt?

Shop somewhere else: a case example

A client I worked with was given this advice by the constable who was working on her case. Her stalker was an ex and often turned up at the same local shops and supermarkets she went to, those being the ones they had visited together as a couple. Her ex's claim when questioned was that the shops were local to him too, and convenient, and of course his 'favourite' items to buy were in these shops. My client was told *shop elsewhere*. She was perturbed by this to begin with, and found that she was the one who needed to change her behaviours, which she did to feel more comfortable. She was okay with this to a degree, as she could quite easily go to the shops after work on her way home rather than from home to the local shops. This resolves the real-world issue for now. So we move on to her presenting issue once more.

Her ex-partner began to watch her behaviour on social media, and he would comment in groups they were both a part of under posts she had already commented on (so she would receive notifications about these new comments and who they were from) and this began to become the new 'local shop' scenario. She had blocked him after they separated. And this account was indeed blocked but could be seen in groups they shared (an aspect of groups on this particular platform allowed for this). In due course, his slightly altered name, picture and sometimes her maiden surname would be used on the new 'accounts' that would be commenting on the posts. She was literally playing 'block-a-mole' with each new persona that came into the space, using small personal details to let her know it was her ex (e.g., specific holiday destinations, romantic phrases and sayings). She knew 'in her bones', as she told me, that it was him, and I advised that she should report this (again keeping my eye on the research about exes and crimes of passion, as they are called), and when she did she was told by the investigator that they would look into it, and to effectively *shop elsewhere* (leave that social media group and platform).

My client found herself in tears as she felt she was the one who was having to change her behaviours, and the resulting investigation revealed that the police didn't have the resources to 'trace people on the Internet in a Facebook group' who could be or might not be him. She should collect screenshots and consider going to see a solicitor. My client was 18 and could not afford this, having only recently left education. She didn't have the internal resources to fight this or put a complaint to the police.

What would you do, what would you advise and what would be your safeguarding superpower in this situation?

What is known to a degree (as we discussed earlier about the difficulty of measuring these issues) about people who engage in stalking post-separation is the likelihood of violence increasing, and the links to serious assault, kidnap, murder or, in the case where there have been children in the relationships, the harm or homicidal tendencies towards the ex and their children (Haye & Jeffries, 2015).

Given this aspect, my client was well within her rights to complain, and rightly so, regardless of her age or sex. The crime rate of recently separated couples and stalking behaviours cannot go undocumented, un-actioned or ignored, because there is a great deal of anxiety, trauma and fear involved on the part of the stalked person. Behaviours that have been reported in my therapy room consisted of not sleeping, paranoid thinking, deletion of social media accounts, changing phone numbers, getting new jobs, moving and depression, that resulted in not sending children to school for fear of 'what could happen'.

This is very serious. We need to take these situations seriously.

In the world of psychotherapy, we often 'treat' high-end anxiety as an irrational set of beliefs or thoughts that are tied to unlikely outcomes such as planes crashing; we also call it paranoia. However, in the scenario of being cyberstalked, there is the unknown and constant worry and thinking about all actions they take with a smartphone or computer. It is known that some partners download software to devices in order to monitor, to remotely stalk where the person goes (GPS) or what they are doing (keylogging) or whom they are talking to (spying) and these all form, for the client, a rational unknown expectational process about the mights, coulds and what-ifs.

And who are we to say what can and can't happen online in reality, if we don't know the terrain or understand the online spaces?

The victim suffering from cyberstalking anxiety is constantly playing these many scenarios out, and they might not be as irrational as the outsider would initially think. They have merit, and often the stalker does things to let the victim know they are online and watching.

Cyberstalking anxiety is akin to micro-PTS and macro-PTS on a daily basis. Micro-PTS is like the worry that gets associated with each ping or buzz of the smartphone and who it could be or what it might say or what they might see. The macro-PTS is the considerations that the person must go through when going out of the house, only this is about the spaces they go online too.

Education settings as the micro and macro

Now add in the factor of education settings for young people, and you can see that they can end up on a macro- and micro-PTS, stalker-anxiety roundabout all day long. For example, in the days before the Internet began, separating from a partner who was also in the school would mean having to see that person in the education setting, and often the person could make enough changes to avoid seeing the ex outside of lessons (if they shared them). However, the physical measures and distance never go away when the stalker is able to follow you online. And if the cyberstalker is the kid in class *x*, then home is no respite from this, and education settings become places of stress and anxiety for young people who are suffering from this issue.

Young people have no 'space' with which to be able to definitively move away from the threats online, as they are always there, like the iconic cursor that blinks, waiting for your next move on the word document, and somehow it is always there waiting even when you're not online. If you don't believe me, open a word document at any time of the day or night and you will see it. Eerie, and ever present.

Screw that, *they* can shop elsewhere!

As the practitioner speaking with a young person about someone who stalks them online openly (overtly), this can become quite terrifying for young people who may not have the resources to manage this feeling. I find, when they speak to me in therapy, the stubbornness and defiance of a teen is most frequently the first port of call as an offence hidden as defence, with which they claim that they will not 'shop somewhere else' because why should they? They are going to keep posting on Insta, Snap and elsewhere, and the other person can go screw themselves. Whilst also looking terrified as they say this to me. It must be so conflictual because this is their social space and there is no way to keep people out of it. There is no door staff with a guest list. But what is reassuring for some of these young people is their friends often speak out in these spaces. But not always.

Giving generic advice about this means that you will need to stop, think and consider what they can do with the tools they have and what tools the platforms and social media spaces offer. This means you will have to use the platforms like they do or a stalker would, or find a guide to help you navigate the space before offering a young person a set of to-dos. Young people often expect you to know what the sites are and how they work, and are often looking to us as the adults to help, and of course we don't even know how surreptitious the behaviour of the stalker is by liking certain posts, or being on the same Twitch channels and using certain memes. So how can we advise them?

Take this lollipop. But don't

Over a decade ago, a film director (Jason Jada) created an interactive Facebook app that, in essence, creates a stalker to follow you based on the information you have and share on your profile. Not only would you see the person using your content to find out who you are, where you live or what you have shared that they could 'blackmail' you with, but the ending of this film is a lollipop that hides a razor blade in it. Mchugh (2011) discussed this many years ago, and now this app is now no longer available (since 2018).

These types of films, or social media stunts, are created by people wanting to 'show you' what you're doing wrong and how you should have protected your identity, content and presence online. Done with the best of intentions, but perhaps not the best of methods?

References

Besharat Mann, R., & Blumberg, F. (2022). Adolescents and social media: The effects of frequency of use, self-presentation, social comparison, and self-esteem on possible self-imagery. *Acta Psychologica*, 228.

Black, M. C., Basile, K. C., Breiding, M. J., Smith, S. G., Walters, M. L., Merrick, M. T., Chen, J., & Stevens, M. R. (2011). *The national intimate partner and sexual violence survey (NISVS): 2010 summary report*. National Center for Injury Prevention and Control, Centers for Disease Control and Prevention: Atlanta, GA.

Burrow, A., & Rainone, N. (2017). How many *likes* did I get?: Purpose moderates links between positive social media feedback and self-esteem. *Journal of Experimental Social Psychology*, 69, 232–236.

Haye, S., & Jeffries, S. (2015). Romantic terrorism. In *Romantic terrorism: An auto-ethnography of domestic violence, victimization and survival*. Palgrave Pivot: London.

Kaur, P., Dhir, A., Tandon, A., Alzeiby, E., & Abohassan, A. (2021). A systematic literature review on cyberstalking. An analysis of past achievements and future promises. *Technological Forecasting and Social Change*, 163.

Knibbs, C. (2022). *Children, technology and healthy development*. Routledge: Abingdon.

Lembke, A. (2021). *Dopamine nation: Finding balance in the age of indulgence*. Headline: London.

Lieberman, D., & Long, M. (2019). *The molecule of more. How a single chemical in your brain drives, love sex, creativity, and will determine the fate of the human race*. Benbella Books: Dallas.

Mchugh, M. (2011). *Take this lollipop makes Facebook stalking personal – and horrifying*. www.digitaltrends.com/social-media/take-this-lollipop-makes-facebook-stalking-personal-and-horrifying/.

Office for National Statistics (ONS). (2022). www.ons.gov.uk/peoplepopulationandcommunity/crimeandjustice/datasets/stalkingfindingsfromthecrimesurveyforenglandandwales.

Short, E., Guppy, A., Hart, A., & Barnes, J. (2015). The impact of cyberstalking. *Studies in Media and Communication*, 3(2).

Siegel, D. (2010). *The mindful therapist. A clinician's guide to mindsight and neural integration*. W. W. Norton & Co: New York.

Women's Aid. (2020). Why don't women leave? Femicide Census (2020) *The Femicide Census: 2018 findings. Annual Report on UK Femicides 2018*. www.womensaid.org.uk/information-support/what-is-domestic-abuse/women-leave/.

Zuboff, S. (2019). *The age of surveillance capitalism. The fight for a new human future at the new frontier of power*. Profile Books: London.

6 Bodies, health and wellbeing

Every chapter, topic and section of this book can be seen through the lens of one or more of the other sections, chapters and topics.

Health as double-edged swords. Help or hindrance?

The health, wellness and fitness space online is a sword with two edges.

Add to this the beauty and cosmetics industry and we have a potential tsunami of: ' "You're not good enough" for all who enter the vortex of "shoulds and musts"'

This chapter will look at health, body issues, body dysmorphia, body ideals and eating disorders related to social media, why males can be overlooked in this domain, as well as why disordered eating and eating disorders are more complicated than image-based influences. We will look at quick fixes, ideal outcomes and promises to ensure you are 'attractive', 'healthy' and 'irresistible', how the influencers and systems in place promise this will 'enhance your self-esteem, self-worth, confidence, longevity and likes on the platforms' (and much, much more).

Better than a school education?

Social media, websites, forum training and apps are fantastic domains with which to learn about the wonders of the body, its inner workings and what you can do to be 'healthy', with all of the meanings that go with this word. So why don't we start there and begin with the topic of health, and what this means for us here in this chapter, and our lives and understandings as practitioners?

In school, we learn basic definitions, and the approach to health usually consists of food or science-based topics such as biology or food technology. We have lessons in physical education, exercise lessons, physical training and sports lessons. These are all aimed at and relate to the physical element of health in education settings. Many children are taught the food pyramid and healthy eating approach in the early years of schooling. For example, children under five are often given milk as a daily part of their school life. School lunchtimes and breakfast clubs have had a reshape on what they now offer to children, as the UK and US currently have many children who are classified as obese.

DOI: 10.4324/9781003289210-7

This obesity crisis may be more to do with the unrelenting access to junk food in supermarkets, deliveries and accessibility afforded by technology or conveniently placed food emporiums on the junctions of main street spaces. It's all too easy to overeat and eat foods that may trigger unhealthy responses in our bodies or are just downright toxic. It's said that many of the junk food producers create foods that are satiating and tap into our drive to eat more than we should in perhaps one sitting, and that have a 'bliss point' or 'sweet spot' set into them and have taglines like 'You can't stop' (Moss, 2013).

Hypocrisy?

Before we go on, and as many of you readers will be over the age of 18, how does this last paragraph feel when I interchange food for alcohol in the sentences? Given the harms you know about this substance, how many adverts do you see with the message lined up to sell you the 'cure' to your ills, and how many of these are seen by young people, have childlike flavours, bottles and parties in them? How much of this space of health are the yin and yang of doing as I say but not as I do, and you *can't have that* but you *can have this* (all dependent upon who is selling what to whom!)?

Let's start with the word *health* and how this is one of the most viewed categories of online spaces, as it encompasses so much. This is the most prominent aspect for both adults and children, and is the most prolific conversation I have in therapy aside from the illegal-harms conversations (volume 1).

Health

Well, for a simple overview, we can start with the World Health Organisation (WHO), where it is stated:

> Health is a state of complete physical, mental and social well-being and not merely the absence of disease or infirmity.
>
> www.who.int/about/governance/constitution

We also have explanations (far too many to cite in this topic) of, let's say, how 'total health and fitness' is the culmination of all things: physical, mental, emotional, nutritional, medical, social, skill-related and adaptability-related (think survival intelligence). So this version of what health or fitness looks and feels like may well be a good 'fit' for this space to think about the areas in which we can focus for this chapter.

And of course, when we think about health, we have to consider the offshoots of fitness, beauty and lifespan, as promoted on social media as part of this industry. We can see further separations and delineations, meaning we have: medical models, psychological models, emotional models, biopsychosocial models, fitness-industry models, alternative-industry models, cosmetic models, functional models, family models, cultural models, historic models, corporate models, epidemiological models, women's and men's models, nutritional models, developmental models, brain models, sexual models, spiritual (financial, planetary and more) models, and even as I discussed in my last book, the idea of nervous system health and body-budget theories, in line with renowned writers like Lisa Feldman-Barrett, Mona Delahooke and Stephen Porges lending their knowledge to this space. See the bibliography for more texts and reading in this space also (which is now becoming the world of trauma-informed care and well-being, huzzah!).

Overload!

If you go to any social media platform or space on the Internet, a quick search will send you to a plethora of advice forums, websites, people and ideas for each one of these topics, and therein the advisory overload begins. Whom to trust?

Health and well-being, together. Do no harm?

Firstly, when we consider the well-being and the unrelenting, high level of information online, we could take a philosophical approach to this topic. We have, for those in the medical practice and those regulated by the medical model: the Hippocratic oath, considered to be directly from Hippocrates and states "primum non nocere"; it was and is sworn in the early days of practice to ensure that the practitioner does not harm the patient, client or customer. Herein this model approaches health as a way of life, a being of health, a homeostatic balance and a whole-istic approach to a human. It is also an ethical framework with philosophical roots and, unfortunately as we will discover, only with accountability to those with certificates in this model such as doctors, nurses, paramedics and certain health professionals (within the UK). The health of the patient also deems the well-being of the practitioner's profession, and I suppose we could say vice versa.

And so, the young people of today, and many adults to be fair, can end up in many of these unregulated online spaces or following gurus, charlatans and cowboys, or they can find a well-researched, evidence-based and ethical practitioners such as Layne Norton PhD, Peter Attia MD, Derek More Plates More Dates, or the Podcast host Andrew Huberman PhD who are sharing advice based on many years of dedicated learning, embodiment and application. It is very difficult to say how many other, of these well researched, balanced people exist online, as there is no way to 'vet' their level of knowledge against a system of unregulated 'professionals'. The only systems in place for this are often the academic degrees someone holds or a professional regulatory body that oversees their practice, with which a complaint can be made about that professional after the harm has been inflicted, carried out or has occurred.

To work out who these people are, whether their intent is good and their knowledge is evidence-based or otherwise, means that the visitor to those spaces is critically analysing the content, spends time researching the research cited for themselves, and it requires that they can understand research to be able to apply it to their lives. And, as a reader familiar with these chapters now, I feel you will not be surprised to read that people don't do this, less so the younger busy adolescent brains who don't have time to take a course or spend time checking facts, and so, if 'this' influencer says it is so, then so be it?

But! And there is always a happy side to this space, which is one of the times I will write a positive aspect in this book. When young people take a positive approach to living well, being well and well-being, as we often advise them to do, then they are likely to find helpful knowledge in this space. Given the reflection I made about obesity, and add to this substance abuse, self-harm issues, disordered eating and bodily health in terms of exercise and nutrition, then there is hope for our children not to follow our footsteps of 'unhealthy' and chronic illnesses, and to find information that keeps them on the right side of not needing medical interventions for what can be and are called self-made illnesses (not my words, but ones I have heard uttered and seen online written by medical professionals).

What is positive is the information is now readily available in a space that would have otherwise been controlled by lengthy waits to see a medical professional, and this now means there are preventive actions that people can take for their health: something they can control, adapt, improve and more. It can be so positive in a time of crisis, and the recent pandemic and learning about taking care of yourself were good in an overarching way when you take out the inflammatory posts about scepticism, infodemic misinformation and conspiracy theories.

Yet, it can also be a toxic cesspit of overbearing, inconsistent, conflicting, confusing, mis, dis and skewed information. There can be an overwhelming number of experts and idiots, and the filtering of this takes time. As discussed earlier, critical thinking in the online space is the most needed form of enquiry and belief system, and course it only takes one meme to change the path of least resistance!

The space of potential ill health and death, in favour of popularity?

What about the impacts on health and well-being if the outcome heads in the opposite direction? So, if we just revisit the chapter on trends and hoaxes, I would like to introduce you to a phenomenon called 'mukbang', which is the online visual (and sometimes auditory) process of eating in front of a (usually) live audience. This has become popular with varying nationalities sharing their cultural foods to educate people around the world. So far, this doesn't sound too distressing.

And of course, our televisions are full of programs about food, with national competitions based on creating the best of [insert your favourite type of food program]: for example, *Bake Off*, *Celebrity Chef*, *MasterChef*, *Ready Steady Cook* and the biggest names behind these shows like Gordon Ramsay's *Kitchen Nightmares*. Even the adults like to watch the culinary delights of new foods, disastrous baking, cooking errors, the momentous part of the 'tasting' of the food and the reactions to the food: good or bad.

Now the etymology of mukbang is suggested to be, according to the Collins dictionary, the parsing together of two words in Korean to mean 'eating broadcast' www.collinsdictionary.com/dictionary/english/mukbang.

And in this process, even the dictionary explanation refers to a 'large quantity of food' being eaten. And herein lies the problem for some young people who engage in this experience.

Several young people place themselves as potential streaming influencers, and to gain the numbers required to become influential, it becomes necessary that they create content that 'sells'. To do so, the exploitation, the lols and bullying that can occur around this issue can (and do) create spaces where the young person is goaded into and does eat a large quantity of food on stream, and this results in several issues.

These range from the financial impact of perhaps ordering 'the entire menu at' [maybe the Golden Arches food emporium], sickness and vomiting after consuming all of the food as well as a fast-track route to obesity in a short period, resulting in rapid subcutaneous fat deposits and risk of cardiovascular diseases or more.

Furthermore, this issue can fall under trends, exploitation, ridicule and cyber-bullying, abuse, self-harm and sexual-based gratifications if the person is asked to record or provide the audio of the eating of the food, as in the chapter about porn (I know, but that is a thing). And so this is where, as discussed earlier, each of these issues overlaps many of the chapters in this book and volume one.

Practitioner pause for reflection

Often you will see, in the safeguarding literature, about abuse and how food can be an aspect of this category from starvation and neglect to overeating. And we often have to consider the fact that many adults are not aware of the nutritional value of food, are often buying highly processed food that is cheap, on offer at the supermarket and buying the latest fancy meal at fast-food emporiums (who make the affordable food choices hit that bliss point so you return) only to be met with a low-nutrition meal. Time-poor parents and carers, as well as easy-to-access and cheap food options can and do result in health issues for children, but what would you do in this situation, for example, where a young child is streaming their eating for popularity at the expense of their health, and what can you do to help the parents, carers or children in this example? Especially when one of the influencers they follow is selling a 'high-energy drink' with their name on it (filled with food groups that young children ought not to be consuming, for example). Abuse, neglect or naiveté?

Marvel-male physiques, gyms, supplements, dieting and damage

This section begins with the males who are pressured by the expectations of the media, film, TV and social spaces, to be: built, stacked, henched, ripped and/or the gym 'roid heads'.

Over a decade ago (Knibbs, 2012) I was giving a workshop regarding the use of Facebook by young people at the time, when indeed it was popular for people aged 13–17 to be using this platform (though apparently, this is an old hat for them now). I was discussing users' profile pictures and how many people could see them, and the process that young people would go through to get the best-looking image. The answers were so interesting and sometimes comedic, sad and shocking, but overall there was a consensus there had to be a number from which to choose. This issue has been discussed by South West Grid for Learning at a conference I attended some time ago when it was discussed that young people take, on average, 42 selfies before uploading the one that's 'just right' (personal communication, 2015).

Now the goldilocks profile picture, according to my clients and students over the years, when posted on any platform, must have some elements in it that are almost nonnegotiable. These are correct lighting, filters (if required) and often the setting. Several years ago, these would be selfies in front of mirrors in bathrooms, bedrooms and perhaps even hallways, so that: a) the device could be seen in the image being held by the person taking the picture, and therefore 'not a professional one', which may be too grandiose; b) just enough information in the background to look like it was spontaneous and perhaps not 'performed; and c) have taken many to choose the perfect one (after maybe sending it to friends for voting and deciding which is the best one).

Young people who shared this with me declare they know they are doing exactly this and know that others are too. All with plenty of practice to get the image perfect to meet the previous criteria so as not to look like a 'model', 'whore' or 'poser'. Who knew taking a picture was so complicated, time-consuming and important?

Reflexons, six-packs and chests

If you read volume one, you will know this issue of chests 'on show' is beginning to sound like a child-sexual abuse issue, and you would be right to be considering all of that information here, whilst also considering and appreciating the laws around males and chest bearing, because this often appears on profile pictures and photos shared online, and not in the CSAEM or self-generated content space where they are traded between peers. Again, not an insular issue but one that needs the rest of the chapters to appreciate fully.

What is interesting is the male in these images, often spotted at the gym I might add. As they move around the physical space looking to get the best angle for the muscle development required of an adolescent male 'puffing up his feathers' and showing himself to both the desirable sex and to the competitors, there is a lot of movement in the smartphone to capture that perfect shot. Facing the mirror, to one side, from above, seated at the mirror whilst 'lifting' or getting their gym buddy to take the image as though it was snapped 'unawares'. It's fascinating to watch, and all ages of male gym goers seem to do this; at times I feel like David Attenborough watching a new species of animal 'peacocking'. This is what might be called the domination or sexual prowess stance, and the 'bigger' you can make yourself look, the better? And if this is the case, where to look for ideas, advice and the correct process for building up muscle and the images that make you look hench, built, stacked and how to do the perfect reflexon (showing your six-pack through strenuous stomach tightening, and keeping a straight face)? That's right: the gym. Oh no hang on, that would be gyms . . . on the Internet. And where to start?

Bodybuilding to acting

Maybe those who have heard of this guy might know he was Mr Universe (on more than one occasion) and so has major lived experience in the world of bodybuilding and exercise; he's called Arnold Schwarzenegger. And of course, muscles must mean fighting power perhaps, and in that case, the world of MMA fighters is the next 'masculine' physique space to look at, with one of the most famous being Connor McGregor, or perhaps even Joe Rogan who has a podcast too, maybe they go to the world of sport such as rugby, football, cycling or one of the spaces that's most popular right now for information and directions about muscles, physiques and health; acting and gaming, say what?

Yes, the male influencers taking to the screens and parading their physiques through gaming and comic-related shows, films and gaming-based fantasy programs are also on the Internet sharing their training regimes, supplement sponsorships and partnerships (whether they take them or not).

Many of the young people I speak to watch the Marvel and DC films, with the main actor always being 'ripped' and of the 'perfect' body, and they follow them online somewhere. This influence is often overlooked in the mainstream focus of body-orientated conversations, because training your body to look like Spider-Man, Iron Man, Superman and all of the hero 'mans' is considered – wait for it – healthy. Or, could it be obsessive, strenuous and costly? We can certainly say the chasing of the ideal masculine body is creating an issue for males, in many areas of functioning such as self-esteem, as Kimmel and Mahalik discuss at length in their paper (2004), however, I am struck by the lack of research in this area since this time.

When does it become too much, as in the issue of overtraining? Yes, this is possible and yet this is a term that is undefined and robust (Matos & Winsley, 2007; Winsley & Matos, 2011). Could it be an issue of eating too much 'whey protein' because the bodybuilders online recommend it, and not enough real food is consumed in its place? What about too many influencer-sponsored supplements, steroids, training schedules, diets ranging from keto to vegan or pushed into the spotlight by documentaries on Netflix such as *The Game Changers (2019)*, featuring Arnold Schwarzenegger and friends https://gamechangersmovie.com/ 2019?

Injuries inside and out

What about injuries to organs, muscles or bones, as the young person aims to 'build fast', and damages their growing body or hormone-based substances to increase muscle mass damaging who knows what? There is some evidence that steroids affect brain and body development, but there is so much conflicting data and low levels of robust research in young people for obvious reasons, so I am generalising here. Or, as the area I focus on in therapy, as it comes up in conversations so much and was discussed at the workshop in 2012 mentioned previously: the six-pack 'reflexon' and lack of body fat needed to 'see' these six packs in the growing male body.

To visibly see the stomach muscles called the abdominal wall, a person (usually discussed in men's health spaces) needs to be in the lower ranges of 7–15% body fat, see https://rippedbody.com/body-fat-guide/ for an image based guide to this or the discussion by Venuto (2012, 2021), at https://www.muscleandstrength.com/articles/body-fat-level-see-abs and dependent upon which article you read, scientific, health-related or otherwise, you'll find a pretty consistent framing of lower body fat for seeing the six-pack. However, in the research for this book, I was swamped with findings and can say genetic disposition, skin thickness, body mass index and more have an impact, but generally the lower the body fat index, the more these muscles can be seen (fairly observational finding, but nonetheless overwhelming on the Internet!).

On average, this will show the average six-pack of this muscle group, and this is often what is being aimed for in terms of: trying to gain the gains, to achieve the Iron Man and Superman physique as quickly as possible, and to show it off on images. And where do young people get this advice? Yes, the Internet, where a 'personal training' qualification (online course over two weeks versus a university level 5–8 course) can lead you into suddenly being confronted by hacks, tips and advice, ranging from well-informed PhD-level trainers to the young and inexperienced using all manner of hacks, cheats and ingestible substances to get you there quicker. What can be injured in the process of wanting and needing to be the next elite?

What about men, when it comes to body conversations?

What is interesting about the body-ideal debates is that males are often over-looked in this way, because we tend to see exercise and training as health-orientated practices, especially when it means the junk food diet is reduced or condemned. Yet this cohort is under immense pressure akin to the females, but more surreptitiously and subtly. The glamour-magazine narrative often cites that females are condemned to perform, achieve and be 'perfect' under the mainstream media offering of what a perfect or beautiful body looks like. But what about men, be that a masculine or gay man's expectation?

Is body image different in men, and is the pressure to be perfect similar or different? And who controls this narrative? What is showing off versus showing up, given the conversations in volume one about sexual images, genitalia and chests? Why do men feel the need for this chiselled, six-pack, 'clearly didn't skip leg day' physique. And what is this doing to the industry of supplementations, quick-fix muscle-building proteins and grab-a-snack health bars? And if you haven't ever paid attention, have a look in your local supermarket, next time you are out, at the shelves of whey protein, snack bars and vitamin drinks. And notice how many females loiter in this section versus the males.

When it comes to having this perfect body type, the males are seeing just as many images and influences as the females, and the new surgical expansions of removing fat, adding in muscle and training to gain gym memberships have been steadily rising in my newsfeeds over the last few years as I watch the health industries online (surgery discussed later).

And this does not subside in the spaces of LGBTQIA when we start to see the influence of makeup, hair and clothing.

Made up, makeup and maxxed up

It seems, without a shadow of a doubt, that the Internet has exacerbated the idea of beauty to an incomprehensible level. Children as young as seven in my therapy office have commented on what they need to look like if they are going to have any images online, beginning with the makeup of a 'Disney princess' and the application of bright, sparkly and shimmering 'accessories' from the local popular boutique. The young people I work with are amazing artists with makeup, following online tutorials that sometimes leave me open-mouthed at the 1–3 hour step-by-step application to the perfect and flawless 'face', with contouring to rival the Hollywood stars MUAs (makeup artists), and this has been for both males, females, trans and anyone else who wants to make up.

TV programs with MUA competitions bring the artistic side of stars, flashes and at times animalistic creations, bringing the eyes to life and making the colours 'pop'. These are actual terms from the programs, and I am still none the wiser about what this means for the average person applying makeup.

In my continuous research, i.e., watching, of the trends online regarding the world of what a perfect face should be, I have been confronted by videos of the routines for face health ranging from UV lighting, light masks, electrolysis, peeling (literal burning of the skin to peel it off), exfoliations that would make a pumice stone look smooth, charcoal-based products, machines that suck, laser or spray gosh knows what and more. Only then for it be replaced with layers of toners, moisturisers and skin rejuvenators, and then onto the products themselves to make one self-transform from natural to immaculate, and your sex or gender doesn't matter in this space.

The downside to this level of products applied on the skin is this is the largest organ of the body, and this contributes to the absorption of some of the most harmful endotoxins in some of those makeup and skin products. These are having health effects that are only just beginning to be understood, and the effects are likely going to be studied in due course over several years. As a functional health practitioner, I am aware that women I work with in their 40s–60s currently have a large total of endotoxin accumulation from their many years of applying products to their skin, and I certainly know they didn't 'layer cake' their faces in the way the young people are today, probably due to the lower numbers of products and what makeup consisted of as a bag of goodies, so to speak. It seems that today's makeup bag requires four wheels to carry about. I may be playing a tongue-in-cheek game, however, listening to my client's list of all things necessary leaves me thinking they must carry it about in a suitcase.

Look younger, feel younger; you're worth it?

What was once a targeted advertising space on glossy pages, aimed at the intolerable fact that people age and need to 'look younger,' the Internet is now a competitive space for eternal youth, natural exquisiteness and always on-point faces and bodies. If you can't make it up, then you can get something to add to it or change it permanently, for example, cosmetic surgeries, enhancers, lip fillers, makeup tattoos, plumper, contoured cheekbones and more. Skin can be grafted, spliced, removed and bones inserted to create new shapes on your face. You can sign up for rhinoplasty, a surgical procedure to change your nose, you can have breasts or bum cheeks inserted (or reduced) and you can adjust the genitalia to a certain degree, as in the case of vaginoplasty. All procedures that carry risks, infections and side effects many years later can and do go wrong, and if they do, on the back of this, you can apply to be on TV programs as the star of the episode whilst your horror story is fixed (e.g., *Botched, Nip/Tuck, Extreme Makeover*).

This is huge in the adult space, where working can supply the individual with the money to pay for such procedures. But what about the young people doing a quick Google search and finding an unregulated cosmetic clinic offering Botox, lip filler or stem cell 'rejuvenation', cures and all? Where are they going to get the money to pay for this? What about the online sellers of do-it-yourself kits, and ones who sell saline, knock-off and harmful chemicals in place of clinical-grade products? What about the use of harsh chemicals on places like the lips being used to create fuller-looking ones, that happen to be toxic? What tests would we need to run on a person to find out if they had applied toxic chemicals, and is this something we need to consider in today's world of knockoff makeup and products? What about the glues used on the eyelashes that can result in eye injuries, other areas of the body being glued together and more?

What about the young person who is determined to speak to a medical professional and request some of the previous procedures that relate to bodies, health or even gender, to feel they are whom the Internet tells them they need to be? Are the medical staff you work with aware of these cheaper, toxic and harmful 'ingredients' and substances, and would they see this as self-harm, self-help or a self-esteem issue? Are we giving out surgeries to support mental well-being, and has this influence or decision considered the influencers and information overload from this health and well-being space? And where do they get their information?

This brings us to the space of podcasts helping you achieve maximum health, wellness and fitness through biological and medical hacks, appliances and accessories that can cost, literally, an arm and a leg for you to be considered 'acceptable' among your peers. This cohort is increasing in popularity for those who are over 30, and some of these podcasts are listened to by the very young adults and adolescents mentioned previously, as they get their advice from scientists, gurus and great marketers.

Obsessed, informed or driven by stats?

Now I am a user of some of these health-related trackers because I value and utilise certain measurements, for example, Heart Rate Variability Biofeedback. I use this in my therapy office and have done this for over a decade, as this helps me help my clients with that nervous system health I mentioned previously. I use HRV tracking to monitor, not obsess, over my health and well-being, though this can easily become something I could be obsessed over by checking the apps on numerous occasions, as this is about ease of access and they sit at the end of my arms. Now whilst I use these tentatively, I tend to monitor my internal weather check of how I feel, because not one system can tell me or has been able to tell me, to date, how 'well' I actually feel. And to be honest, they were not particularly quick off the mark to notice the day I came down with the COVID-19 virus. I felt ill before they noticed a change in my physiology. These devices were said to be 'on point' for detecting COVID symptoms, but my evidence was not as quick as I was. Furthermore, even with some of the apps and devices I use, they claim to be able to give you an average rating of readiness, which is often in the ballpark, but emotions, feelings, psychology, dream content and *being a human* is not measurable in this way, and so physiology is the only real data set to be reflected to me, and this is what I work with.

However, the more health-related tech we produce, the more the clients I work with seem to be buying it and buying into it, and the more I have had conversations about the Apple Watch informing them they are unwell, their sleep is 'not good enough', their calories (macros, etc.) are not right for the gains and they are using their screens too much (and in exam season no less!). And the list goes on. The tech is beginning to tell them, like an intrusive smother mother, that they do not know who they are, how they feel and more.

The effects of this are just beginning to appear in my therapy room as apps for anxiety, self-harm, wellness, dieting and sleep are beginning to become the daily check-ins for young people to see if they 'measure up' against the rest of their peers. Competition to see who can get the largest, or lowest, numbers or streaks. Those who send their peers the latest podcast, video or advice about health because 'some random dude online said' and, of course, this becomes gospel in the new trend of how to measure, adapt and overcome the routine, food choices and knowledge that your parents have.

Which health apps are helpful, and which don't spy?

I have often found when talking to parents that when I discuss apps and ways to help clients, I will often say that you have to find the one that is right for you and your family, the one that isn't aiming to spy on you, the one that doesn't cost a fortune, is reliable and functions for the process we are discussing, and I often recommend that they visit Orcha Health, https://orchahealth.com/ for researched apps and not to 'just download' any old one off the online store.

> This is also a pertinent time to remind practitioners not to suggest apps without checking their background for age restrictions, where the app was created (and by whom and what it does), where the data is collected, etc., because the child can in effect come back to you years down the line regarding their data protection and rights if you were the one who suggested this option. Furthermore, do

not recommend YouTube as a place to go and watch videos, as discussed in the chapter on the harms professionals can cause.

However, parents and professionals often do not know what apps, influencers or podcasts their child is using to manage their health. For example, My Fitness Pal (aside from the issue of being hacked in 2019) is an application that provides a space in which they can track their food intake and monitor calories, alongside exercise advice and more. This is neither good nor bad in itself, however, there is a function to add the calorie count for a food item into the database, and so the accuracies of each food group, junk food item or individual piece of food may be inaccurate when added in by a well-meaning user to the systems. Calorie counting, then, is likely to be somewhat inaccurate by this default error and bias.

Calorie tracking, which, on the surface, is not a bad thing to do for some circumstances, does not necessarily denote a disorder, obsession or actual issue because someone is tracking this. Calorie counting is used in all sorts of programs by medical staff and therapists to get clients to measure what they have been doing all week, and often is surprising, as many people don't know what their daily intake looks like on a plate, so to speak. If you consider the process of monitoring what you eat as an exercise to pay attention to your daily and weekly schedule, then this can become an illuminating process of surprise.

Rather than obsessing over calories and noticing what food types you consume, you can see what it is you're eating and you can then adapt accordingly over the week to ensure that you are in or close to the 'healthy' space many of us aim for (if there is such a thing). For example, how many times during the week do you add in some butter or add a sauce to something and not notice that you are doing this, because you have focused on the jam, spam or ham sandwich? It's easy to miss those little extras, and these kinds of exercises handed out by professionals are for this purpose, as with awareness comes change (when it's wanted and actioned upon).

However, for young people, if this becomes the only thing they do and follow, and is almost to the point of carrying scales around with them should they go 1g over their daily allowance, then you are beginning to look at obsessional and potentially harmful behaviour that is being encouraged by the data contained in the apps, platforms and podcasts. If there is no room for flexibility in calorie counting, food choices or measurement, then in the words of Dr Dan Siegel, those 'rigid' behaviours need a careful and close eye kept on them. Often this is where the focus of discovered eating can stem from, and working with some young clients who become aware of a calorie, but not what that means for their body, their health and what a calorie actually is, it becomes a somewhat arbitrary number that they believe is the only aspect of health and nutrition worth paying attention to.

And this is the narrative that social media often drives about food, health and weight, again without substance as to what those words mean for a young person when nothing is known about them or what is good for the goose or gander, so to speak!

Many adults I speak with (usually these are parents, carers and professionals involved in a young person's life) don't realise that the social media apps, advice and information their children are using and taking in information from is not directly from their education setting, teachers or textbooks. This issue is as wide as it is long in determining whether it is good, sound and robust information, backed by evidence, science and peer review, or whether it is a snake oil salesperson luring in the customers of today and tomorrow.

However, they may be getting really good information, given that, as I make a contentious statement, some of what we learn in school is not always fully accurate, without bias and omitting important factors based on the time, curriculum and culture in which we learn; this means that today's child can find out most things about most things on the Internet, and in doing so can fill in the blanks, or perhaps have the blanks filled in for them by the people online, and be able to make choices that are *good for them.*

Practitioner pause for reflection

What apps, platforms and spaces do you get your information from regarding your health and well-being, and what books, podcasts or videos have influenced your level of knowing what healthy and unhealthy looks like? Would you know how to check out what a young person is listening to or reading, and whether this is scientific research or anecdotal influencers' behaviour and aim to get 'merch' into the hands of their fans? For example, a well-known YouTuber or two now 'dabbles' in energy drinks, whey protein and healthy snacks, or advises on the use of substances to enhance thinking, performance or 'performance', and so the young people you are working with may well be buying some of this stuff, as they have been told by *X* it is good for *Y.* Consider how you can ask a young person about their consumed content, who it is, what qualifications, expertise and lived experience they have, and do you have the time to research this for each child you work with?

Eating, not eating, fasting, dieting, and disordered eating patterns, what's the difference?

'Fit, fat or frumpy' was the name of the presentation at the BACP private practice conference (Knibbs, 2019), where I discussed the influence of social media, websites and forums on the developing person exposed to the knowledge of what is considered the 'right' form of sustenance for the human being. This brings us back to the level of information, misinformation and disinformation out there in the formats of podcasts, YouTube shorts, TikTok advisories, fitness and health gurus selling the latest product, hack or invention. The plethora of sales teams employed to sell the influencer's merch to the young and well as the older generations, such as energy drinks containing high levels of caffeine and other chemicals. The information is not always great with trends and hoaxes and snake-oil remedies and there are hidden harm spaces afforded to eating, or not (these websites both pro or anti eating and health still exist in spaces and places out of sight, and are not being named here for obvious reasons).

In the diagnostic criteria manuals; the Diagnostic and Statistical Manual-V (APA, 2013) and the International Classification of Diseases-11 (WHO, 2019), eating disorders have become more complex than ever before, with changes to the issues that can present. Many of these relate to the lack of physical ingestion or expulsion of food or other substances, providing us with categories about food intake, processes before, during and after food intake and the most well-known issue, of zero intakes of nutritional substances, which is commonly misunderstood as the refusal to eat.

To give you an overview of the categories of feeding and eating disorders in the DSM-V: 'those in which persistent disturbances of eating or eating-related behaviours result in the altered consumption or absorption of food, and significantly impairs physical health or psychosocial functioning'.

These are listed as: pica, rumination disorder, Avoidant/restrictive intake disorder, anorexia nervosa, bulimia nervosa, and binge eating disorder.

And one is called Eating Disorder Not Otherwise Specified, which is not in the DMS-V, but I have seen it on referral forms, child protection plans and other documents.

Practitioner pause for reflection

Looking at these categories and knowing there are TV shows about 'fussy eaters', I wonder as a professional what your knowledge about these processes is, and what you consider an eating disorder, or issue, phase, liking for, distaste and avoidance of would look like and what words you may have used yourself as a parent, friend or professional to describe someone's eating habits? What are your preferences and opinions about food and how it is approached by a child or family? What about the recent issue of foodbanks, cost of living, the ability of people to be chefs versus cooks and what you would advise a young person that could talk to you about the 'Krebs cycle' and what nutritional value a food group is and was and what diet plan they followed? Would it be classified as one of those named disorders too if they had a level of knowledge that surpassed yours, and how can you critically analyse what they tell you if your approach to food has left you a little over or under your 'ideal' weight?

What do you know about fasting for positive intentions, such as autophagy, gut resetting and other aspects versus the anorexia diagnosis afforded to some young people who are in this space? What questions would you ask to know if this was a phase, intentional process or diagnostic issue requiring immediate attention? Anorexia nervosa is one the most debilitating issues I know of as a therapist, and at times I struggle with these questions. The young people of today are often well versed in what we need to hear, need to know and what they know about eating or not.

Gluttony or lockdown: an obesity crisis and the pandemic of 2019 to date

In direct opposition to the under-eating issue, we can find on almost any news outlet, social media space or magazine that we are facing an obesity crisis overwhelmingly blamed on the western diet, which is being referred to as the SAD (Standard American Diet). The NHS who have been suggesting the past few years the UK ranks among the worst in Europe https://www.longtermplan.nhs.uk/online-version/chapter-2-more-nhs-action-on-prevention-and-health-inequalities/obesity/ pledging to reduce childhood obesity by 2030.

Obesity, which is the prolonged intake of food resulting in excess body fat (visceral and subcutaneous), is not considered in the diagnostic manual under the eating disorders section, as this is attributed to a lack of energy expenditure balanced with the intake of food (no way, really. You mean to say excessive calories and lack of movement contribute to gaining fat, weight and inflammation?). It is suggested that obesity could be genetic, physiological, behavioural and environmental in its cause, although some medications may influence the propensity to become obese. Not to mention the type-2-diabetes crisis that is being named on social media or on the National Heart, Lung and Blood Institute in the US as a metabolic issue, called metabolic syndrome, as designated by the clusters of issues present see NHLBI – www.nhlbi.nih.gov/health/metabolic-syndrome, that creates an illusion that overeating is not the sole cause of this medical issue. I wish we could think like this about all of the diagnoses, for example, if we took a look at all the contributing factors we might be able to see a person as a product of their environment and not one sole cause.

> My reflection here is this is not news or developing research. We know from studies on animals that excessive food intake results in higher body weights and is linked to all causes of mortality, and we know that the field of epigenetics shows us that environment influences gene expression, and so all of the above is true, with no one direct 'cause', but a way that everything about a person is influenced. I am already seeing influencers suggesting that in due course we will be adding the Internet and gaming to this list of 'possible' causes of obesity, due to lack of movement, because people who watch TV are possibly active more than Internet users. And the common phrase being used nowadays is 'sitting is the new smoking'. I think we need a radical intervention in care homes and hospitals if that is the case, pronto.

Could obesity be down to several factors, for example, as I mentioned earlier, the access to junk food, processed cheap foods in the markets and supermarkets, the cost of real food farms being out of the reach of many people as living costs spike year upon year, results in the intake of foods that may be associated with the accumulation of body fat, which also is said to include drinks such as sugary fizzy pop (soda to US citizens) and alcohol? Could it be that we are quite literally behaving in opposition to our historic Neanderthal tribes, and convenience is a contributing cause to this obesity epidemic?

What is it that draws us to play less outside, sit more and eat foods that are created for us to hit that 'bliss point', and what is it that makes this so appealing? Is it the advances of technology and our ability to not need to hunt the mammoth, run away from the tiger and work in a changing environment with the development of furniture that supports this, rather than the industrial hardworking climbing, pushing and pulling that our bodies are 'designed' for? If so, then technology in its purest form is the demon, and this includes homes to keep us dry and safe, chairs, weapons to keep away tigers and bears (often not found in the UK), planes and boats that enabled us to move away from dangerous areas of wild animals and environmental disasters, famine and war. Oh, and the Internet?

Pandemic, epidemic and permacrisis

We have an epidemic of food-related issues, with obesity at a crisis point in the US; and shortly behind is the UK, with a figure from the NHS of two-thirds of people being overweight or obese www.longtermplan.nhs.uk/online-version/chapter-2-more-nhs-action-on-prevention-and-health-inequalities/obesity/. We have more people diagnosed with prediabetes, metabolic syndrome disorder and type 2 diabetes than ever before, and this is according to many dietary experts. Resting glucose levels and insulin resistance leading to diabetic issues measured through diagnostic tests (HbA1c) is often the first sign of these issues; these levels are climbing for the public, and yet we continue to focus on the eating disorders mentioned previously when it comes to discussing social media and the harms online: a point I will come to later in the chapter.

There are so many books on the health crisis, and, of course, during the COVID-19 pandemic, food and health-based advice has been awash on the Internet with many well-educated people condemning people's choices about food in a time of crisis when 'home delivery' for groceries was often the only option for many families (those who were isolated due to autoimmune conditions and immune-compromised bodies would be in this cohort). Access to the supermarket and the quick-delivery food apps meant that during the two years of restricted movement, many people increased their body mass, weight and fat stored to produce something called 'lockdown lard', which in a time of actual physically restricted movement meant many people could not go to the gym, or take more than an hour outside activity in the UK under the orders of the government, and this resulted in the slowing of physical activities for all citizens. As a result, because we couldn't go to spaces where we might breathe on each other, we didn't take our movement health seriously. As a result of that, I now sit with client upon client who 'CBA' (can't be bothered) to rejoin the gym, and finds sports too much or overwhelming in terms of the numbers of people (a direct result of not being around that many people for some time perhaps, and a fear of the next bout of COVID-19?). I have noticed that many of the child clients and adults I have worked with in the last two years would be classified as overweight, obese and often have junk food diets. I have watched and listened to versions of a muckbang, a term to meaning eating broadcast in the Collins dictionary accessible here: www.collinsdictionary.com/dictionary/english/mukbang as I witnessed the gorging of food, consumption of fizzy drinks, milkshakes, biscuits, doughnuts, crisps, junk food deliveries and processed foods straight out of packets in the fridge, on camera or with participants bringing their unfinished fast food to the clinic. Food has become comforting in so many spaces and places that it seems that people carry food around like Charlie Brown's blankies, and I wonder if this association is to do with the lockdown associations and emotional valence with food.

Has lockdown changed our movement, diet and health habits? Yes. Have we become nations where food is an issue for many of us, where longer-term health issues will increase and where we are no longer bothered about taking ourselves off to exercise for fun and to our body's benefit? Have we zoned in on this as a public health crisis? I don't see the evidence yet, but it's speculated on social media, that's for sure. And online, there is a large cohort of discussion about the impact of the vaccine on our health, but less so about how exercise is the linchpin of health.

Returning to the point about total fitness, the physical fitness and guidance from the government was severely quiet, with the guidance given on what you should wear should you need to go into public spaces, but little guidance on exercise and keeping your body healthy, which is, as far as I can tell, the regime offered by those who run diabetic, obesity and healthcare clinics. So I found this intriguing, to say the least, at a time when we were initially told we could exercise outside for an hour a day. So, like good citizens, we abided (even when we know about the benefits of the outdoor sun in all seasons)? Aside from Joe Wicks who went viral with his lockdown exercises for school kids and parents, carers alike (reportedly not so slim as he was during lockdown, and yes this was media reporting). But, I ask you to ask people how long they kept this regime up, and you'll likely find the same answers as I find: 'I did it at the start, but then . . . couldn't be bothered. It was too much, it was too energetic for me, it was too early' and so on . . .

It is interesting how we focus on health when it comes to bodies, food and illness. What is the permanent crisis that evolved out of this space?

Comfort blanket, emotional eating and the issue with complicated behaviours

If I talk to a client, friend or family member, food is often quoted as a 'comfort'. We have phrases like comfort food and comfort eating; when you look at the disorder 'manuals', you can see that food intake is more than disturbances and is rooted in emotional and psychological processes. Food intake is often related to emotions, time, money, cultural diets, beliefs about food, myths, access and cooking ability and independence, and sometimes correlated with early births (talk to me about pree-mies and eating disorders and beige brown and boring diets, as I don't have time to cover this here in this book), and it's complicated!

Diet antidotes?

And so, where can you find the antidote to the issues named previously?

In the world of fitness, health and wellness online. So let's talk about food, intake and the issues of misdirected knowledge.

I am a functional health practitioner as well as a psychotherapist, and this means that I have studied and continue to learn about areas such as nutrigenomics, which is the influence of nutrition (food), environment and by testing bodily functions (hence the 'functional' part of this approach) this enables me to provide a pragmatic and actionable view upon health for the people I work with. It is an approach that addresses (and is said to be protective) by focusing on prevention rather than a reactive and symptom-management model. However, it does seem more people in this area have the post-diagnosis effects, such as people with irritable bowel syndrome, or thyroid issues. This is not a mainstream health approach to date, as it is considered 'woo woo' or 'alternative' to the medical model, but seems to be gaining in popularity, though I would personally say this is a private medical model, out of the financial reach of many, which means that this is still an elite space. It is aimed at reducing and mitigating the likelihood of what is often called the four big killers, which are cancer, heart disease (CVD), Alzheimer's and diabetes. It does not have the answers to all the worries and ills my clients bring, and so I feel very lucky to span the world of biological health with the psychological and emotional (and other pillars such as spiritual, movement, intergenerational and other areas of that tricky word health). It is, without ever being called this, a trauma-informed approach to health, given I suspect that all people seeking out this approach will have some form of trauma in their past leading to the illness they present with, as supported through research in the ACES study (Felitti et al., 1998).

In taking on this training, it meant that I was thrown back into the world of biochemistry at a deep level, and in doing so went much deeper into epigenetic processes and how nature and nurture influence these (the study of the genomic markers and how they are influenced by biology, environment and of course stress and trauma, and in this case food). And whilst doing so got very excited about the space and carried out a behaviour online that I would like to tell you a story about.

I lead by example, where I can, but also can make mistakes

Quite sometime before the pandemic hit us, I was learning about the benefits of fasting (called time-restricted eating, intermittent fasting and eating windows) and alongside a group of colleagues decided to engage in a version of extended fasting, not for religious reasons but to see what the experience was like. I announced this on a social media platform, as the group of us were providing support to each other through this space (we were from many countries). One of the people in this space has many qualifications and years of experience in fasting and its benefits, and is a medical professional. On the back of this announcement, I found myself in conversation with another therapist colleague who suggested that this was promoting eating disorders. They happen to have been someone with a history of this. To a point, they are correct. My intent was announced to the people I was doing this with, and I understand that someone who may have been looking for an in-group, wanting to reduce their weight, looking for connection, be influenced by any one person in that group or have a proclivity to eating disorders may well have made the choice to follow the group, and it could have been an issue for them.

I do not absolve myself of the blame for the people who would be negatively affected by my behaviour and process, and at the time had, but hadn't considered the responsibility afforded to me by being on social media and making public posts when it came to fasting, because there's a difference in fasting for health and food restrictions, on purpose. After all, that's what the DSM-V and the ED courses I have been on told me. I was not thinking at that moment about the two processes looking the same to outsiders, and the overlap of food restriction versus food reduction for a short time. Did I have an eating disorder under this guise?

This is one of the reasons I think we all have a personal responsibility for our behaviours, and we also must take care of our young people who can see these kinds of posts at any time. Imagine if a child had copied my fasting without that expert knowledge I have been consuming from that medical professional and others. I am steeped, like the great British cup of tea, in the world of research and counter-research to make my decisions, and realise lots of people want the quick fix without the hard dedication to learning being the foundation that supports these decisions. Children may not even know that fasting and food restriction are different in intention, and belief as the process looks the same.

Practitioner pause for reflection

As a practitioner, what is your level of commitment to learning, and knowledge of these issues appearing in this chapter? Therapists don't give out advice, but other professionals who work with children do, and if a child spoke to you about these issues, what would your take on it be, what would your advice be?

Anyone with a propensity to fast for varying reasons would have been encouraged to see this as perhaps a fix, a new fad, but may not understand the what, why and how of this approach, and this got me thinking about this space.

We have many fasting and food-restriction cultures and religions around the world. People fast for many reasons, and of course, we can be directed to do this by our surgeons before an operation or procedure, doctors or diabetic clinics to measure your resting glucose and of course, many of us announce this on social media. So what does this do in terms of promoting, influencing or encouraging those who have a diagnosis of disordered eating, or eating disorders?

Where do we draw the line at health, support, advice and adoption of new practices such as time-restricted eating to facilitate health (TRE is often used for some types of diet, bodybuilding techniques and to help obese people lose weight)?

You see, food is a daily need, rather like water and sleep; we cannot avoid its necessity. Those who are informed about the nutritional values of foods, herbs and spices may be perceived as being 'holier than thou', as this advice is literally 'shoved down the throats' of those who do not eat and sustain their bodies in the way of 'health' (there's that word again). Advice is offered up on a plate as to what you should be eating, when you should be eating, how much you should be eating, how often, what you should avoid and what is good, bad or indifferent in this space. Cruel memes take hurtful digs at those who cannot afford the versions of food considered to be 'the best for your body' and look down upon those who eat according to their culture, religion or beliefs. Images of 'my fridge' are imposing what healthy looks like, and of course those in low-socioeconomic-status areas could not afford to stack their fridges with many of what the full American-style pantry fridges have with their supplements and additions.

Vegans, vegetarians, pescatarians, fruitarians, meat eaters and all in between attack each other's way of sustenance and diet. And which diet would some of them suggest?

These are the most common: keto, paleo, plant-based, low sugar, low fat, dairy-free, gluten-free, vegetarian, flexitarian, FODMAP, anti-inflammatory, carnivore-only, intermittent (TRE), sirtfood (high in sirtuins), IIFYM (basically anything that meets your macros in one day) and balanced diet, as suggested by the NHS good food pyramid or plate (the one often taught in schools). And what about the WGAF, weekend binge and gin diet?

So how on earth is a developing child, exposed to all of this information on so many channels, platforms, apps and in their ears, supposed to make sense of what foods to eat? What advice are they given in education versus what they can find online? And what about allergies, incompatible diets, food choices that they can be exposed to, mukbangs and all in between, from bodybuilding to weight loss, foods to help your gut to foods that heal, hinder or harm? How would you decide, and of course where did you get your food knowledge and what is in your cupboards and fridge? Phew – a lot to consider there is!

How do you discern signal from noise in a world that's loud and clear about 'the best approach' if only you follow 'my' advice? Imagine being at a market where you were being pulled by voices screaming out, 'Come to my stall, I have the magic pill, potion and remedy'. It's akin to watching Pinocchio.

There is just too much noise. And of course, those selling this advice often want you to buy into their subscription models, which children and young people cannot, do not and perhaps would not, opting for the free memetic tribes who can advise them in a quick shot image or soundbite, and of course deep learning can be avoided then because children and young people are time-short with all of the other information and 'stuff out there' they need to read, listen to, absorb, consume and learn. And so the metaphor is to think that parents, staff, teachers and professionals in the real world are climbing a hill made of sand when they tell young people that the information online isn't always correct, on point, has biases, may be skewed to sell you something, might be misinformation, disinformation and more.

Eating disorders, mis-orders and disordered eating.
How the online space offers images of the body beautiful and encouragement to change how one looks, from eating to body dysmorphia and body hatred

ED, DE, EDNOS, not eating, picky eating, fussy eater, over eater, comfort eater?

Tara was underweight and she was in my office for what had been diagnosed as anorexia nervosa. She was a tiny, framed female, engaged in high-activity hobbies and 'hanging out with her mates'. She was not menstruating, which is a common side effect of low body weight and often is one of the main noticeable symptoms of AN. Whilst undertaking my assessment and work with her, it became clear that Tara was not using advice from her peers about how 'not to eat', not using advice the chapter here suggests and not getting advice from those websites or forums that promote AN (often called pro-ana sites) as she was not an avid user of technology.

As a practitioner who always discusses the space of social media, gaming, tech and how this appears in a young person's life, I was a little stumped, to begin with. 'Where did this young person get her ideals about body image, weight and eating habits?'

Memes, billboard images, TV. It was an amalgamation of many spaces that a young person is exposed to, and not as I had thought at the outset, 'down to the social media space'.

However, social media is more prevalent, toxic and overwhelming, and unfortunately as we are learning, those algorithms drive young people to images about bodies, weight, eating, self-harm and more on certain platforms, and most young people (and adults I may add here) are convinced that emaciated-looking bodies are 'healthy' and desirable, given that most fitness and health industries online tell us so!

How body image is portrayed and what is the undercurrent of the 'Hollywood bod'

For those of us who have watched the celebs on TV over the years, it will come as no surprise to hear that people in the public eye have needed to 'watch their weight', and some have battled with 'yo-yo' diets such as those allegedy reported by Oprah Winfrey, or where other celebs look, at times, skeletal, such as Nicole Kidman, and yet in the last decade, the posterior has become a valued asset with accolades such as 'rear of the year' and the Kim Kardashian 'booty', alongside trends such as the 'twerk' (a robust twitching of the rear into the camera lens, akin to the moves dealt out by pole dancers in adult-only clubs).

And so body-based images are among the most prolific image type that a young person will encounter online today, given the enormous category as mentioned previously of health, wellness, fitness and beauty. And in this, they will often 'see' those who are celebrated as being beautiful with comments, headlines and memes telling you so. Adolescents are often easily influenced by the narrative of the social setting, this being the most prevalent time in their lives when group belonging, peer acceptance and discord within the families are most rife. This is a normative maturational process of leaving the nest and moving into the world of independence, and is accompanied by identity formation and sexual development.

So, the brain's plasticity at this point is focused more on 'whom do I need to be to be accepted by society', alongside a 'who do I most want to be surrounded by' kind of thinking. This often means that adolescents often look like those aptly named 'rebellious teens' that are so often demonised by adults as fads, and doing things to upset teachers and other adults in their lives. This, of course, is true, and this is so they can create a space with which, when it comes time to leave when there is discord, it is easier 'to do' (Siegel, 2014).

Influences on achieving that body. Purge, starve, obsess and eat the elephant

One bite at a time. Just enough to quell the noise. Sip water. Eat cucumber. Eat paper. Chew gum. Chew ice. Take laxatives. Vomit after ten minutes to hide suspicions. Feed the dog/siblings/throw it away in the compost heap. Wash a bowl and spoon. Give your food away on the way to school. Work out during the night doing sit-ups and press-ups. Wiggle your legs constantly and say it's anxiety. Walk and stand – always. Take pictures more than twice a day.

These are some of the 'interventions' that many of my clients have revealed where restrictive eating patterns and attempts to lose weight and body mass are in play. They may sometimes eat with their parents, only to purge or work out excessively during the night to keep suspicions low, resulting in sleep deficits and exhaustion, confusing the parents around them. Sometimes they eat only small amounts, claiming they ate at friends' before coming home, or asking to eat at friends' to alleviate needing to eat at home. This is very common, as parents cannot see what was served or consumed unless they ask the other parent, carer or guardian.

But here is the point that has changed the landscape of body-based images that are present in my clinic over the years: the selfie. Often taken more than once a day, this allows the person to zoom in on those areas they want to make changes to, with faltered thinking about the fact that a person can target a tiny section of their body with the previous interventions. There is distorted thinking about fat and what this is, as many young people do not know about adipose tissue, water weight for females around menstruation and perhaps bloating caused by excess hydrogen or methane production in an issue called SIBO, and of course why would they as this is outside of the normative health information we are all exposed to, let alone young people?

So practitioners, when you work with issues around health and wellbeing, there needs to be a consideration of the words, language and direction we focus upon with young people, because one piece of advice can lead to a search and end up in any one of the spaces mentioned previously. As a functional health practitioner as well as a therapist, I negotiate this territory very carefully in sessions, because the world is now one click away.

References

American Psychiatric Association (APA). (2013). *Diagnostic and statistical manual of mental disorders* (5th ed.).

Collins Dictionary. *'Muckbang' definition.* www.collinsdictionary.com/dictionary/english/mukbang.

Felitti, V., Anda, R., Nordenberg, D., Williamson, D., Spitz, A., Edwards, V., Koss, M., & Marks, J. (1998). Relationship of childhood abuse and household dysfunction to many of the leading causes of death in adults: The Adverse childhood experiences (ACE) study. *American Journal of Preventative Medicine*, 14, 245–258.

Game Changers. (2019). https://gamechangersmovie.com/.

Kimmel, S. B., & Mahalik, J. R. (2004). Measuring masculine body ideal distress: Development of a measure. *International Journal of Men's Health*, 3(1).

Knibbs, C. (2012). *Sex, lies and social networking*. Workshop for UKCP CYP Conference, London.

Knibbs, C. (2019). *Fit, fat or frumpy? The effects of social media (writ large)*, BACP Private Practitioners Conference, 28 September, BACP, London.

Matos, N., & Winsley, R. J. (2007). The trainability of young athletes and overtraining. *Journal of Sports Science & Medicine*, 6(3), 353.

Moss, M. (2013). *Salt sugar, fat. How the food giants hooked Us*. Random House: Croydon.

National Health Service (NHS). *Long-term plans for obesity*. www.longtermplan.nhs.uk/online-version/chapter-2-more-nhs-action-on-prevention-and-health-inequalities/obesity/.

National Heart Lung and Blood Institute (NHLBI). *Metabolic syndrome*. www.nhlbi.nih.gov/health/metabolic-syndrome.

Orcha Health. https://orchahealth.com/.

Ripped Body.Com https://rippedbody.com/body-fat-guide/

Siegel, D. (2014). *Brainstorm. The power and purpose of the teenage brain*. Jeremy P Tarcher: New York.

Venuto, T. (2012, 2021). https://www.muscleandstrength.com/articles/body-fat-level-see-abs.

Winsley, R., & Matos, N. (2011). Overtraining and elite young athletes. *The Elite Young Athlete*, 56, 97–105.

World Health Organisation (WHO). (2019). *International classification of diseases and related health problems* (11th ed.). https://icd.who.int/.

World Health Organisation (WHO). *Definition of health*. www.who.int/about/governance/constitution.

7 Self-harm

Every chapter, topic and section of this book can be seen through the lens of one or more of the other sections, chapters and topics.

> Self-harm is complicated. It has many forms and many reasons for being. It occurs in many spaces and is carried out or enacted in many ways.

Much of the space online is focused on certain types of self-harm. Rather than trying to define the full scope of behaviours here, because that would be an enormous task, I will endeavour to cover the most common types, whilst thinking about the legal AND harmful side of this issue. The Online Safety Bill is not focused on *some* of this topic as a primary concern, and it cannot be, as it is impossible to manage successfully with the borderless world on a subjective matter. This means not only do you need to read the whole of this chapter, but also the volume preceding this and other writings about this topic, but also stay up to date on online trends in order to keep abreast of the new forms of harm carried out upon a person, and the harms they inflict upon themselves.

This chapter is more detailed than many of the advisory spaces online, because as a practitioner you may find that you happen upon a newer form of an issue, and one where there is not a plethora of robust research. At the time of the writing of this book, some organisations were forming online-harm advisors, specialists and guides, however, this may not include all of the issues here, and the ones I find out about in clinic as and when they occur. There are no self-harm experts or specialists when it comes to online spaces, but there are organisations who have dedicated much of their work over the years to this, sitting alongside content such as suicide (see the Samaritans for some helpful guidance on talking about self-harm and suicide – www.samaritans.org/about-samaritans/research-policy/internet-suicide/talking-to-your-child-about-self-harm-and-suicide-content-online/ and www.samaritans.org/about-samaritans/research-policy/internet-suicide/guidelines-tech-industry/understanding-self-harm-and-suicide-content/),

The self in self-harm

Firstly, identifying what and who the self is can make the idea of self-harm easier to understand, but this is not a psychotherapy-theory book, rather, one in which,

DOI: 10.4324/9781003289210-8

in this chapter, I am not going to take you too deep (into that theory), but I endeavour to give you the reasoning behind the why of *self*-harm. This may be one of the most important aspects and concepts you can then use as a practitioner to understand the young person engaging in this behaviour.

Then I will discuss the issue of online presentations of self-harm, cyber self-harm, cyber-based support for self-harm, and then the overlap of eating disorders and self-harm, sexuality, gender and self-harm, and trends in self-harm.

The self is, depending upon whose theory you read, an aspect of 'me' or 'I' that can be described, felt, known and has a sense of separation from others. It is said that through the process of infancy, and toddlerhood – which includes stages, often discussed in psychoanalytical literature as separation, individuation and some other developmental processes such as rapprochement, self-awareness (consciousness) and more – a baby learns they are indeed singular, unique and an individual (Cozolino, 2006; Fonagy, 2001; Gerhardt, 2014; Panksepp, 2004). This can be heard in their language with 'me want' and 'molly want', soon replaced by 'I'. For some of the children and young people you work with, these stages may not have 'completed', so to speak. For example, some of the children and young people I work with are so needed by their parents, they cannot think for themselves, do not know how to make decisions and are often poorly, sick or may never leave the nest, so to speak.

These children have only ever known the co-regulation of being with the parent: for example, when they have a tummy ache, they can only be soothed by sitting on dad's lap with a blankie. There is no space to manage things 'by themselves' (not on their own or alone). If this is the case, then the process of self-regulation may not have developed or matured. This may also be something you see in the adults around you too.

In the theory of emotional and psychological self-soothing and self-regulation, this becomes very important when we see what is going on for the children and young people you are working with.

In many trauma theories, you may have seen the idea of the 'window of tolerance' (Siegel, 1999) and is a way to describe the zone of 'optimum arousal' (Ogden et al., 2006). The Polyvagal motorway of wellness video that I created in early 2018 and updated in 2020, see www.youtube.com/watch?v=QGBv1KrJ5Pk&t=102s is an explanation of this theory, made as simple as I could for young people in my clinic. It is a way to understand how someone can be pushed out of the nervous system 'comfort zone' (a space in which they can manage stress) by an event that is excessively stressful to that individual (this does not always ring true for everyone facing the same stressors).

For example, for readers who have not learned this theory, the threat of being eaten by a bear can create an immediate present-danger reaction from us to run away or play dead. Stress doesn't always present as a bear, and the stressful situation becomes less about a bear and more about the people around us. For children and young people who live in homes with trauma, abuse, violence, emotional or psychological issues, the equivalent bear might just be the angry parent, the slamming door, the swearing, the neglectful feelings they encounter on an evening, the fights that happen around the dinner table, the impending exams and the friendships that turned sour, and now result in dread about going online and so on and so on.

Rather than fill up the page here with excess theory, let me keep it simple for you and explain my understanding of self-harm and how I would like to explain this to you. Using my lanes analogy, I see how self-harm occurs as an attempt to get out of a blue or red lane and 'back into the green lane'.

This may well make more sense to you if you see the acts as self-helping, self-soothing and self-directed behaviour with the harm *as the intervention, not the symptom* (as far as the child is concerned). This may well be in direct opposition to what you may understand currently as to what, or why self-harm. Many people focus on what, i.e., the method and what is the background story, e.g., the child has a diagnosis of some description, rather than how they manage anxiety, stress, rejection, feelings of loneliness, heartache, abuse, trauma, caring for an adult or sibling, death, sexuality, growing pains, social pressure and so on. If the intervention is an attempt to feel better, then you can see when we move this thinking into an online-harms perspective that the issue can be understood with the same lens and approach.

Whilst this may not make sense to you as you are using your logical and analytical brain and thinking, you can direct the idea to a meta-perspective. When we look at cyber self-harm, we can see the same process, but not self-harm to the body as such, but the concept of self (a presentation I gave at CYP Now in 2017).

What is it?

Self-harm is a concept often used to mean 'cutting' of the body, namely the arms (in most cases). Self-harm is sometimes said with a scorned face by those who misunderstand the issue, do not have the patience to deal with it, call it attention seeking and think it's all just a phase. The term is misused and misunderstood in this context.

It is a form of self-annihilation, although the person does not want to completely obliterate themselves; it is a process of the psyche, the uncontrollable feelings (known and out of awareness) and is driven by the need to feel better. It has many forms, and like the idea of the devil, ghosts or vampires, is understood by certain age groups as a set of behaviours they can relate to. For example, toddlers cannot think rationally beyond, 'I want *x* right now', and when they do not get *x*, this leads to what we commonly call a meltdown (dysregulation), and in response to these intolerable feelings, the toddler will kick, bite, scream or throw their body in an exasperated and uncontrollable state, and we see heads being banged on floors, walls or legs. We see the biting of the other and the biting of the body that belongs to them. Often the response from the adults at this moment is the one that children can introject, swallow whole and believe about themselves. For example, a parent shouts, 'Stop it and go to the naughty step', and the child learns, 'When I have intolerable feelings I am sent away'. They do not know how to manage their feelings by themselves.

They may learn to hide their distress going forward, or they may decide to show it to someone else. They may even make it so visible that they are hoping, yearning and expecting their parent to 'take notice' and soothe their pain. But what if these 'solutions' do not work?

Why is it?

So to use the analogy of my motorway, I ask my clients, and have done for many years, the following question: do you harm to feel, or to stop feeling? This leads to my next question, which asks about the length of time the intervention works for, e.g., how long does it last and when does it go back to being the opposite of their solution (e.g., when pain stops and numbness returns?).

Knowing whether children and young people (adults too) are trying to move out of a blue, down-regulated, withdrawn and numb state, or a higher up-regulated anxious, activated and heightened state, or both, can help me work out what is going on in their nervous system and how they try to manage what is going on internally for them. We have a starting point, and I can adapt my questions and interventions to them from this point.

> Examples and discussions below are discussing actual harm, so please take care of yourself when reading! As per the caveats in this book, please ensure you are in an environment where you can take necessary self-care breaks, put the book down if needed and stop reading when you feel you need to.

Down-regulating

Let's take Sally for example, who cuts when she comes home from school. Sally has been tormented by another pupil about her sexuality, and she is angry because she never speaks out against this pupil. She carries the anger all day, and when she comes home she heads to the bathroom and cuts. The depth is dependent upon the pain she feels, as she tells me, 'in my head', which translates as 'psychologically or emotionally'. When I ask her the 'what are you cutting for' question, she replies to stop feeling what's in her head (and later tells me her heart and tummy).

To make it go away, she tells me she watches the blood leaving her body as the release of this pain (metaphorically). I understand what she is telling me and explain to her 'the anger, being a hyper-aroused nervous state and heightened feelings', due to her internalising the teasing, ridicule and outcasting she is receiving from the other students, seems to be the feeling that she is 'releasing'. The intervention reminds me of the bloodletting that used to occur in the times of the plague, and she agrees this is a sensible option, getting rid of the disease this way. Sally's thinking is logical here. Her intervention of choice comes from a place of trying something to help, and now associating it with 'feeling better' for a short while. I ask her how many other types of trying to feel better she has tried in the past, and she lists lots of things from punching herself, punching the pillow (one advised by adults around her so she doesn't cause injury to herself), shouting, journaling, breaking stuff, ripping paper, stamping on the floor, having a 'paddy' (a Yorkshire word for a temper tantrum), biting herself and pinching. She even tried snapping elastic bands on her wrist and ankle, to no avail. She found the cutting 'did the job, it was the only thing that worked and med me feel better', she tells me.

When she cuts, her blood pressure is lowered temporarily. She says this lasts for about 20–30 minutes before she begins to feel the self-harm site pain and then she can focus on that instead of the anger. This translates to it taking her approximately 30 minutes to become aquatinted with her interoceptive pain and to be in the here and now. Her naturally produced endorphins have been working to keep the pain at bay, and these can feel invigorating to her, and she enjoys the sensation they bring. As a releasing mechanism, this is her drug of choice.

> (I, as a person with a body full of tattoos carried out over many years, can understand this endorphin rush and the associated mind-body connection with, what is without a doubt, infliction of harm to the body; my version is (mostly) assessed differently by the public and perhaps seen as artwork, and does not receive the same stigma associated with it, though as a teenager my tattoos were perceived by many around me as the destruction of my body. I do not encounter this so much nowadays, but I do still see 'that look' on many people's faces, but less so than over many decades of these becoming trendy and accepted.)

Sally wants the emotional pain to go away and so substitutes it with pain to release her nervous system 'stuck' response (which may not be fully attributable to the anger of bullying; more on this shortly), and in this case 'down-regulates' and lowers the body budget associated with rumination and pent-up anger.

Up-regulating

Now let's change it to Sally wanting to feel something, rather than nothing, because she *feels numb with the daily mockery resulting in shame.* So when she cuts herself she immediately feels the sting of the cut, and perhaps even puts cold water on it to strengthen the pain while keeping it clean. She is now hyper-focused on the pain in her arms, leg or stomach as she holds the site to stem the blood flow (more on cutting location sites later). She is now focused on physical rather than emotional pain. This translates to her having increased blood pressure through focused attention on the cut site, heavier breathing and slight anxiety about the cut. She is now interoceptively paying attention to her body, where pain begins to subside once the throbbing of the cut lessens, and she returns to numbing out. Again, this can take perhaps 5 to 30 minutes, for her wound to coagulate and stop bleeding and for the pain to reduce.

Sally wants the emotional pain to go away and so substitutes it with physical pain to release her nervous system response and up-regulate (a term to mean to raise arousal, raise activity and raise the body budget associated with this) as an invigorating way to be present in the here and now, and move away from numbness and nothingness.

Changing lanes, over or undertaking

In the scenario of my motorway lanes the self-harm, cutting in these examples is an attempt to get out of the red or blue lane respectively, and the aim is to get to the green lane, with the expectation the intervention will result in a consistent 'middle-lane driver' position.

This is difficult for children and young people who don't know how to self-regulate and find mechanisms of self-soothing. To be perfectly honest, many adults are not very good at this either, and we have our versions of how we self-regulate (I'll leave you to think of your own examples here). Many children and young people often do not have the foresight for healthy self-soothing activities, as they may not have been shown, or in the case of Sally, have tried other options, but as it didn't resolve the issue immediately, they opt for ways that are more extreme, and this results in a more permanent association and 'quick fix'. They don't know how to stay in the green lane and so rely on using these types of behaviours to do this.

The adults around them may not have ever shown them how to self-soothe and regulate using other methods, behaviours or even self-talk. This likely stems from early childhood where, for example, small children can be seen carrying out behaviours like this when they have a 'meltdown', or what adults sadly call a 'temper tantrum' and 'toddler terrible two's behaviour'. Toddlers do not have the language to express how they feel, so in the shaming words of the adults around them (often struggling to manage this dysregulation), they become 'naughty' and bite, hit, kick, throw themselves on the floor screaming, bang their heads on walls, floors or other surfaces, become rigid or floppy, whine, cling or run away. Their expression of their emotions is communicated in their behaviour. And so what is learned in this stage of life becomes the 'go-to' when they are emerging into adolescent processes. Their dysregulation strategy is held deeply in their bodies as a belief about getting their needs met, being seen when they struggle, not having the skills or words to seek out assistance and so opt for self-directed solutions. They are looking to move from the lanes of distress into the middle lane of health and well-being, but often overshoot, overtake and undertake, and end up 'back where they started' with no real and full-time solution to their issue.

They may not look like logical interventions to the adults – they may look like childlike behaviours – and often my clients tell me their parents and guardians tell them to 'grow up' when they are brought to me with these kinds of self-harm behaviours. If only their brains had the capacity to think like an adult and be grown up, perhaps this would help. However, I think that co-regulatory capacities are missing here, and so the adults saying grow up is reminiscent of their capacity to manage the distress of the child.

Moreover, if a child was harmed in a particular way, such as the example of a toddler who was abused and pulled by their hair (by parents, siblings or other children) they may then go on to use this as a familiar regulatory sensation for themselves when they become scared or worried as an older child. What worked previously and is familiar then becomes a useful tool now, though the word often used in the psychological literature is dysfunctional, maladaptive and abnormal as ways to describe these behaviours.

A question for you to consider: is it really any of these terms when you can see the root cause? Could it be seen with less discriminatory, pejorative and pathological language, and seen as a self-misdirected soothing mechanism? Could there be another way to self-soothe that's more helpful and long-term, and that may need the help of another person to teach them how to do this? And if we introduce the concept of compassion here, then seeing the distress in another person can evoke in us a feeling of wanting to help (not rescue) and to be that co-regulator. As a parent it is distressing to see your child in pain that you cannot take away, and I often see this helplessness growing in parallel with a self-harming client, and so the co-regulation often begins with the adult as well as with the child.

Descriptions of self-harm, self-injury and mutilation follow

This section discusses self-harm sites (locations on the body), depth and frequency and why this is an important aspect to know. I am also keeping the level of panic in the reader to a minimum but not discussing these with extreme examples to prevent and reduce the likelihood of trauma. I am sharing the very very basics and peripheral knowledge here. Please do not take these comments to be *the* way to 'assess' how serious a person is about self-harm, as *all self-harm has the potential to be fatal depending upon the location and depth*. The location, depth and frequency of a cutting site is a question I always ask in practice, as is the self-care and reparation process used, as the location of the cutting is usually, but not always, indicative of shame, secrecy and escalating injury. For example, if the site is on one arm only (using the dominant hand to cause the cutting) and uses a horizontal movement, I am as a practitioner less concerned at this stage than if I am working with a child who is cutting their thighs near arteries that can result in death in a very short period of time, or perhaps the stomach where stemming the bleeding can be very difficult. Arms are often cut on the lower part and towards the wrist, which can be seen by others (adults and children around them) and often this is the one called 'attention seeking', as it can be attended to visually. Having worked with children who have needed plastic surgery and long-term medical care post-cutting, I can say that nothing is ever 'superficial' about these processes, as the use of implements is also of concern, where parents remove blades and children find or make semi-'sharp' objects themselves to continue the behaviour. You must seek the help of a professional versed in self-harm knowledge to work with self-harm. This requires an understanding of neurobiology, anatomy (for safety) and self-care advice, and the reasoning behind the self-harm with a care package in place that can be managed by the child as well as the parent. Cutting can take many forms, and self-mutilation is the most serious and requires immediate specialist knowledge.

So why would they look at it online?

Many children feel alone in their distress. Think about any event that you experienced, and when you hear someone else say your thoughts out loud, you often have that, 'Oh, I thought it was just me' moment. This is why the trend of #metoo was so prevalent and resulted in such a large, shared experience for people who had been sexually assaulted. We don't like to feel alone, so we seek out others for both validation and to know, in the words of my adult clients, 'we are not crazy?' This is often why therapists, social workers, teachers and other people around you sigh with relief when you say that 'it's not just you'.

Children may also seek to understand this phenomenon by looking at this material online for several reasons. So let us think about the versions of self-harm, not cutting, that have also fallen under the chapter about challenges, trends and hoaxes. Children are curious about what others are doing and want to be included in many things, even if it means at times doing things that could harm them.

There have been challenges that appeared as mentioned, such as those like neknomination, where concoctions of high-level spirit alcohol were mixed with all sorts of chemicals and compounds found in kitchens and swallowed on camera, and I wonder how many of these children found themselves vomiting or in hospitals with alcohol poisoning?

There was the drinking of sanitiser fluids (before COVID-19) because they contained alcohol at 70% ratio. And then cough mixture was placed into an upside-down child, doing a headstand or handstand, and the bottle was in the anus because this has more absorbable tissues than the stomach. And the cinnamon challenge, where a spoonful of cinnamon is often swallowed and breathed in at the same time, due to its fine texture, resulting in a major coughing fit. And these are just some of the versions that are both a 'challenge' and self-harm. Unfortunately, some of the other versions of self-harming have resulted in death, such as the 'staying awake for days challenge', 'masturbating nonstop' and 'choking' challenges.

Legal and harmful

Self-harm

Definitions

So when we talk about children viewing self-harm images, it is largely impossible to define what that actually means in practice, given that the previous examples are some of the ones I have seen over the years. And what about when harm is being done to another person or sentient being and a child finds themselves looking at this regularly (for example, abuse, fails and prank videos)?

When I worked with victims of the Manchester Arena attack in 2017, one of the conversations that regularly took place was the use of social media to seek out video and images of the attack, including using sites where the images had not been edited for news commentary and contained detailed images of the scene. Each time my clients watched this, it resulted in a re-experiencing of the event that traumatised them. I have also found victims of child sexual abuse and sexual exploitation use Google Earth to visit the 'crime scene', and this can also be a hidden harm in the digital-life-story work offered to children who were adopted, fostered, removed from the home, lived with relatives and more. In the description of self-harm, this would repeat harm to their healing journey, and each viewing was harmful to their 'self' (this was not necessarily the case in all these examples, and I don't have space to discuss this here).

Thinking about harm, but not engaging in the physical?

Another version of self-harm is: there are sites dedicated to images that look innocuous, such as images of clouds, underwater scenarios and deserts that result in conversations about death and dying. Sites are dedicated to the process, discussion and 'role-play' of varying forms of dreaming and dissociation, and another form of creepypasta-type forums. So would we count the psychological versions of talking to others as though we were writing our obituary and 'imagining' being dead as self-harm, or would we be classifying this as suicide ideation?

Scarification, tattoos and body modifications

What about sites that show tattoos, body modifications or scarification being carried out? The post on Instagram of the newly formed image or surgery that is inflamed, sore and can still be seen to be oozing plasma? Or indeed the modifications of tongue splitting and the use of items to make a person look like a vampire, werewolf or another animal? Is this harmful if it results in those mirror neurons and empathic resonance with the images?

Condemned videos

I will keep this brief, as this is a distressing subject for many. There are videos and images that any of us can be exposed to that are about certain harsh, abusive parenting interventions and discipline, and include capital and corporal punishment – interventions acceptable in other countries and not in the UK, for example. Other content will be discussed in the next volume, as this is a preliminary introduction to a specific topic, and where cybertrauma was first conceived with my clients. These videos are often not in conflict with platform regulations where the videos are condemned. For more information on this, see my interview with onlineevents (Knibbs, 2014), www.youtube.com/watch?v=fyUyM-eW0L8&t=1908s.

Body beautiful, body toxicity, body dysmorphia and that health chapter

As was discussed in the health chapter, issues around body shapes, ideals and food are often very distressing to look at when you can see the impact of long-term eating or health-related disorders. For example, the most well-known imagery is that cited about anorexia nervosa, as discussed in the health chapter. But diabetic ulcers, lung cancers and other health-related issues that can affect eyes, bones and posture are also a version of distressing images to the viewer. Think about how cigarette packets used to be on display with their 'warning' images visible. If a child keeps going to explore these images, would we say self-harm or not?

The mainstream media, platforms and written reports often mean *cutting* as the self-harm that is under discussion

Now as I get into this aspect, it is difficult to explore due to the nature of the act, the forums and spaces, because these apps, platforms and social media spaces are now removing this material from the main areas on their platforms and so this may complicate the searching and viewing of this material by determined users. For many years, children have accessed this material outside of the main social media companies that now dominate, and I personally have captured some of this since 2014 when discussing this with my clients, who were adolescents at the time. The use of 'code words' and changing hashtags has been rife for over a decade, and at the time of writing there are a number of cases against social media companies taking place, yet the forums and sites my clients visit are still busy with visitors. Some of whom will be children, adolescents and adults in distress.

Furthermore, the classifications currently used in education settings, child support services and online (including media outlets) are kept simple, such as self-harm is 'injury to the body and results in damage to the tissue or death'. As discussed previously, this is intentional cutting for non-artistic results, such as a scarification-based practice. Every other version or description of self-harm is perhaps up for debate, as discussed previously.

This is then going to complicate the matter of who is watching what and where. This act of viewing is likely to be hidden in shame and secrecy. It may not be on the social media apps where we have been led to believe this stuff exists in the highest amounts. And of course, addressing this issue is complicated, because self-harm in children really does make a lot of people worry (and rightly so in a lot of cases), not want to talk about it as it could open a can of worms, think that this is a fad, think it's only cutting, not know about the spaces where this material is and listen to the mainstream media articles and what is called outlier examples often given in the media.

So how do we assess phenomena for which we can only really look at large case examples of small sample behaviours? This is like looking at harm itself as discussed in volume one. How and where do we even begin? Knowing the viewing of this material is going to be a mixture of happenstance, or deliberately sought out and is always tied to the real-world issue a child is facing, where do we start? Do we teach the practitioners about the modus operandi of why a child may view this material, for example, depression, anxiety, loneliness, looking for a solution to emotional distress, copycat behaviours and more, and where they may go, and which precedes which? The answer here is yes, and that is why you are reading this book, I hope.

Practitioner pause for reflection

Given that you may have only considered a small number of versions of self-harm, I wonder if there are clients you are now thinking about in terms of their online behaviours, and where they visit and why? Have you ever asked about the platforms they use, other than the big ones? Have you considered the impact of real-world issues as a precursor to seeking out this material, or if they happen upon it, what this may do to their thinking about potential interventions for distress, and have you worked with the adults around them to think about co-regulation and working to help them manage to see the child in distress? Were you focused on the big news items about self-harm and were you aware that there are so many forms of this material and how a child can harm themselves by viewing all sorts of material?

Back to the start: history of self-harm on the Internet

For many years, websites and forums have discussed the act of self-cutting, self-injury and self-mutilation (think levels of danger to life with those statements and you can get an idea of the material hosted/viewed/shared). Harm to the self (body) has been hiding in plain sight for over a decade, behind various ways of writing about this act. For many years, spaces on the Internet have wanted to keep many of these sites hidden, deleted or removed. Self-harm images are contentious and polarising, and can ruffle the feathers of the participants on the forums, and so the people who engage in this behaviour often behave like criminals, reinventing the wheel by changing the way they speak about this issue and finding an underground space with which to meet in. Going undetected by those in opposition is the way to be able to continue in your quest. If I am 'in' with the crowd, then I know the secret code to enter those spaces.

Rotten? You bet!

There are the sites that portray harm to the body (self or other), such as traffic collisions, people having accidents, surgeries that went well and not so well, infectious diseases, war crimes, autopsies, animal abuse and many other forms of actual harm to a body. They began when the World Wide Web did. There was once a website that – like Ripley's Believe It or Not! – began to share images of animals that were born with perhaps anomalies, like two heads. The site was up and running by 1998, and I visited this website as a person with curiosity in bodies and biology, and because *I had been given the URL* by someone who said it was interesting (this word is still an interesting way of describing it, that's for sure). The site had many other images on it that were not two-headed animals.

TV in the early 2000's also began to share the weird and wonderful oddities of biology (that you can now visit in person). I was an intrigued fan of Gunter von Hagens, with his plastination techniques and live autopsies on channel 4. Yes, the TV channel shows the same kind of material I just discussed. Also his artwork appears in a James Bond movie (*Casino Royale* as James makes his speedy way through this exhibition) and can be visited in the real world at Bodyworlds https://bodyworlds. com/exhibitions/human/. But the autopsy show did have a post-watershed showing time, so that's okay surely?

However, the website I mentioned previously soon added more macabre stuff, and to date is still sharing the more heinous side of human behavior, as are some others that I am also not going to name directly here.

Curiosity piqued? I thought so.

This is an example of why children click through to these sites. They are given a URL or site name, or sent a video with a short, intriguing description. Read on and I will explain why.

The site I am referring to still exists today along with so many others like it, though they are more macabre than the initial outset in 1998 due to the technological advances of video and live streaming. However, the act of looking at harm to 'A. N. Other' can be considered a form of self-harm. The desire to do this is quite innate in many of us, and if you don't think you have this behaviour in you, then do check what you do next time you are passing a vehicle incident on a road, an ambulance at the side of the road or perhaps even a crowd of people around a fight.

You might not get to the actual point of looking at bodily harm, or it may be hidden in the back of the ambulance for example, but your curiosity is to view it. Why do we do this? Well, there are lots of theories, but the most accurate one to date that I can find is for our brains to warn us of the dangers of x behaviour causing y injury. We want to understand, deeply, what can go wrong and how. This is the negativity bias that I talked about in the first book (Hanson cited in: Knibbs, 2022).

We are intrigued by images like this: the most famous of these in the last few years is the Alan Kurdi photograph that so many of us found ourselves staring at (and in all likelihood, parents who looked at this felt so many overwhelming feelings) that we couldn't take our eyes off it (for me this was a heart-wrenching photograph and one that still results in me feeling so sad, I even walked away from writing this for about two cups of coffee after typing this).

Why do we harm ourselves by looking at, and not looking away?

When we don't understand something, we tend to focus in on it to try and find a way to understand when the event unfolded, as well as why, how, what and which. We look at the harm, and for each one of us, there is one specific body part that makes us shudder if we think about hurting it. For example, a broken leg under some jeans makes us think of unbearable pain, maybe because we have had that happen to us and can empathise and imagine the pain thanks to those pesky mirror neurons. But to see a squashed toe, or nail . . . well, urghhhh! We are fascinated and repulsed by varying forms of bodily injury. How many medical programs are on TV that are watched by so many? So to look at what another person has willingly done to their body can defy reasoning. We want to know 'why', and that fraction of a second of looking is enough to wake up those mirror neurons.

Many people think the self-harmer is weird, detached from pain or doesn't feel it, can't understand why they don't cry out when doing the harm, and it is certainly something that many people do not 'get'. For some of us, there is a feeling of wanting to vomit when we think about this act, or to shout at the harmer; for others, there is a drive to find out more. For example, I was once teaching some police officers (about a cyber-related issue) when a female officer said she loved attending traffic collisions, because there was often something good about getting stuck into the event. This could have been a superhero complex, a drive to see blood and gore, an altruist drive to help and save people or something more sinister, and I never asked anymore about it because the answer could have traumatised people there. Each person has their own response to seeing another person's distress or bodily damage and, of course, many adults know that cutting leaves visible scars, which can also drive others to judge and stare.

So knowing these drives to look, stare and judge are in us, being able to take our time, explore in depth and consider the act of harming oneself, we can begin to see the process of why a child or young person may want to look at someone else's scars, process or 'artwork'. Yes, I just compared this to art, and in the same way that one would spend time in an art gallery taking each piece in and trying to get the artist's meaning, aspect and message, it can quite easily be transferable to considering these types of images and looking at what other people have done to themselves, especially if you are a younger person looking to find that regulatory intervention and find the answer that someone else might just have.

> And of course, Rosie told you about this account, so it wouldn't hurt to take a look, would it? if Rosie can bear to look at it then maybe, so can I?

The sites that share and host this material are spread out on the Internet, and I know that Molly Russell's father was, along with the Children's Commissioner at the time who was Anne Longfield in 2015–2021, determined to highlight the images of self-harm as something that needed removing off the Internet and social media as quickly as possible. Unfortunately, the issues around what this actually means in practice are far more complicated than issuing a direction to 'remove it all' and naming the site where Molly had been browsing the material. This material is rife, and in so many spaces, that the analogy to finding a needle in a haystack is quite apt here. However, this does not mean we should not take any action! The young people you are likely to work with who engage in this behaviour will find these images all over, on many sites, with the constant moderation teams and programs fighting to keep up with it: there is that much of this kind of material and, as previously, some of it does not get removed because it does not break community guidelines.

It is not just Instagram that has these accounts, images and videos present, though the algorithms may feed these to you very quickly, as some research carried out by 5Rights (2021) found that these images were prevalent to young users of the platforms within 24 hours, if not minutes, of opening an account (https://5rightsfoundation.com/in-action/new-research-shows-children-directly-targeted-with-graphic-content-within-as-little-as-24-hours-of-creating-an-online-social-media-account.html).

Many young people I talk to that are actively self-harming, i.e., those who do not view Instagram alone, are looking to be part of a community and often do not use these major platforms, as their material gets taken down quickly. They also don't use the formal or well-known hashtags or identifying markers for the same reason. These images are so often hidden in plain sight, and the landscape changes quickly. One client told me she thought like drug dealers and how they navigate the space of minimising detection. There will always be those who aim to be open and say 'cannabis', and those who use street names, and she said this is how her friends used the online spaces.

Often the conversations I have in therapy are about how young people found the name of a website dedicated entirely to the form of self-harm art, guidance and support, as each client uses these sites for differing reasons. And this is the aspect as a practitioner we need to pay attention to. Even giving you some of the ways in which S3lf H## or SeLfH***, or any other way to describe this issue, has used or is being used is outdated (these hashtags were in use in 2014 and from Tumblr, so they will not likely be ones in use today). The disguised naming is constantly changing, and keeping up can be difficult. You are likely to find a version of this on social media, but the forums and contact between harmers keep many of us out.

And these sites are often hosted elsewhere, set out for adult use where access to the sites is hosted in a way or time that does not require age verification, making this a tail-chasing exercise a lot of the time (that is not an issue you as the practitioner need to take on, it is more for your information).

The self-harm support network, it's not necessarily what you have been led to believe

Not all sites have a 'how-to' manual. This is the common misconception that these images and sites are said to include. Some do, so we need to keep that in mind, and some have a 'how to safely', and instructions for keeping wounds clean and free from infection (lack of knowledge about how to do this without causing lifelong damage or threat to life is the biggest conversation I have with clients and guardians. Not knowing how to be safe before, during or after the harm has resulted in some serious injuries requiring medical surgeries in some cases).

Some of the sites have a community of helping each other not do it (for example, adult males have a no-fap forum for stopping, what they call self-harming masturbation). Members support each other as the AA does, and it is this aspect I want to highlight here as a part of our analyses, interventions and how we work with young people. You wouldn't say to an adult, 'Oh, no you can't go to AA, it's full of alcohol users, abusers and addicts', would you?

In 2014 I found myself reading a Tumblr blog that a client was visiting, looking at the self-mutilation that a young girl carried out on herself. To keep the trauma to a minimum here, the blogger needed severe medical interventions after each episode of self-harm, and had developed surgical skills and anatomical knowledge that would rival a plastic surgeon. I was reading this blog as I was discussing with my client at the time what was behind the reasoning for them reading this blog. They told me that they learned how not to hurt themselves seriously. They were able to reduce the self-harm episodes by talking with others in the comments, and found a way to substitute her behaviour with the knowledge she could reach out to this community when she was feeling the need to harm.

The girl in the blog was wise about her own trauma and was finding support from the community too, and so this became a metaphor for AA for my client and me.

We talked about the other forms of somatic work they could do (and did some in the sessions), and what this was like as a way to help them self-soothe. This was not an intervention for them to 'replace' the self-harm with 'my wonderful new intervention' (we were being facetious with this phrase). They were learning to recognise the signs of wanting to self-harm and the new body self-soothing was a way to slow down the previously fast reactive process, and to give them space to make more conscious cognitive decisions about the type of harm they engaged in.

What was a really great conversation with my client, and an eye-opening experience for me, was the levels of harm a young person could go to in major distress. I learned from several clients, and the blog here. Working with young people who have marked their bodies for life, and the underlying reasons for doing so, has given me much more of a deep understanding of the process. My clients' open conversations in the 2011–2022 period, so far, have led me to be more aware of the spaces they visit and the reasons why. I also know that viewing these images is not necessarily the mainstream media's interpretation of a complicated issue.

In this time, I have worked with some cutters who cannot find support outside of the education settings (high school and higher education) because they are talking to their friends who engage in this kind of behaviour without ever really being able to talk about it in a once removed disinhibited or anonymous way, as the online space offers. Young people are often accused of it 'being a fad' or a trend or 'superficial', and there doesn't seem to be an approach in schools to discuss this issue, as 'it will open a can of worms and encourage them to do it' (the most common response I have had, and a common misunderstanding). Also, parents are likely to remove their children from subject matters they are frightened of, as we see this with sex education lessons, religion, gender discussions and specific online issues, such as porn viewing. So how does a child find support or help, especially if they haven't told an adult, or are carrying this out privately and/or secretly?

The double-edged swords of self-harm spaces: support, ceremony or health activity gone wrong?

Given that the hashtags are the target words used by social media companies for the removal of this material, then using the metaphor of drugs, the names and handover points went underground. We know that information about drugs and alcohol can result in more conscious decisions and safer choices. For example, there are organisations that test your 'street drugs' at festivals and events. And we have education packages in schools and youth settings giving out information about sex, drugs and alcohol, which is said to be reductive in medical interventions and lowering the numbers of deaths (if not, why do we do it?). So why does this not exist for self-harm in the same way? We actually *need* some of these support spaces for young people, whilst discouraging the imagery or detailed reports of how being shared. You as the practitioner are likely to find this difficult to support if you are not versed in the why of self-harm, or signposting when those robustly monitored and moderated spaces don't really exist. Self-harm is, in many cases, a very difficult topic to talk about for young people in the real world, and so they may need a well-regulated, moderated space with which to seek support in a non-shaming way.

And yes, in doing so, with the creation of one of these supportive spaces, they may and likely will learn other methods, as the alcoholic learns ways to hide their issue by listening to others speak. There needs to be a way to create this space, safely, and robustly, and that has levels of support in and around this space from well-trained adults, and perhaps even other young people. What may happen, though, as with all well-intended interventions, is, if this is created, the space results in an unofficial offshoot, becomes a space where the vulnerable can be exploited, is created by some person or service wanting to be helpful, grab funding and be seen to be dealing with the latest 'buzzword' bingo trend (politically motivated) or come from a place of good intent who doesn't know or understand the depths to which people will and can go to in bodily harm, may not have knowledge of anatomical structures, deep biological or medical knowledge, alongside psychology and human behavior, with which to have considered conversations and provide guidance and advice, maybe judgmental, may not understand how self-harm feels, may be directional – and this is why this issue is complicated.

It's why young people tell me the hospital staff are often confused, disconnected, shaming, don't use painkillers or anaesthetics, are harsh, cold and quick to send them away, and so they do their best not to end up in the A&E departments. If we could start here, this would also be a fantastic outcome.

Compassion and a great deal of understanding are required for this issue. Some of these images are not on self-harm sites per se, but appear in videos of religious ceremonies, and cultural rituals that also provide the world with ways we can do ourselves harm (think coming-of-age rituals here) and of course, some of these images fall into the space of 'health' interventions that are taken to excess. For example, I watched Joe Rogan in 2021 take an ice bath for 20 minutes, which was both amazing (to see his self-control and psychology) but also terrifying, as that length of time would be harmful to a less fit and healthy person no doubt, which could result in a tragedy when hypothermia is a real potential outcome for those trying to 'outdo' others. Like Spider-Man, those with power carry a lot of responsibility, and these ice baths (which are a current trend) can self-harm if not carried out in a responsible and informed manner.

Let's begin the conversations of what self-harm is in the minds of young people, how we approach it, converse with and help them understand the space online as to what constitutes harm in this space when viewing these kinds of images and videos.

And what about slow and deliberate, slow and accidental harm?

When does self-harm become something that is innocuous and so subtle we don't recognise it? What about the idea of a child staying up late to watch their favourite TV show, streaming the latest box set, playing a game till they have a bursting bladder and, in the words of a 14-year-old, 'power piss' it out (Knibbs, 2016)?

Practitioner pause for reflection

Do you know about the harms of a shifting circadian rhythm, the lack of sleep resulting in the lack of glymphatic draining occurring in the brain, and the likelihood of increased brain fog and decreased cognitive functioning over time via what is called the sleep deficit (Walker, 2017)? All of these are concepts in neuroscience and are often discussed in health spaces online. Have you heard the rumour about blue light being detrimental to health (and how this is unlikely, given eyes do not filter out 'just one wavelength') and that the misnomer here is now almost an urban legend? Have you been advising young people to avoid blue light, and turn their screens darker? I used to when the data first came out, and I once did this at a convention when I turned my phone filters to red and then couldn't read anything, straining my eyes even more. Talk about an oxymoron! Then I did better and read some more and now talk about the blue-light myth, a lot.

Brain health is important to young people, and knowing about the adolescent's phase-shifting patterns of wakefulness and tiredness leads to lots of arguments in houses when the parents want to go to bed before the young person and find themselves in a heated discussion about smartphone, devices and lights out. Knowing that young people don't feel tired till later hours than many of us 'boomers', they want to find something to do, such as being on social media, watching TV, etc., but find themselves falling into a state of relaxation that inhibits their awareness of needing to turn it off, switch off, notice they are tired, and perhaps they even lack the foresight and knowledge with which to do this. A recipe for disaster, you say?

Indeed, this subtle form of sleep deprivation, high light levels (lux) in the evenings, lack of the AM natural light intake, and missing the (late) PM dusky light sources through their eyes is resulting in sleep-wake patterns that are not healthy for many of them (and adults too). Inhibiting the hormones cortisol and melatonin in the circadian rhythm balance is what is getting 'teenagers' a bad rap for being constantly tired and forgetting stuff. This staying up later on devices and lack of interoception and bodily awareness around sleepiness and cognitive functioning is a form of slow self-harm, akin to cigarette consumption or shift workers who can be classified under 'carcinogenic work conditions'.

The advice to many parents to date is to take the damn things off them, or saying no tech in the bedrooms means that young people are becoming more resourceful at finding ways to circumnavigate the rules, and doing this behaviour as a way to 'naff off' parents. Rather than being educated about looking after their brain health with helpful conversations, advice and tips they are punished, denied certain activities or have their devices held to ransom because of a media-driven approach that is being used to condemn the young people. It is no wonder they rebel.

Good, robust and research-backed education about brain health is the way to help parents understand the evolving and growing brains of young people and what they need, why their sleep can become disrupted and measures they can take to assist, guide and inform, rather than what was mentioned previously. I find, more often than not, young people I work with *know* that staying up too late on their phones is 'bad for their health' but they don't know exactly what this means or how to do anything about it. 'Put the phone down' messages are unhelpful; rather, the clients

I work with need support around recognising what they are actively engaging in and why, and that requires a conversation about understanding their needs and body budget, emotional state and the psychology of why companies are exploiting their adolescent brains. Usually, the latter part of this conversation results in them rebelling against big tech rather than a big adult at home.

I find knowledge about how sleep 'works' and what it is for, how and why young people's brains need this process and what it does for their weight, alertness, intelligence and longevity and using the idea of brain health as a route to less stress tends to be the factor that creates the self-directed change the adults are enforcing on young people. Also, when they hear how the tech world exploits their brain development, they tend to become rather protective over it. What we certainly know about young people is: tell them and they will ignore, resist and switch off, but give them autonomy and tools to manage their own health and they can begin to choose to do this, and that is the way to create change – alongside patience in the realm of 'they stayed up too late again' and knowing when this is an issue to really get worried about, versus knowing young people like the rest of us don't actually like being (over)tired! They just don't know how to use sleep to their advantage, nor do their brains ask for it in the same way ours do (or is that just me?).

You can find more about sleep, brain health and adolescence via the bibliography, as there are quite a number of sources that informed my reflection for you here.

Deliberately? 'Do me a roast' as a form of self-harm or indeed self-ing the roast?

One of the terms that has evolved over the last ten or so years has been to give someone a roasting, which is similar language to the 'rollockings' of the years I was a teen. And so now the term roasting, following on from being 'burned', 'merced' and the more recent version of wrecked as rekt (this is also used in other contexts) is to 'go full on and hard at someone with insults, criticisms and banter'. This is akin to watching the comedians on TV joking with each other to see who can get the 'below the belt' joke and banter closest to the mark of 'crossing the line'. There is a very famous comedian who does this and has a high-gross Netflix show, of which he constantly reminds us in the show.

When celebs or comedians do this, or as in my blog about banter and memes, you can see that the jokes are obviously a form of (allegedly consensual) abuse dressed up in the form of a joke. And to quote Jimmy Carr from his Netflix special, 'they are jokes and not really how he feels', and this is the secret sauce, so to speak, as to how someone can say something that borders on hate speech, crosses the line of hate speech and indeed meets the criteria for those -isms and -ists we so often find ourselves facing. Banter, jokes and –isms, and telling apart the nuanced differences, are difficult.

This is a point to note, when you work with young people, and you are facing what will be the Online Safety Bill legislation that discusses this kind of language, meme and abuse online. How do you investigate intent and how do you 'prove it', especially when you might be faced with children and young people with learning and social difficulties or disabilities that mean they really don't have the intent of someone cognizant and fully present to the harm they intend to inflict on another person? We seemingly will go around in circles for a while.

So when we look to the concept of 'asking to be roasted', we can see that this is a form of self-harm that doesn't have bodily wounds, as in cutting, but can leave psychological scars and can cut deeply. Imagine asking to be a part of a friendship circle and someone throws a curve ball and 'attacks your weakest spot' as part of the initiation process. Would you face it and jokily laugh (what is called the discounting gallows laugh in transactional analysis) or will you go and muse, ruminate and become saddened to the core by the 'roasting'?

And imagine if you joked and said you wanted to be roasted, and images of a sexual assault against you became the target of that roasting? And why would someone open themselves up to this kind of 'game'? The answer lies in the attachment: the wanting to be a part of the group and part of the society that cares or gives you attention. Again, this is not attention-seeking but attention-needing behavior, and don't we all engage in this? Sally, whom we looked at earlier, may not get any attention at home, so this is for her by far a better version than the silence offered in her home. She feels seen by those who roast her and tries to laugh it off.

And some children would rather have the negative kind of attention than nothing at all, and when you consider traumatised backgrounds, you can see that these children often don't think they deserve any of the 'good stuff', and so resort to getting something rather than nothing, and this is a surefire way to be noticed and for people to pay attention to you.

Looking at this through the 'to feel something' or 'to stop feeling something' lens, you can see that all self-harm behaviour is a self-misdirected way to feel better. And how difficult it must be for these young people to speak to someone about what their real needs are. As I say when talking about young children, look behind the manifested behaviour and listen for the unspoken needs. Interpret the behaviour to hear what is being asked for.

Behind the behaviour: self-self harm

When you look at the versions of self-attacking self-harm carried out online, it can be even harder to understand that a young person can create a persona or fake account (sometimes called sock puppet account) to bully themselves with. Meaning they use the fake account to roast themselves for what seems to be two purposes.

Firstly, so others can see them being attacked and roasted and perhaps come to their rescue? Many young people will attack the attacker if they really care about the 'victim', who in this case is seeking to see if anyone cares or indeed doesn't. For example, if Gerald is struggling with his identity and sexuality, and is looking to see how this will be accepted by his peers, he can create an account to attack him publicly, calling him gay, bent or weird. He can then see what his friends do with this information and whether they stand up for his rights, such as defending his gender identity, right to be whom he wants and so on. If they join in with the attacker, he can tell himself that it is not safe to reveal his sexuality, as he will not be supported by this group of friends. It is a way to test the water, so to speak, which is not nearly as easy to do in the real world, as you cannot create a fake avatar or clone with which to do this . . .

Yet.

The online space gives us opportunities like never before to see how we fit into society, and the versions of self-harm that can occur online mean that, as with every other aspect in this book, we need to look at what is going on underneath and what the modus operandi is, what the intent and drives are that a young person is seeking. This ought to be common practice and, sadly, online issues get labelled very quickly as the behaviour alone without understanding the why.

Secondly, a person may believe they deserve punishment because the house, home or institution they grow up in has conditioned them to feel worthless and useless, and the sentence most often uttered denoting this to the young person is they are a 'waste of space'.

So, akin to the inner critical voices we all have, the young person can write these online, save or download them in spaces that they can revisit time and time again to reaffirm their beliefs. They can even attack their own profiles as a way to feel soothed because, for example, today no one is talking to them, and online someone might join in, even if it's negative.

Given this, a young person can collect a 'board' of memes about how useless they are, just like those of you collecting inspirational quotes on your social media feeds.

Looking at children's behaviour with a 180-degree flip to our behaviours can often help us understand what they are doing and why.

So a quick thought experiment for you imagine living in a house or institute and being in your room where, the moment you leave, the other people in the space mock, jeer, laugh, humiliate and abuse you in a myriad of ways. Perhaps you wake and realise you hate your life, your body, your voice, your very existence. Sadly, this happens so often that these children and young people find a way to manage and cope with this. Their way of doing so may not make sense to you logically, but it does to them.

Practitioner pause for reflection

As the practitioner finding out the roasting of the child you work with turns out to be them disguised as another person online, I ask you to consider the previous scenarios and look behind that moment of 'What are you doing?' to '*Why* are you doing?'

And with the last example here, the 'self-harm by proxy' may just be a call for help to tell someone what is happening to them, such as sexual abuse. Imagine if you could say online, 'You're a slut/gay/homo for shagging *x* person' and what this may be attempting to achieve. If a child or young person can be the 'other' who outs them for what is happening at home, school, in institutions, etc., then they can disclose in a way, that allows them to stay safe with or to the abuser, that it wasn't them who told, which is a logical, safe way to keep themselves from further or physical harm from the abuse/abuser.

And so, before moving on to the next subject, please do consider this when you see websites like 'everyone's invited'. So many readers of that site may be looking at disclosures from other children trying to 'do the right thing', and this may be a way for disclosures to happen in the online space in a way that has never offered children a get-out clause, so to speak, by offering them the opportunity to 'be someone else'. *This is a huge change in disclosure discourse* and we as practitioners need to be aware of this.

And finally, know that this roasting, whether it be direct, indirect or self-self-harm, can also fit under the umbrella of 'online' sexual violence and assault, and so look back to that chapter to consider the overlap here.

Legal and harmful

Suicide and self-harm content online

Suicide and self-harm are often discussed together as similar typologies when it comes to online harm. Both are versions of legal and harmful ideologies in the UK, but may not be in other countries. Suicide may also include the events such as Christchurch and other mass shootings where the perpetrator knows the event will conclude with their death. It can be self-harming to view or read about these events, and the Samaritans have great advice for the journalists and public listed at the ends of the chapter and in the bibliography. Sadly, some forums do not follow this advice, and often they are faster than the news outlets at sharing information (not mentioning the sites here) and some children use these sites for this reason.

Suicide sites and live streaming of such events

Suicide is perhaps the scariest of all the safeguarding processes that a practitioner deals with and is the outcome most parents fear. The idea that a young person has the cognitive capacity to decide they want to end their life leaves many adults confused, fearful beyond sensible actions and distressed and disconnected from the child or young person. Given that self-harm-based responses from professionals have tended to be full of heightened anxiety, anger and what can often feel like a 'You fix it, Cath, this is beyond my level of knowledge' referral process. Then you can see, feel and hear the utter panic behind suicidal intentions, ideologies and threats. No practitioner wants to get this safeguarding call 'wrong', because they fear their employment, judgement, failures and prospects will all be focused in on that phrase, 'How could I, or did I miss it?' or what they feel will occur, which is, 'How did *you* miss it?'

Questions that often come up in this space are:
Can a young person understand the permanence of death in the same way an adult can?
Do they consider all options before this one?
Do they say it for many reasons?

Do they mean the same as us adults when they say to end their life?

What policies and procedures do we have in place, and what do I say when I think this is happening or could happen?

And why don't they tell us?

Well, they perhaps do, and maybe the truth is we don't see them, understand them or have enough interdisciplinary conversations about these young people to piece together the patterns. Perhaps the truth is also practitioners are not skilled enough in this area, due to it being complicated, and perhaps practitioners are so overworked in a society that demands so much of them that they don't recognise it, have ample time to consider it or read their notes, reports and type up their thoughts for others. Perhaps the truth is parents, carers and guardians are so busy working as many hours as they can to house, feed and clothe their children that they are missing those important conversations and connections in order to see what's really going on with their child. Perhaps some don't know how to have those conversations, and some are scared to because they would feel like a failure, confused or like they have to seek out support, which will cost them money they may not have.

And given that some recent research found that a very small number of parents who responded to the survey were even worried about their children feeling sad after being online (Online Safety UK, 2022), it can become an invisible issue and, of course, how can we see the invisible and action it?

Conversations, conversations and conversations. All of us, all the time

Do we really all have the time for this?

Given that this chapter is about online spaces discussing self-harm, then suicidal content, intentions, plans and existential crises that parallel the adults, dreamy spaces of what it would be like to be dead, promotional memes, bullies and many taunts to 'go kill yourself' suggest why a child may feel the need to end their life in the first place.

We need to understand the entirety of the two-volume book before getting here, and therefore this chapter and topic is last in the book, relating to children and young people's behaviour. This is a saddening subject and one so many of us want to change. This issue of children ending their lives, making plans to and actions towards is considered to be on the rise, and perhaps the age at which this is happening is also getting younger (but as with many issues that become visible, we do need to question whether rates are rising or reporting is easier to measure the incidences).

Papyrus suggests this is the biggest killer in under-35s in the UK (www.papyrus-uk.org/) with 200 school-aged children ending their lives each year.

Although, figures pertaining to suicide linked to social media, cyberbullying, sextortion and other online issues are not counted for reasons discussed in the stalking chapter about reporting issues. Often there are a multitude of reasons for suicide, with depression, anxiety, grief, abuse and trauma being a part of this, if not a defining aspect. The contribution of online issues to suicide will be difficult to provide robust research for, and so as practitioners you need to be aware of all in this chapter and these volumes as antecedent to the problem, such as looking at the why, what you need to be aware of in the digital spaces and to what extent suicide material online may be in the spaces children visit.

Minecraft. **Fall damage and the world of creative 'flying'**

Whilst not entirely about suicide, this world of gaming offers young children unrealistic expectations about what happens with their avatar (gaming figure) when they die. Akin to the respawn effect discussed in Knibbs (2022), children under nine or ten years of age don't necessarily understand a person's end of life, death, what death is and that you don't get to come back alive. So, when they are playing a game like *Minecraft* and can literally jump off a building, mountain or high level and incur some 'fall damage' (reduction of their life in the game) or die and respawn, then what and how do they make sense of this?

Client: It's okay, Cath, cos I can just fly over that, swim in the water without needing to breathe, fall off the highest tower, go into the lava and it's okay cos you can't die in this mode (meaning creative mode).

Me: That's interesting, do you think you have modes like that where you can't get hurt?

Client: Well, I suppose I can hurt myself if I fell off the chair like I did that time, but it didn't hurt that much so maybe I would just be scared to jump, but it's alright as the hospitals would fix you like and then you could go back to climbing in a week or so.

Me: Hmm, that hospital sounds great, and they are very good at fixing people. I'd like to get fixed in a week for sure if I broke my bones or got hurt jumping off stuff!

Client: Someone told me in chat on their server.

Me: Oh. I wonder what else they told you about getting hurt and how come you were talking about that?

Client: Oh, they said you could do this at the park on the climbing frames and you wouldn't die, but the hospitals can fix you in a week cos they have things to fix you if you get fall damage, but you can't have too much or they have to respawn you and your mum would be mad.

Me: I bet she would be, and she would be worried about you getting respawned. And I wonder what that would be like.

Client: Well, I was gonna do it when I go to the skate park with my brother, and we can do some dares and jumps on the scooters and see if we can do like Steve (*Minecraft* character) when he's got his diamond armour on.

Me: 'Hmm, sounds like you want to have a lot of fun at the park, and I'm wondering what scary jumps *we* might want to speak to an adult about, so they can make sure you don't get really hurt. I wonder if you know that here (pointing to my chest and body) that we humans can't respawn, and that could make people around us sad. We can get hurt though, like when you fell off the chair, and yep, some doctors are really good at fixing broken bones and stuff, but our heads really are very delicate so we need to take care of them. Is it okay to ask mum to get you a helmet for your scooter and skateboard tricks so you can be cool and also safe?'

Mum: Oh, he does it all the time, he's got no fear and really, I think he's trying to kill himself at times with the stunts he does ha ha ha, he's a menace and the other kids egg him on too, so I just give up and let him get on with it. I reckon he will break his leg soon enough, and that will teach him, eh?

Mum is not an uncaring mother by far, in fact, she was keen to support her child in therapy from day one and, of course, this conversation here was about something away from gaming. This is normative play and parenting for most parents. It sounds like fairly normative boisterous play and exploration for a seven-year-old, and looking at movement skill sets, risk-taking and child development, this does not seem out of the ordinary to a child growing up in the 1900s and especially 1980s. So why am I so concerned in 2019 as I was here?

I cannot tear myself away from the thinking around these issues that are overlapping with maybe the spaces online and how children are now incorporating all the things they do, learn about and embody into their play and development as having another influence (not causation) as to their understanding about death, injury and harm. Conversations about being able to 'come back from being dead' used to be in science fiction novels based in descriptions of cryogenics, fantasy and speculations. However, the influence of games where death is no longer finite might just be changing the cognitive understanding of death and permanence in children. I wonder what Piaget would do or say now.

Unalive versus suicide

Words are changing how young people see their world. This is a small introduction to help you understand that you may be looking at what *you call suicide* and in some online spaces is *called being unalive*, which also encompasses the greater feelings of dissociation and not wanting to be fully alive in all of its glory and passion, because that has the underbelly of pain. Being unalive is a concept that young people and young adults discuss in forums as a way to comprehend their feelings, rather than it being explicitly about being 'UN-alive', and so this is a space to create the awareness that words we use as professionals may not match a young person's experience.

Social media, gaming, bullying and suicide

Going back to my decade of blogs, writing and teaching, and here in this book, the earlier chapters: the intentional intent to hurt others, what we call cyberbullying, and what that might do to the psychological health and well-being and emotional regulation of a young person in distress can be easy to see here. The connection lies between the depth of sadness and hurt, with wanting to die by suicide, self-harming and emotional dysregulation resulting in perhaps both of these behaviours. Sadly I have seen too many newspaper articles and online-media news reports of children who ended their lives, and the resulting finding was the cyberbullying that took place beforehand.

Cyberbullying is one reason children end their life, and often cyberbullying is related to another issue. More often than not, even when children are frequenting spaces online that contain harmful images, they are doing so in order to resolve those feelings of dysregulation that we label as depression, anxiety, loneliness, education struggles, friendship fallouts, frustrations, deaths in the family, separations, abuse, neglect and more. The digital landscape exacerbates the issues as discussed throughout this book.

If we take all supportive forums away rather than create moderated spaces, they will be left in a further deficit because they often do not speak to their parents or guardians. Recent research showed that young people will ask Google or their friends before their parents if they had an issue (Online Safety UK, 2022) and if this is the case, Google – or the versions of 'new bff in the house', e.g., Alexa, Siri – and other large platforms would do well to provide robust, research-backed, peer-reviewed guidance using lived experience and randomised controlled research showing where and how to get help, rather than the children happening upon suicide and self-harm support groups or sites run by people who are not necessarily informed to the degree that professionals are, or are glorifying the content.

> Google, Amazon, Apple and Meta could signpost responsibility in this matter. I believe they should. If one of their children needed to speak to a guidance counsellor and this could prevent suicide, I am sure they would want their search engines to do this responsibly, accurately and quickly.

Why?

It is the biggest question, and often I am struck by the logicalness of a child in my therapy office with suicidal intent, ideation and thinking as to the outcome of the 'it stops this' feeling. This makes absolute sense, but to the child, there is often no comprehension of what the full extent of ending their life means for everything else. It is what is called an escape hatch in TA language, and rather than hurt others, the self is destroyed to prevent any further pain. This is the intervention to halt being in pain, distress or deep sadness that is seemingly beyond words. Thus, suicide seems to be a way out of suffering.

So how can we tell when a child or young person is suffering so deeply that the only logical solution to them is to end their corporeal life?

> This is the whole reason behind this book and the explanations of the real cost to children and young people who suffer harm in a world of technology.

Changing landscapes. My children as my guides

The pressures faced in a world of technology have changed the lives of children and young people, and unless you are under the age of 25 reading this, you are likely not to understand this at your core being because you didn't and haven't grown up with this space always on and present in your life and head. You have never had to comprehend what young people face, and even I, writing this book, become overwhelmed when I think of my children, now adults, having to face this. Given, I introduced them to computers before they were five years of age, thinking that this would facilitate their learning and play environments in positive ways. Given this was way before Facebook was around, it seemed a great idea as I saw the potential for systems-thinking approaches to life and solutions at their fingertips. Gaming was a fun activity. Then came the beasts of online gaming and social media, and my thinking continues to be updated weekly as this space evolves to create new worlds for brains and bodies not ready for this. At least I don't think we are ready. We will find out in 50–100 years I suppose.

Post the 'friends reunited' platform as I was using the Internet, and the invention of Facebook, into the realm of online gaming and consoles, they have been my guides in what children can be exposed to, how normative real-world child development has changed online and how this has given me such an in-depth awareness of what growing up in a world of technology looks like – I can write this book here for you the practitioner, as to what to be aware of when working with children. I am by no means the expert, I am learning as I go, but what I do have is 30 years of this world to share with you, as I am aware some of you are almost 20–25 years behind.

We must keep our eyes open to the ever-changing space and how the children feel, because ultimately it is the feelings of despair, sadness and suffering that lead to them ending their own lives, and we need to be their eyes and ears by getting 'tech savvy' and learning about this stuff here.

Sextortion is the biggest shame-inducing killer. From Amanda Todd to now

One of the most prevalent forms of shame that a child can be exposed to is the threat of exposure of something they did, and the belief they will be rejected and abandoned by parents, peers and other people they may feel are important. Mostly children will say, 'My parents are gonna kill me' or, 'Whatever happens don't tell my mum and dad'.

Just over a decade ago the viral story of Amanda Todd spoke of her cyberbullying about the fact she showed her breasts to someone online. However, the original threat came from the coercer who blackmailed her upon the capture of the photos, and the cyberbullying inflamed the issue, resulting in her suicide.

Shame is different to embarrassment or guilt, and the way this is experienced by children is the reason they often comply with our demands.

For example, the thinking behind these feelings goes a little like this:

Embarrassment – I did something silly, or something silly happened that I know may encompass guilt, but I can see the light at the end of the tunnel and know this won't be with me for life, and one day I can look back at this and laugh about it. I am still okay.

Guilt – I did something wrong/bad or hurtful to someone and I know I can take responsibility for that, make amends by apologising and atoning and I know that I can even rectify the situation with compensation to some degree, and this will bring me a feeling of self-forgiveness in the process. I will be okay, I may not feel that right now but I can trust I will be okay and I am okay.

Shame – I am bad, I can never do anything to resolve the issue, the person(s) hate me and don't need me, want me or even like me, let alone love me. I am toxic, useless and no good, I am rotten to my core. I am not okay, I may never be okay. I can't even believe there is hope that I will be okay.

Children don't always have the cognitive capacity to see beyond the incident as discussed in the chapters and volumes here, and as a result, they feel like they are the ones that will be ejected from the tribe for something they did. It's why shaming a child works in the way that it does, they believe that the milk they spilt, crayon drawings on the wall and biting of the dog means that they themselves are rotten in their humanness. You don't even love them, so how can they love themselves?

Cue harm to others or self. Most children know if they hurt something or someone else, this will compound this feeling, so they opt to hurt themselves with self-talk that is harmful or self-destructive.

Sextortion and suicide

If a child is threatened with the exposure of an image that a perpetrator tells them will result in people 'never wanting them', 'getting arrested by the police', 'Mum being so angry that . . .' or 'sending them to a naughty boys' or naughty girls' home' for a picture that 'they themselves actually did take', then it is likely that children will hop over the first two feelings of embarrassment and guilt and land right in the pit of shame. Children do not cognise the image that they took was *coerced from them*. *They did not choose willingly*, but the perpetrator tells them so, and the internal voice of 'why did you do that', heard many times as they were growing through toddlerhood and childhood comes flooding in with those feelings of, 'My parents will kill me for being so bad, so rotten, so useless, so horrid and so stupid'. It is said that our response times need to be swift when this happens, as many young people have been sextorted in this way; reports in the media have disclosed the time from the threat occurring to suicide as being within a 24-hour window, or very close to that. However, I am still researching this issue, as this seems to be a sex difference, and I am looking at the issue of gender and sexuality in this space, and research is sparse at the time of writing.

A thought experiment: can you feel what shame feels like in your body, and would you tell your partner, or their parents, about the worst thing you 'ever did', and be able to do that without 'chugging a few' alcoholic drinks first?

Why is Brene Brown so popular as she discusses shame, and why is shame the biggest emotional response therapists should learn about? Because it's the one feeling we all fear, hate, run from, feel sick with and, of course, know so very very well.

It is so deep that there are often no real words that can ever convey how sickening this emotion is to deal with (it was a rhetorical question about Brene, by the way).

So why on earth do we have an unrealistic expectation that children and young people will come forward and talk to us about something they feel ashamed of, when:

a) We might use this emotion to create behaviour change in the house or other setting
b) The governments, schools and society use this emotion to punish
c) They may be too frightened about being rejected or believing that anyone would understand
d) Services like social care, police and teachers have and still do react with a facial expression, noise or language that further entrenches this feeling
e) We lie and tell them that the collective 'we' does not react in this judgmental, pejorative or dismissing manner?

They see our hypocrisy, they see the results from telling the truth, and they see the resulting output online for people who have taken incredible steps to talk about some of these issues and how the media and public 'react'. For example, the responses to Amanda Todd, some of which you can still find online. I am with the kids: I would be saying, 'Not on your nelly, nope, not happening'.

Can we challenge this behaviour in others? Especially online?

Next time you see someone's dog take a poo and the owner walks away without cleaning it up, see what you feel and want to do. See what you say. Or, next time a child engages in a behaviour that you would not let your children do or 'get away with', see how quickly you judge the other parents or carers.

We all do this, and children know this. *Inherently.* They hear us, see us engaging in this online, watch us, and they know by the age of about three what shame feels like, deeply, and we, the adults, put it there. Why would they share something a perpetrator says will get them killed, hurt or rejected forever?

How about we start focusing on changing the behaviours of those who do this harm? I think the work of Stop It Now! (Lucy Faithfull) is the most commendable service doing this for adult perpetrators, and the services helping to prevent bullying in children and adults are amazing at changing this landscape too. We all need to take a stand in speaking about the crimes mentioned in the volumes to prevent the feelings that result in children wanting to end their lives.

If a child discloses they have shared intimate images, then they are courageous, not stupid.

Given that disclosures aren't always being brought forward, you can see that this shame festers and grows daily, with unknown numbers of victims, with perhaps no foreseeable light at the end of the tunnel. And the truth is the perpetrators are often correct when they tell children these images are going to be shared, never be fully removed and may haunt them for the rest of their lives. Children know this is a fact too because they (over the age of 12) are beginning to understand how digital data works, and of course the perpetrators are more than happy to explain the sharing, uploading and spaces where their images will be, forevermore.

I hope that, at this stage, this gives you some insight into a child's thinking behind self-harm and suicide when it comes to this particular issue. Logical to them is an absolutely 100% cause-effect relationship, and out of all the issues in the books, this is the one that can be tied to the pernicious type of trauma ever suffered by children in today's world, with the worst possible outcome. This has never existed in our history in the way it does now. It is increasing, according to the services that remove this material, and this is the most worrying aspect for me writing this, as I haven't even covered newer technologies in this chapter.

Suicide: you don't get to respawn after this decision

We must and can do better, and perhaps the bit that the practitioners are looking for here is how, and in a short recap of the entire book, you must grab your cape, get on your trusty steed and head for the world of tech to understand it, embrace it and learn the language. You are already an adult who survived childhood and that puts you ahead of the young people in terms of knowing life, its ups and downs, and you are pretty good at it, not a wise old person sitting in a rocking chair yet, and so our job is to use the information provided in this book to meet the young people where they are.

And as a small note at the end of this chapter that envelopes into those spaces of professionals who harm, and suicide as a Venn diagram overlap: when we are in public spaces debating assisted suicide as in the case of places like Dignitas, and sharing information about suicide capsules that have been built and how we feel about them, we often forget that our posts can be and are read by young people.

Be Spider-Man. Be responsible. You are not on the Internet with 'just' adults.

References

5Rights. (2021). *New research shows child accounts directly targeted with graphic content within as little as 24 hours of creating an online social media account.* https://5rightsfoundation.com/in-action/new-research-shows-children-directly-targeted-with-graphic-content-within-as-little-as-24-hours-of-creating-an-online-social-media-account.html.

Cozolino, L. (2006). *The neuroscience of human relationships: Attachment and the developing social brain* (2nd ed.). W. W. Norton & Co: New York.

Fonagy, P. (2001). *Attachment theory and psychoanalysis.* Routledge: London.

Gerhardt, S. (2014). *Why love matters. How affection shapes a baby's brain.* Routledge. London.

Knibbs, C. (2014). *Cybertrauma: Past, present or future.* www.youtube.com/watch?v=fyUyM-eW0L8&t=1908s.

Knibbs, C. (2016). *Cybertrauma; The darker side of the internet.* Self-published and available on Amazon Kindle and Blurb Books.

Knibbs, C. (2020). *The polyvagal motorway of wellness* (updated version). www.youtube.com/watch?v=QGBv1KrJ5Pk&t=102s.

Knibbs, C. (2022). *Children, technology and healthy development.* Routledge: Abingdon.

Ogden, P., Minton, K., & Pain, C. (2006). *Trauma and the body: A sensorimotor approach to psychotherapy (Norton series on interpersonal neurobiology).* W. W. Norton & Co: New York.

Online Safety UK. (2022). *If not now when report.* www.onlinesafetyuk.com/.

Panksepp, J. (2004). *Affective neuroscience. The foundations of human and animal emotions.* Oxford University Press: Oxford.

Papyrus. www.papyrus-uk.org/.

Siegel, D. J. (1999). *The developing mind: Toward a neurobiology of interpersonal experience.* Guilford Press: New York.

Walker, M. (2017). *Why we sleep. The new since of sleep and dreams.* Penguin: London.

www.samaritans.org/about-samaritans/research-policy/internet-suicide/talking-to-your-child-about-self-harm-and-suicide-content-online/.

www.samaritans.org/about-samaritans/research-policy/internet-suicide/guidelines-tech-industry/understanding-self-harm-and-suicide-content/.

8 Professionals who harm

Every chapter, topic and section of this book can be seen through the lens of one or more of the other sections, chapters and topics.

Harms that professionals cause, contribute to or have no idea about

This section looks at complexities of what you don't know about digital spaces until you know, usually through a safeguarding event or by reading books like this. Then, we can and must do better. This also means that you may not be aware of the issues in this chapter, until you read it and may feel several emotions about it.

I considered that this chapter should be towards the end of the book, should this create discord, get the hackles up or create panic in people who consider their behaviour impeccable, ethical and/or would be soul-destroyed to think that they caused harm in this world of technology.

I find that, when teaching, I can touch upon a topic only to see startled faces in the audience who then get caught up in the finite details of that subject matter, and this can be rather like emotional contagion, as people suddenly find themselves questioning their practice, and often questioning me, moving us all away from the presentation at hand. The biggest 'culprit' of this is the dreaded Data Protection Act, as well as four letters that spark fear in most cases (discussed later in the chapter).

In digital spaces, this unintended harm is often not due to direct malice but naiveté. No one in the following scenarios discussed is deliberately intending to cause harm to people (I hope). As you read this, if you feel a situation is familiar, please take a breath and stay with the topic for the information you need. You didn't know what you didn't know until you read this. That's how education works.

The following examples (which are vignettes where needed to protect identities) are all cases I have worked on in the last few years. I have worked with these issues for longer than this time; however, to give readers an insight into how current these issues are, I am using several examples where I have been required to attend meetings in local authorities, schools and education settings to explain why the following issues are of paramount importance to our fields of child protection and safeguarding.

DOI: 10.4324/9781003289210-9

Shock and awe, caveats, and trigger warnings

One of these is the traumatisation of audiences by well-intended professionals, through the showing or in-depth discussions of material that is traumatic and does not contain a *trigger warning* or *content warning*. These are now popular terms to denote that content that follows may be distressing. And herein lies the issue as to these spaces and the potential harm caused. The caveat here, like in the rest of the chapters and volumes, is to look after yourself, where you have the awareness of needing to. For many people, we don't necessarily know we are re-experiencing something until later or perhaps not even at all. Furthermore, there is research supporting the idea that the words 'trigger' or 'content' can evoke a response of 'getting ready' for something that may not be triggering to you (Jones et al., 2020). However, your nervous system does not know this in advance and so gets Amy R ready! (My previous book discusses her at length).

The title of the conference is enough?

At a large trauma conference early in my career, I saw a presenter show a film about his work. He did not 'prepare' the audience (as is now common to do so) and proceeded to show a film about a woman who was in group therapy and revisiting her trauma.

As we broke for tea and biscuits, one of my fellow colleagues was talking about how this content should have been communicated beforehand to the audience. I was initially confused because we were at an event about trauma, and this had been marketed toward therapists. My thinking was, of course, where there are therapists, then you can bet your bottom dollar that we will be discussing the trauma as we do in training, where sessional videos are often shown. This is how we 'show and prepare' the next generation of practitioners.

However, I began to muse over this and considered that, pretty much on a daily basis, I, along with other trauma therapists, may be so 'used to hearing this stuff' that we have developed many mechanisms with which to hear but not be penetrated by these traumas. A term is often known as self-protection in empathy, connection and compassion to prevent vicarious trauma. However, some of the audience had not been through this training process, were not that far into their careers, had not done their work or were just impacted by the video and its contents. I sat for a few hours that evening considering that, during my training, we discussed our own potency and robustness to hear others' trauma and how this becomes our way of being able to sit with the clients in resonance and alliance. But something was bugging me about it.

Why do the presenters, and I have included myself in this cohort in the past (and now try to do better in this aspect), set off with the PowerPoint or list of things they want to convey and head right down the road of fact sharing and examples to illustrate their teachings, without checking in with the audience? Just because we are therapists, teachers, trainers or whatever profession does not necessarily mean that we are impervious to being triggered, traumatised and affected deeply. We don't necessarily have to hear about every aspect of the depravities of the darker side of human beings and their behaviours to learn.

I got spooked!

As with most of the things in the world, when it's experiential, we learn faster, and only then do we say we have 'deeper' understandings of such things. At a conference I attended in 2017 with one of my heroes, he was talking through the neurobiology of trauma and referenced an experiment conducted on animals in the early 1930s. As I listened, I was sitting next to my friend, and we had been so excited that morning to know we had two days with this person. I was in a 'ready to learn' state and paying attention to every word. I was seated mid-row and had just finished my coffee (all facts that are important, not just to fill the page). I listened intently, and as he described the experiment I suddenly found myself feeling hot and ill, my temperature rising quickly, and I was sweating; I thought, 'Oh ****, I'm going to have to move fast to not vomit everywhere!' I was aware this event was being recorded, so I found myself stuck in the process of: move or don't move? I knew that I would have to move quickly, and I would need to be subtle in 'getting out of here'. This was terrible! What should I do?

I took a breath so that I didn't vomit (amazing the things we do to try and stop these body processes). And suddenly I realised what was going on as I heard my own narrative. This was a familiar voice, which was panic, and was not related to the here and now, this was a flashback to my childhood of a terrible event. I had seen the image on the screen behind the presenter and my mind extrapolated, generalised and, before you could count to two, had associated said image with my childhood. My friend who was a therapist had clearly picked up on my energy and asked me if I was okay, and like the good child that I was, I answered yes. Whilst internally trying my best to get this feeling to subside and breathing like I was about to do a deep-sea dive, using a technique I learned with the Flow Genome Project only a few months before. Two minutes later (I think) I was back in the room and looking at my hero on the stage, thinking, 'You absolute git'. Why would you show such a terrible image? The anger from my past was now present and, of course, as an adult here and now I can write about these things, whereas the child in the past was paralysed by power, the associative memory and the event unfolding.

A type of cybertrauma had now happened to me, experientially in a way that reflected the definition of cybertrauma *a la perfection!*

Isn't this just your problem?

I am sure you can see how the image was a problem for me, but what really is the issue of showing films, images or sounds to audiences if they are attending a lecture, seminar or workshop aimed at understanding trauma, grief, attachment or any other 'psychology' topic? Or perhaps the world of cybersecurity where stories of harrowing scams and hacks take place? Surely people are expecting to hear the terrible and the worse? And what is the issue if you say upfront, 'This content may be triggering for some of you'? Is this not like the warnings we get on TV programs before we chose to watch a film, program or video?

Ahh, there it is: choice. We can, if we wish, leave a program, turn off the TV or even leave the room, hide behind our hands or a pillow or whatever safety behaviour we want to use. Outside of the home in these conferences, workshops or training, it's the lack of escape. The social judgements of others keep us glued to our seats even when we are having a full-on internal meltdown. And on the back of this, I use a fun and playful version and an example of this in training around CSE, and each and every time I do this, the adult does not leave. Why? Well, they don't want to be seen as rude, weak or to be ridiculed.

Because?

I sit at many conferences, training and events, and people will say, 'If you would rather leave the session, or if you feel uncomfortable please do at any time'; some even add in, 'No one will judge you', which is a bare-faced lie and we all know it but play along accordingly (talk about peer pressure and social norms). And this underpins the caveat, the trigger and content warnings' useless side.

Many traumatised people cannot leave!

If you have read anything on trauma, you know that a trauma response often happens out of awareness, is a reaction rather than a response or choice and bodies do whatever they need to in order to survive, which makes the point absolutely moot, for a trauma professional to think someone in their audience is suddenly going to do it differently because they are teaching and have given the permission. If only it were that easy in therapy!

Their bodies often freeze – trauma, shame and vagal tone roots them to the spot – they are paralysed by the fear, and inherently know they will be judged if they move, exacerbating these issues, or in the case of a well-learned trauma response: anticipate being killed if they move.

> We know these are trauma responses; we teach it and we ignore it in the case of expertise, professing to the masses.

And before the professing even begins, the very statement suggesting people need to physically leave on its own, with no other options given, brings up a history for many victims that goes hand in hand with the topic (see my statement shortly). For example, a professional lecturing about domestic violence at a DV conference brings up slide number one, smiling and saying gently, 'Anyone who feels distressed with the content can leave, and we won't judge you'.

'*Crock of shit*', *says Sharon to herself, sitting in the fourth row, 'if I make a move, they will all know I'm a victim*'. This is a socially aware and cognizant moment. Meanwhile, the trauma memory is now evoked in the background, and whilst she does not hear a voice loud and clear, her body does: '*You move, and I'll kill you*', it says. Sharon stays rooted, hardly moving in that freeze response, which is not passive but active and is like the 'spider on the carpet'. No one notices her.

I have also been at conferences where the lecturer does not give this caveat, launching straight into the case of Sally. Blah blah blah, she drones, as she recalls the story of Sally's assault, the court case and the victim blaming. Sharon is still rooted to the spot but may not understand why she is so.

Options, what options?

And so she stays put, experiencing terror at the hands of the professional. Not very trauma-informed and applied?

Doing it differently?

Perhaps as you get ready to speak to the audience you could say something like the following statement:

> Some of this content may be uncomfortable for some of you, but not all, you may find yourself feeling things and I know that this may be a stress and, or trauma response, or the content may not feel nice to hear about, I get it, I rarely talk about the nice stuff. If you need to daydream, look out of the window, scribble notes and doodle, stop listening or jiggle your feet, please do so. If you wish and are able to and you want to nip out to the loo, grab a quick puff, go for a walk, I don't mind as we all need to take a comfort break that's not scheduled – I know my bladder doesn't run to the timing of the conference!
>
> If I see anyone that seems to be struggling with the content, I will try and adapt the content. At the end of the session, before questions, let's have a quick toilet break for people to move, or (if it's the end of the day) please look after yourself and do what you need to, even if that's the kind of activity or behaviour that is advised against, like having a glass of wine, sweets, cake or chocolate or all of them!

I am not saying this is the only solution or these words must be copied verbatim, but people need permission to check out psychologically and cognitively for all or part of the session, to leave for reasons that they can empower themselves with (even though they may overpower this internally with the social-judgment thinking), they need a language that is empathic, resonant and compassionate. And most of all is the understanding of trauma responses in a crowd. My understanding of this came mostly from my inability to 'do' anything, when came my flashback and the work I did with the Manchester Arena victims. The image rendered me *powerless* in that moment, and if there is one thing I hope I can alleviate in my sessions, it is that, because that's the most common feeling in trauma.

Online-safety examples of harm

Now the previous examples were from conferences and workshops where professionals attending are likely to have been therapists, or people who are studying trauma or use it in their practice. However, other types of conferences also seem to promote this kind of shock-and-awe tactic. I have seen an ex-head teacher display a picture of self-harm to the audience, clipping it with a phrase about 'attention seeking behaviour', I have seen online-safety professionals using videos, images and stories that are harrowing, police officers scaring the bejeezus out of the audience as they tell them hackers will get into their Facebook account and share images of child sexual abuse, I have seen the cybersecurity sector utilising the hardships of a victim's crime to explain to the audience what not to do and I have seen professionals design 'programs' to use with young people that will show them the effects of crimes, knife crime, sexual exploitation, drugs and county lines, and one that shows children how they could end up murdered if they speak to people online. These resources are scary and do not have the intended outcome because of how trauma and stress shut down the brain.

Documentaries, films, videos and the sharing of distressing images

After watching one of these events unfold at a sexual-exploitation conference, I was maddened and asked the professional why they showed these images, and was met with a shrug of the shoulders and a comment about the audience now knowing what self-harm and exploitation looked like.

> This is not how we learn, and this individual may need to read about trauma and have some empathy for the audience, or we need to speak out more about this kind of harm that professionals cause by doing this.

The person I was sitting with at this conference had a history of self-harm, as she was a victim of exploitation herself and was furious that her coping mechanism as a young person had been so 'glibly dismissed' by someone she said 'needed a slap' (this is the polite version). Fast forward a few months and I was sitting with a good friend in the world of e-safety at another conference, when the ex-head mentioned earlier was speaking; all of a sudden, they produced this image of self-harm and my friend looked at me and said, 'Oops' (as if they read my mind!).

I spent the next few days musing over why professionals do this, and in the spirit of sharing, wrote a blog about the kicks that some professionals get from watching their audiences react to these kinds of stories and images. Some do it to shock in the hope it will cause a change in behaviour (this has never really worked for the masses), and some do it because they don't understand trauma at all.

Moreover, when these images and videos are created, they are rarely if ever vetted by a trauma-informed individual versed in the impact of this kind of cinematic and vicarious trauma. I am quite unique in this space, and cybertrauma is still an unknown issue, even with the slightly different wording of online harms and 'legal and harmful', as I call it. These kinds of videos, images and stories have been shared for many years in schools and youth settings with little understanding of 'cyber' trauma (even if you call it vicarious).

I have been challenging this behaviour for some time in spaces like social media, and this has led to conversations where TV shows, police forces and children's services have created material to be shown to children that is graphic, and often suggests the victim should have done something different (victim blaming), depict actual crime conversations and are triggering. I have asked where and how these videos were assessed, and to be fair, the responses I received were lacking in being able to define this, but boy did some of them have other types of impolite content (the charms of being challenged on social media).

These films would likely be regarded as 15 or even 18 by the BBFC if they were in cinemas, yet they are taken into the education settings and shown to children, without being watched by the schools, because when a service (third sector, voluntary or statutory) is brought in to teach, they are trusted as adults, often without checking their resources. Even if the resources were checked, would staff know what to look for in terms of cybertrauma?

I am suggesting that as part of the education framework (for any settings with children and young people), the new media-literacy programs being developed discuss and satisfy the requirements that content to be shown to children is assessed for the effects of cybertrauma. To do this effectively, ethically and with robust research there would need to be a standardised way of carrying this out and this will require a consultation process and assessment using some of the approaches here in this book. If we had, in place, legal AND harmful guidance regarding cybertrauma in the form of an ethical body, bill, legislation, organisation, service etc., then we would be able to apply the ideas to this type of content, protecting and safeguarding children. The Online Safety Bill is not suited to this type of content because it is not technically an online event if it is a lesson or event in person, but could be if it was a webinar for example. This is a requirement that perhaps the Department for Education, Ofsted or even an international standard bodies would need to cover, such as UNICEF, as the rights of children to not be traumatised by content shown to them is really about their rights, and not the adults who want to teach them a lesson.

> Immersive technology: a point to note is that immersive technologies are going to exacerbate this issue tenfold, and we already have services that have created these kinds of films in VR, and have been using them with children without ethical bodies approving their use (see my website for a handout on this particular issue).

For you, the practitioner, here's a way to think about this: I once appeared on a daytime-TV program alongside a professional from a charity that supported the showing of CSE films to young people. The interviewer said to the professional, 'So Cath thinks these films can be traumatic and should not be shown'. The professional replied, 'They can be'.

In which case, why are we showing them?

I'd also like to refer people back to the chapter in volume one on imagery around pornography, and how this is processed as to why this issue is so broad and needs the changes I am suggesting.

And these resources can end up on video-on-demand channels where they are not rated, protected or carrying warnings about the content, and can be seen by children of all ages (at the time of writing I can still find a number of these on YouTube). These are not likely to be censored under the current systems in place, because they are educational videos and do not contain some of the characteristics of censorship-worthy content.

A well-intended professional suggests a video for a child

She said, 'Here's a video I want you to watch outside of sessions, and we can chat about it next week, okay?'

'So off I went, and it was awful, there were loads of them slating us and I can't believe people speak like that, what happens if that happens to me when I'm next out?' Michele was explaining to me how her therapist had advised her to watch a video outside of therapy sessions, because it would have taken all the allocated session time if they did it there and then, meaning that they couldn't do much after the video. Michele explained that, like always, she went home and did what the therapist asked because she was the expert.

Diligently, Michele played the video in her bedroom. At the end, it went on to play the next recommended video, as this was how she always used YouTube. The video that followed had inappropriate language (sexist, racist and more) about her issue, which was about sexuality in the communities of black and brown people. She was facing a video that had religious overtones (and, I think, a very conservative and punitive message, from what she told me), and this set Michele back on her understanding of her issue. She spoke to her mum about it, saying that her therapist had told her to watch. Michele was angry that the auto-play video created confusion, had some terrifying images about surgery in it, had an overarching message about what God would do to her and what the consequences were to changing gender (this was not the US-based video showing the health impacts of surgery, as this was not where my client was at in her journey, and thankfully hadn't been looking at surgery videos, as these are very graphic).

Michele and her mum went and spoke to the therapist, who allegedly took no responsibility, citing to the parents and the school that she was aware young people used YouTube and, yes, she knew what they could be exposed to, of course! But this was 'not her fault'. She denied any culpability or wrongdoing on this issue, stating that this was a parental issue of 'non-supervision' and that her telling the child to watch the video was not unprofessional, unethical or worthy of a complaint against her.

Would this have happened in therapy, and would she deem showing the film as an okay intervention? Possibly, and certainly if the therapist took it upon themselves to deem what was appropriate education for the child, based on what they thought was good information. Would this be tantamount to illegal activity in a therapy room? Perhaps not, as this material is unrated, and therefore at the discretion of the professional as to what they consider good material in order to psycho-educate a client. And that leads us back to the previous issue.

Practitioner pause for reflection

Moreover, if we were to show children and young people propaganda, misinformation or disinformation, a hoax or indeed put upon them our values and ideals by the showing of such videos, where does that lead us? Are we citing evidence-based and research-based information, or are we showing them the latest influencer, TikTok or reel? Is this professional of us, to think we can show these children videos we feel are suitable, and based on what? When did this practice become so common that it went mostly unnoticed?

We as the professionals may actually be the problem here. I have seen many therapists, social workers and youth workers using videos from the Internet as part of their intervention work with young people. To quote Shoshana Zuboff (2019): 'who decides and who decides who decides'. And where is this framework? I cannot find any guidelines, recommendations or ethics about this issue for professionals.

Where is the ethical framework covering this for those professionals working with children, and how do we evaluate the videos created for use in schools, or those used from an online source, given the speculative nature of trustworthy sources? Are we being directed to use content from certain websites, and if so, how is that evaluated in terms of usefulness, impact and evidence? Where are the long-term studies on the use of online material used in professional settings?

Misuse of apps

Professionals use 'apps' in settings where these are not evaluated, evidence-based and may well have been created by bad actors. Again, I have watched, for a number of years, many therapists in social media groups advising each other on the various apps they use with their clients. These can range from breathing apps, to drawing ones, notetaking, self-harm, mindfulness and so on. And the recommendations come from a place of the professionals using them or seeing them advertised, then downloading and utilising them for their practice. However, when I ask, challenge and point out issues with doing this, I am shot down, asked to leave groups (or kicked) and silenced with my 'ethical hat' on. However, as you are reading the chapters and volumes, you may now be able to see that there can be many issues with asking a client to use an app on their smartphone that could have been created by a bad actor, has an unsuitable age rating, is for over-13s, pilfers an inordinate amount of personal data and tracking, hacks their smartphone, could be giving out mis and disinformation on the app, spreads propaganda, advising about health that is lacking evidence or is dangerous and the list goes on (into other areas that are more nefarious). And in all of this, there is a system already out there (and has been for several years) that can advise about these apps, that have been rigorously checked, for many of the issues mentioned here, and that service is Orcha (https://orchahealth.com/). This service is not on many recommendation lists or suggestions for some professionals, and I wonder why. This is not because this service is small; they contract with the NHS for practitioners. Why do I get asked to leave groups when bringing this into conversations? Well, I can only assume it's like the time a professional in the world of online therapy said to me about DPA, 2018, and 'the dreaded' the GDPR EU and UK versions (2018), we just want to use these services and platforms, it would be complicated and I don't have the time to learn.

So in the spirit of the book, let's start looking at the Data Protection Act (2018), privacy rights and freedoms of children, which, at the time of writing the first book in 2020, was culminating in this issue, becoming front and centre for worldwide organisations. However, the filtering down of this information to the singular practitioner leaves people looking like rabbits in headlights when I start to talk about protecting data and information (that's another book I am creating, on its way for you)!

Other harms

Smart-TV monitors at the local authorities, third-sector organisations and hospitals, social media, emails, reports, client disclosure, and health-related platform use, where full privacy laws are not understood, because the GDPR EU and UK versions (2018) created a whoo-ha of panic, and now this is seemingly the only law we feel we need to follow? Again, see the next book I have co-edited as this law has changed, has very important additional aspects, is both UK and EU and is not the *only* law we need to follow.

Pretend case study

Sam is a child in protective measures. His father has fled the home due to violence and taken up living arrangements in another city. He takes Sam to the local school after a few weeks and enrols him, hoping that Sam can feel some normality back in his life. During the week, a third-sector company arranges a 'drop-down day' of education. They bring in some sole traders working for the third-sector company to support them in education on all things child-protection, suicide and bereavement awareness. At the end of the day, the school is proud of the students and takes some photos that are shared on social media by both the school and the organisations who provided the training. The school has removed Sam's face, as they are following guidelines. The sole trader has not received permission to take or share photos of the event. Sam's mum is aware that Dad may have gone to a particular town when he fled, and so she spends her time checking the social media feeds for the local schools in that area. It doesn't take her long to find Sam in one of the images: she recognises his frame and slight lean to the left with his hips (even though his face is blurred out). She follows the names of the people involved in the drop-down day to other social media profiles. She confirms it's him, locates the school address, and the following day, Sam's mum decides to make her way to the school to meet her son at the end of the day, creating a very difficult situation for Sam and the school.

Now, this school asked about children in photographs on their data-protection policy; because the GDPR requires this, they considered safeguarding issues as far as they could in the school, however, this was not necessarily communicated with the visitors to the school, who also did not have their own safeguarding and data-protection policies that they shared with the school beforehand. Before we move on, are you working in settings where you share your data-protection policy before going into those spaces, and if not, why? Is it something you think we need to do as practitioners, or is this too far, too much duplication, and is this something you even possess?

These slight omissions and presumptions, that everyone is working from the same perspective and has a knowledge of safeguarding, do not always include issues of child protection in this way, because to date this is often omitted through a lack of education in training. If this is not in your training, perhaps you can ask why not? If you are in, let's say, education, youth settings or training of practitioners, perhaps this is something you need to add to your safeguarding training and child-protection policies. Do you ask to see a DP policy before allowing someone professional onto your premises, and do you share yours with them?

The difficulty with these kinds of moments for children is, for example, Sam didn't want to feel left out by his new peers, or seen to be a 'weird' or 'special case', and so chose to be in the photos, regardless of the fact that school had been informed that he wasn't to be in these for this purpose. The school took the pictures and blurred out his face, but sadly in this pretend case study, the images were stored on a removable hard drive or USB (you can fill out your own ending to this story about the fact that the original photos were not destroyed and were sitting on the drive).

Now, at the same school, it just so happens that one of Sam's newly formed friends, Mike, was in the published photos, and later that day was around at Sam's for tea. He was approached by a stranger on the Internet claiming to be his dad. His biological dad. Mike did not know he was adopted, as the parents had not 'broken this news to him' because they wanted to do this in their own time and under their own family rules about when and how. Mike was given lots of information by the stranger. He was told who he really was and where he was born, his real name, siblings and family dynamics. When he got home (raging, I might add) and explained to his adoptive parents about the message and news, they were angry too and shouted at him, revealing the true story of his birth, his parents being 'alcoholic drug users and being in the nick'.

Not because they were horrid parents, not because they wanted to shock Mike, but because they were taken aback by this sudden contact and had not been given training by the adoptive services with which they worked about these kinds of issues. They were frightened and worried about the contact via social media, and so gave Mike his life story in one sharp sentence rather than the gradual, life-story-based work that is often used with adoptive children.

Both issues have happened in my career, I have also seen issues like this discussed on Twitter. I have worked directly with adoptive and special guardianship cases where these things have happened. On each of these occasions, the guidelines for dealing with these kinds of issues have been missing, or have not anticipated this, sometimes with the families being without input from services for many years, and so up-to-date training on these issues has not taken place, because this didn't really happen that often a decade ago. As technology changes and speeds up, it would seem some families are forgotten to the closed cases on the shelf, and it is not at the forefront of the practitioner's mind to evaluate and consider the issues with technology and the historic cases, in cupboards, boxes and out of sight. I don't know if it is the practitioner's responsibility to think about these cases, but I suspect it is more the responsibility of the service.

Twitter and the arrests discussed in real time

I have seen UK solicitors discussing, on Twitter, the person they are going to represent, who has been arrested and has mental health issues. I challenged this professional (in the past) and it resulted in me getting blocked (and no, I'm not learning at this stage). Not only does this contravene data-protection principles and is risky of identifying a person outright, it also puts into the social media space that a client has mental health issues. This is something they most certainly didn't consent to, for which that person's data about this fact could be mined and used against them. And yes, this person was outed in the respect of a quick Google search, because they went to magistrates' court the following morning, according to the solicitor. If solicitors do this and they are versed in the law, what hope is there for practitioners who do not receive training in what constitutes sensitive data, and information they should not share outside of their practice?

By this, I mean I see a regular set of therapists, some who are quite bespoke in their specialism discussing clients online, in varying ways, but if I were to highlight them here it would be hypocritical of me to do so (and would identify some of them), however, I did share this information with a conference of practitioners in 2018, when GDPR became legally enforceable. I also know complaints have not been upheld about these kinds of issues, and I am happy to discuss this broader online professionalism, the risks of sharing content about your practice and what con artists are looking for and why, in real-world settings where I know there is confidentiality, and the practitioners are bound by a code of ethics. It is shocking that we are 5 years into the Data Protection Act (2018) and 25 years plus for the Data Protection Act (1998) and still this is the most misunderstood area of practice that can lead to breaches and long-term harm, and how the digital space can be unforgiving to this lack of knowledge. I have said before that people think I'm sensationalising or telling horror stories, however, I know from practice that data is worth income many times over for the criminals who exploit this, and I know that data online is traceable, and as such, practitioners need much more training in this area.

Alfie and Karen get married

Another pretend case study here. Alfie is sitting with Karen in the local hospital after she was scheduled for a minor surgery. Her ex-partner knew this surgery was scheduled because the letter for it went to her old address. She had only recently moved out, away from a violent relationship, and had not changed any of her details at the hospital. She was intending to do it today when she arrived. She had been off for her bloods and was now heading back to the reception area. As she headed back towards Alfie, her ex-partner was standing in reception and her name was displayed on the waiting board with the clinic number she was now to head towards. Alfie was completely unaware of this and saw how Karen was looking as he headed over to meet her. Karen was first met by her partner who was agitated and wanted her to come home, and so set about a physical display of apology and pleading that resulted in the woman feeling under pressure to silence the situation.

This is not harmful behaviour by the hospital, as, pretty much, this is standard practice; however, if we consider coercive, violent and abusive relationships, we can see that 'calling out' a person can be difficult. Given that in the last few years, hospitals have moved to digital sign-ins and boards that resemble airport check-ins, these moments can end up being difficult. Imagine you were attending a clinic for sexual-health issues and your neighbour was also at the hospital (I think sexual health is probably more discrete than this, but I wouldn't know if this was the case, it's an example here). I am being completely antagonistic here, and I know these are 'far-out' examples, as health services need to know whom they are dealing with, but this is an example of progress, perhaps without all issues considered.

Communication and other services

James Bond email

Jeremy was a young child whom I had been asked to work with, referred by the school. During my time in therapy with him, it became apparent that he might have some learning needs. As I saw him, as a private practitioner, we talked about arranging a meeting at school with his teachers. As with all my younger clients, I explain that when I send my emails, I use a service that is like a spy service, and the email can only be read by the recipient and, akin to James Bond's work, it can't be tampered with or sent to someone else without me knowing, and so I can say with certainty that his 'data' and information was safe in transit when I sent it.

After meeting with the school and talking with a number of people in senior roles, we realised that home life was being supported by the early-help hub teams too, and in doing so there was a history of some domestic abuse, lots of previous houses and home moves due to poverty (so several settings were shared with other family members as well). We agreed that we would need to arrange another meeting with professionals to understand a bit more about the situation and to ensure we were not doubling up on interventions, and a request for an educational psychologist would be sought for some of the issues that would need testing.

The following day I received an email from the school, with a disclosure at the bottom of it about the confidentiality of the email contents. Attached to the email was a Word document: the report from the meeting. The document was not password-protected. Details in the Word document included the child's date of birth, address, previous addresses, names of family members, the psychologist's request and details of why this was needed, and this email went to a number of professionals. The email was not encrypted, the file was not protected in any way and also went to the parent's email address with all of the professional's emails showing in the CC field.

Now whilst this is not technically breaking the law – well, actually it is, but that's another conversation for the data-protection book in progress. The issue with this is: due care and attention were not taken to protect the data of either the child, family or professionals involved. The email could have been intercepted by what is called a 'man in the middle attack', i.e., criminals could intercept and read, or the email client provider could intercept and read the contents, which most of them have the permission to do in the T&Cs you signed when setting up your account.

The parents now had an email address for me that wasn't the one I had shared with them for my business; the psychologist and the early help hub replied to this email thread and did not disguise and protect the child and family information when replying, and yet three of the professionals had the signature at the bottom of their email showing data-protection-based information (the message that you are possibly familiar with that reads, 'This email is intended for . . .' etc.).

Whether harm has been caused is an issue that I cannot say for certainty; I mean, how would I track the 'interception' on any one of the servers the email bounced through on the many journeys the email took? Also, if any of this data was indeed viewed by anyone other than those intended (i.e., the addresses in the email 'send to' bar), how would we know that?

And at the end of the day, this data and information is about a child whose unprotected meeting notes and conversations about them were shared through the thread over and over again.

This issue is, sadly, not uncommon. Most professionals who work in the space of health and well-being are not IT nerds like I am and don't necessarily understand how technology works. And this is the biggest issue for children's data, information and the issues around cybersecurity. Layers of complexity need to be created in the use of digital technology in order to protect the digital data hosed there or when it is transmitted to others. And it is this complexity that sends professionals running to the hills. But it doesn't have to be complicated. Getting training is the easiest solution, and hopefully you will get a trainer who can translate the gobbledygook from IT professionals to a language you can understand. And when the book on data protection and cybersecurity is out, grab a copy of that too. Every layer helps.

Lockdown and the rush to online continued work

I may have just lost some readers at this point.

This brings me to the issue, issues or potential risks that occurred during lockdown with the rush to work online, via telephone and email. The professions of health, mental health and well-being, child protection, some child services and holistic services did not have prior or adequate training in understanding technology, how to protect electronic and digital data and what the laws of data protection meant for use of technology that could be accessed, hacked, destroyed, intercepted, rewritten, shared. Training in systems and how they work wasn't even on the radar for some services, because they didn't need it, nor did they have business contingency plans in place. I doubt some professionals have one of these as we speak.

Making waves

During the last two years (three by the time this book is published) I have upset and angered a number of professionals in my field because I have questioned advice from other professionals and membership bodies who likely panicked and advised about the continuation of services over data-protection laws. With a number of data-protection, cybersecurity, information security, privacy and international standards of best practice, we have been committed to education and assisting in this sphere, to no avail. On some occasions, I provided training and advice, only to have it tossed to the side because it meant services could not deliver the service they wanted to, especially to young people under the age of 13. I have been contacted in numerous ways and asked to remove posts, blogs and training advice because 'it's complicated', 'it would mean rewriting training' and 'we want to use that platform because it's easy' (some of the direct replies and responses I receive). I've also had services that I am an associate practitioner for asking me to send documents unencrypted, because they don't want to use 'complicated software', a social-care direct services tell me they can't accept email referrals and a police force asking me to send a very sensitive document unencrypted to them because 'they used. pnn on their email address' (this is not secure just because that's the ending on the receiving email address, for those wondering).

Many of these issues that I challenged, and still do, are related to:

The processing of data via text and or voicemails on a smartphone, which often backs up to the cloud and where this phone is used for both personal and client work, and where emails are received on the device.

Platforms used to carry out confidential sessions. Such as the platform Zoom, which, until March/April 2020, had claimed to be fully encrypted, and as was discovered, was not as secure as people trusted, as session hacks took place with some horrific issues occurring.

The use of platforms that move data outside of the EU without standard clauses in place, at the time of DPA (2018) and GDPR when we were in the EU, and now as it stands outside of the EU.

The processing of children's data and use of platforms rated 14 or 16, such as teams used for children and their education.

All of these issues are still prevalent, may incur breaches when practitioners use devices at home that have a shared network and have not understood the privacy policies of platforms and services they sign up to, including their Internet provider.

The list goes on and it's difficult to discuss because it's complicated.

It's not you, it's the training

It is a difficult landscape for many people, and of course, why would practitioners know this? After all, they studied to become a health or well-being practitioner or to design a service for the people whom they serve. For example, social workers are taught to be social workers and not the kind of nerdy geek that I am with a background in IT and the native tongue of cyber-related realms. You might not be trained to use this stuff, or the trainers might not have the lexicon, the knowledge or, as happened during lockdown, the sudden rush of 'technological experts' – for example, people selling courses on how to use Zoom (which Zoom still does for free, and YouTube has lots of videos too) – but the panic to use services meant that a large number of children had their data processed unlawfully, and the rise in online services rose, with little depth to the issues that needed protection.

To date, my biggest challenge is explaining (without making practitioners cry or worry excessively) that the deficit of knowledge about the Data Protection Act – which is not new as mentioned, as it has been around since 1998 – means that the potential for litigation is sitting quietly until we have the same greedy systems that pushed for PPI claims. We can and must do better in our knowledge of technology to protect children, no matter how complicated it is, or how much you just want to use easy systems.

We the adults have been the product, as well as big data collected and mined by services that manipulate our social media feeds, push political agendas, create discord and polarised content and cause fear in us. Let us do better for the children, and that means we have to learn a new language taught by established and recognised services who can make this easy for you, and know the laws.

Zoom rooms and consent

A very brief paragraph here, but one where I have yet to see guidance and application of good practice. Over the lockdown I took some courses, some of which were online and included world-leading corporate companies with many people heading to their training, summits and events. When joining these, we would sometimes be asked to move into 'breakout' rooms. Not once, not ever, did we get a room in which there was a coordinator versed in safeguarding and the processes of what to do if there is a violation of any description in the room. I saw and heard sexist, ageist and sexual remarks being made by attendees to others in the room. I watched those attendees drop off the calls and have no idea how they are or what the impact of this was. And there was nowhere for me to report a concern. I have been recorded in these sessions with no data-protection policy available, or consent form available to read, and accept and I have not got a clue where my data is on some of these trainings conducted outside of the UK and EU.

Viral recommendations for psychedelics onstage and on the Internet

One last element I wanted to end this chapter with is the fast-moving content about psychedelics as a new panacea for trauma in mental health. This is not a new area of investigation, with many organisations and individuals looking at this, from the likes of David Nutt (formerly the drugs tsar) to Rick Doblin (MAPS) and Robin Carhart Harris (ICL), but since the explosion of Michael Pollan's book, the conversations online by professionals in the fields of trauma, well-being and coaching have also exploded with recommendations for all forms of psychedelics. I also saw a professional suggest ayahuasca as a remedy for trauma onstage in 2017, saying that even if you purge all night you will learn something. My adolescent clients have been talking about this for about a year now, and I am worried that some may go and try, forsaking the golden rules of 'set and setting', and of course may not be using the medical-grade formulas. The greats of trauma have been running conferences online (some for free) and the discussions of this new intervention are catching on for younger people, with many coming and asking about them in therapy. Some of them get good information (backed by research I have been reading) and some are getting the 'guru' in Spain, Peru and the Amazon, to name a few locations (these locations have professional settings too, but my clients are not naming these).

As professionals, we need to be aware of all new and emerging ideas, interventions and research directions. You could be sitting with a young person who has just decided to go and try the 'toad' next year based on a podcast they listened to recently where this was discussed (in 2022 there were lots of these).

Psychological games by professionals – the gritty space of social media

Professionals are 'battling' it out in the sector of health, well-being, education and psychotherapy with researchers, journalists and each other. I also see this in the e-safety spaces, as well as law and elite health spaces, as discussed earlier.

As I said at the start of this and volume one: I don't have all the answers, I read research and read the counter research to ideas. I read the uncomfortable texts, books and posts, and I am currently watching a space, particularly on Twitter, of professionals squashing their peers, not in academic rigour and evidence but in rage (and seemingly hatred). I wonder what young people think about our professions when they see this? Some professionals are attacking the health and medical industry, telling people to avoid certain medications and that some interventions and research are hokum, and I am seeing the confusion in the narrative of trust in professions like ours that are here to safeguard and protect children, whether that be online safety, knowledge about autism, trauma, sports or whatever.

> If we can't do debate nicely, then it's no wonder the younger people face this difficulty online too. We are modelling it for them, day and night.

References

The Data Protection Act. (2018). www.legislation.gov.uk/ukpga/2018/12/contents.

The GDPR (EU). (2018). https://gdpr-info.eu/.

The GDPR (UK). (2018). www.legislation.gov.uk/ukpga/2018/12/part/2/chapter/2.

Jones, P., Bellet, B., & McNally, R. (2020). Helping or harming? The effect of trigger warnings on individuals with trauma histories. *Clinical Psychological Science*, 8(5), 905–917.

Zuboff, S. (2019). *The age of surveillance capitalism. The fight for a new human future at the new frontier of power.* Profile Books: London.

Helplines and organisations

www.ceop.police.uk.
www.childnet.com.
www.gloablkidsonline.net.
www.internetmatters.co.uk.
www.iwf.org.uk.
www.lgbthealth.org.uk/.
www.mind.org.uk/.
www.nspcc.org.uk.
www.parentzone.org.uk.
www.safeinternet.org.uk.
www.samaritans.org/.
www.stopitnow.org.uk.
www.swgfl.org.uk.

Services dedicated to the removal of and protection against CSAEM

ICMEC-= International Centre for missing and exploited children @ www.icmec. org/.

INHOPE = The International hotline for removal of CSAM @ www.inhope.org/ EN?locale=en.

INTERPOL = International Crime Agency @ www.interpol.int/en.

IWF = The Internet Watch Foundation @ www.iwf.org.uk/.

NCMEC= National Centre for Missing and Exploited Children @ www.miss ingkids.org/HOME.

WeProtect = Global Alliance for Protection against CSAM @ www.weprotect.org/.

References and bibliography

(13) (PDF) The Impact of Cyberstalking. Accessed November 22, 2022. www.researchgate. net/publication/282201099_The_Impact_of_Cyberstalking.

American Psychiatric Association (APA). (2013). *Diagnostic and statistical manual of mental disorders* (5th ed.).

Anti-Bullying Alliance. (2022). *Cyberbullying definition.* https://anti-bullyingalliance.org.uk/.

Atrill-Smith, A., Fullwood, C., Keep, M., & Kuss, D. (2019). *The Oxford handbook of cyberpsychology.* Oxford University Press: Oxford.

Baddeley, A. (2007). *Working memory thought and action.* Oxford University Press: Oxford.

Bailenson, J. (2021). Nonverbal overload: A theoretical argument for the causes of zoom fatigue. *Technology, Mind and Behaviour,* 2(1). Nonverbal overload: A theoretical argument for the causes of Zoom fatigue.

Baker, P., & Norton, L. (2019). *Fat loss forever.* Amazon print on demand.

Ball, M. (2022). *The metaverse and how it will revolutionise everything.* Liveright Publishing Corporation: New York.

Bandura, A. (1973). *Aggression: A social learning analysis.* Prentice Hall: New York and Boston.

Bandura, A., Ross, D., & Ross, S. A. (1961). Transmission of aggression through imitation of aggressive models. *The Journal of Abnormal and Social Psychology,* 63(3), 575.

Bandura, A., & Walters, R. H. (1977). *Social learning theory* (Vol. 1). Prentice Hall: Englewood Cliffs.

Barret, L., Dunbar, R., & Lycett, J. (2002). *Human evolutionary psychology.* Palgrave Macmillan: Basingstoke.

Bauman, S. (2011). *Cyberbullying. What conselors need to know.* American Counseling Organisation: Alexandria.

Bean, A., Daniel, E., & Hays, S. (2020). *Integrating geek culture into therapeutic practice. The clinician's guide to geek therapy.* Leyline Publishing: Fort Worth.

Benton, D., & Young, H. (2016). A meta-analysis of the relationship between brain dopamine receptors and obesity: A matter of changes in behaviour rather than food addiction? *International Journal of Obesity,* 40(1), S12–S21.

Berne, E. (1964). *Games people play. The psychology of human relationships.* Penguin: London.

Berne, E. (1970). *Sex in human loving.* Penguin: London.

Besharat Mann, R., & Blumberg, F. (2022). Adolescents and social media: The effects of frequency of use, self-presentation, social comparison, and self-esteem on possible self-imagery. *Acta Psychologica,* 228.

Black, M. C., Basile, K. C., Breiding, M. J., Smith, S. G., Walters, M. L., Merrick, M. T., Chen, J., & Stevens, M. R. (2011). *The national intimate partner and sexual violence survey*

(NISVS): 2010 summary report. National Center for Injury Prevention and Control, Centers for Disease Control and Prevention: Atlanta, GA.

Boffey, P. (1987). Infants' Sense of Pain Is Recognized, Finally. https://www.nytimes.com/1987/11/24/science/infants-sense-of-pain-is-recognized-finally.html

Bradshaw, S., & Howard, P. (2019). *The global disinformation order: 2019 Global inventory of organised social media manipulation*. Oxford Internet: Oxford.

British Board of Film Classification. (2020). *Young people, pornography & Age-verification*. Accessed via BBFC directly, Personal Communication: Email, 2020.

Brown, B. (2017). *Braving the wilderness: The quest for true belonging and the courage to stand alone*. Random House: New York.

Burgess, J., & Green, J. (2019). *YouTube* (2nd ed.). Polity Press: Cambridge.

Burrow, A., & Rainone, N. (2017). How many *likes* did I get? Purpose moderates links between positive social media feedback and self-esteem. *Journal of Experimental Social Psychology*, 69, 232–236.

Buss, D. (2004). *Evolutionary psychology the new science of the mind* (2nd ed.). Pearson: London.

Buss, D. (2016). *The evolution of desire: Strategies of human mating*. Basic Books: London.

Buss, D. (2021). *Bad men. The hidden roots of sexual deception, harassment and assault*. Robinson: London.

Cantor, J. (2009). *Conquer cyber overload. Get more done, boost your creativity and reduce stress*. Cyberoutlook Press: Wisconsin.

Carse, J. (1986). *Finite and Infinite Games. A vision of life as play and possibility*. Free Press: London.

Carter, S., & Getz, L. (1993). *Monogamy and the prairie vole*, Scientific American 268, 100–106.

Centre for Disease Control. (2010). *National intimate partner and sexual violence survey*. www.cdc.gov/violenceprevention/pdf/nisvs_report2010-a.pdf.

Centre for Humane Technology (CHT). (2020). The Social Dilemma (2021). *Centre for Humane Technology*. https://www.humanetech.com/ Aired on Netflix 2021.

Children's Commissioner U.K. (2022). *The things I wish my parents had known. Young people's advice on talking to your child about online sexual harassment*. www.childrenscommissioner.gov.uk/report/talking-to-your-child-about-online-sexual-harassment-a-guide-for-parents/.

Christiansen, A., DeKloet, A., Ulrich-Lai, Y., & Herman, J. (2011). "Snacking" causes long-term attenuation of HPA axis stress responses and enhancement of brain FosB/deltaFosB expression in rats. *Physiology & Behavior*, 103, 111–116.

Coles, M. (2015). *Towards the compassionate school: From golden rule to golden thread*. University College London.

Coles, M., & Gent, B. (Eds.). (2022). *Education for survival: The pedagogy of compassion*. University College London.

Coleman, J. (2019). *Why won't my teenager talk to me?* (2nd ed.). Routledge: Abingdon.

Collins Dictionary. *'Muckbang' definition*. www.collinsdictionary.com/dictionary/english/mukbang.

Collins Dictionary. *Information, misinformation and disinformation*. www.collinsdictionary.com/dictionary/english/information.

Consilience Project. *Technology is not values neutral*. Accessed June 29, 2022 https://consilienceproject.org/technology-is-not-values-neutral/.

Cozolino, L. (2006). *The neuroscience of human relationships: Attachment and the developing social brain* (2nd ed.). W. W. Norton & Co: New York.

Crown Prosecution Service. (2017). *Revenge porn. The legal definitions in respect of criminal prosecutions*. www.cps.gov.uk/legal-guidance/revenge-pornography-guidelines-prosecuting-offence-disclosing-private-sexual.

Csikszentmihalyi, M. (1992, 2002). *Flow. The classic work on how to achieve happiness.* Rider: London.

Csikszentmihalyi, M. (1997). *Creativity. The psychology of discovery and invention.* Haprterp Perennial: New York.

Culata, R. (2021). *Digital for good. Raising kids to thrive in an online world.* Harvard Business Review Press: Boston.

Culloty, E., & Suiter, J. (2021). *Disinformation and manipulation in digital media: Information pathologies.* Taylor & Francis Group: London.

Davidson, J., & Gottschalk, P. (2011). *Internet child sexual abuse. Current research and policy.* Routledge: Abingdon.

de Becker, G. (1997). *The gift of fear. Survival signals that protect us from violence.* Dell Publishing: New York.

Delahooke, M. (2020). *Beyond behaviours: Using brain science and compassion to understand and solve children's behavioural challenges.* John Murray Learning: London.

Delahooke, M. (2022). *Brain-body parenting: How to stop managing behavior and start raising joyful, resilient kids.* Harper Wave: New York.

Department for Education. (2018). *Working together to safeguard children: A guide to inter-agency working to safeguard and promote the welfare of children (PDF).* London: Department for Education. https://assets.publishing.service.gov.uk/government/uploads/system/uploads/attach ment_data/file/942454/Working_together_to_safeguard_children_inter_agency_guid ance.pdf.

Department for Education. (2021). *Harmful online challenges and hoxes.* www.gov.uk/govern ment/publications/harmful-online-challenges-and-online-hoaxes/harmful-online-challenges-and-online-hoaxes.

Dick, P. (1962). *The man in the high castle.* Putnam: New York.

Dick, P. (1968). *Do androids dream of electric sheep?* Doubleday: New York.

Dictionary Link. www.merriam-webster.com/dictionary/consent.

Digital, Culture, Media and Sport Committee. (2021). *Second report of session 2019–21.* Misinformation in the COVID-19 Infodemic. House of Commons: London.

Dines, G. (2010). *Pornland. How porn has hijacked our sexuality.* Beacon Press: Boston.

Donovan, S. (2022). *The strange and curious guide to trauma.* Jessica Kingsley: London.

Duffy, J. (2019). *Parenting the new teen in the age of anxiety. A complete guide to your childs stressed, depress, expanded amazing adolescence.* Mango Publishing: Miami, FL.

The Education People. (2021). *Online safety alerts. Think before you scare.* www.theeducation people.org/blog/online-safety-alerts-think-before-you-scare/.

Edwards, D. (2018). *Animal Moves. How to move like an animal to get you leaner, fitter, stronger and healthier for life.* Explorer Publishing: London.

Edwards, L., Stoilova, M., Anstead, N., Fry, A., El-Halaby, G., & Smith, M. (2021). *LSE Consulting. Rapid evidence assessment on online misinformation and media literacy.* https://www.lse.ac.uk/business/consulting/reports/rapid-evidence-assessment-on-online-misinformation-and-media-literacy.

Erikson, E. (1998). *The Life Cycle Completed. The extended version.* WW Norton and Co.: New York.

Ernst, F. (1971). The ok corral: The grid or get-on-with. *TAJ,* 1(4).

Etchells, P. (2019). *Lost in a good game. Why we play video games and what they can do for us.* Icon books: London.

Ey, L., & McInnes, E. (2020). *Harmful sexual behaviour in young children and pre-teens. An education issue.* Routledge Focus: Abingdon.

Eysenk, M., & Keane, M. (2000). *Cognitive psychology: A student's handbook* (4th ed.). Psychology Press: London.

Feldman Barratt, L., Lewis, M., & Haviland-Jones, J. (2016). *The handbook of emotions* (4th ed.). Guilford Press: London.

Ferrari, P. F., & Coudé, G. (2018). Chapter 6 – mirror neurons, embodied emotions, and empathy. In K. Meyzer & E. Knapska (Eds.), *Neuronal correlates of empathy* (pp. 67–77). Elsevier Inc.: London.

Festinger, L., Riecken, H., & Schacter, S. (2009). *When prophecy fails*. Pinter & Martin Ltd: London.

Fetzer, J. (2004). Information, misinformation, and disinformation. *Minds and Machines*, 14(2), 223–229.

Finkelhor, D. (1984). *Child sexual abuse: New theory and research*. Palgrave Macmillan: London.

Fonagy, P. (2001). *Attachment theory and psychoanalysis*. Routledge: London.

Fonagy, P., Gergely, G., Jurist, E., & Target, M. (2004). *Affect regulation, mentalization and the development of the self*. Routledge: London.

Gayle, D. (2017). *Claims of child-on-child sexual offences soar in England and Wales*. www.theguardian.com/uk-news/2017/feb/03/claims-child-sexual-offences-soar-england-and-wales-police-barnardos.

Gazzelay, A., & Rosen, L. (2016). *A distracted mind. Ancient brains in a technological world*. MIT Press: London.

Geher, G., & Kaufman, S. (2013). *Mating intelligence unleashed. The role of the mind in sex, dating and love*. Oxford University Press: Oxford.

Gerhardt, S. (2014). *Why love matters. How affection shapes a baby's brain*. Routledge: London.

Gilbert, P. (2010). *The compassionate mind. A new approach to life's challenges* (revised edition). Constable: London.

Goldacre, B. (2008). *Bad science*. Fourth Estate: London.

Goldsmith, J., & Wu, T. (2008). *Who controls the internet. Illusions of a borderless world*. Oxford University Press: Oxford.

Goleman, D. (1995). *Emotional intelligence*. Bloomsbury: London.

Goleman, D., & Davidson, R. (2017). *Altered traits. Science reveals how meditation changes your mind, brain and body*. Avery: London.

Goodyear Brown, P. (2012). *The handbook of child sexual abuse. Identification, assessment and treatment*. John Wiley and Sons: New Jersey, NJ.

Grant, R., & Naylor, D. (1990). *Better than life*. Viking: London.

Greenberg, D. M., Firestone, P., Bradford, J. M., & Broom, I. (2000). *Serial offenders: Current thoughts, recent findings* (L. Schlesinger, Ed.). CRC Press: Boca Raton.

Greenfield, S. (2014). *Brain change. How digital technologies are leaving their mark on our brains*. Rider: Croydon.

Gregory, R. (1997). *Eye and brain. Fifth edition. The psychology of seeing*. Princeton University Press: Oxford.

Haidt, J. (2012). *The righteous mind. Why good people are divided by politics and religion*. Penguin: London.

Hanson, R. (2018). *Resilient. Find your inner strength*. Rider: London.

Harding, D. (2006). *On having no head. Zen and the rediscovery of the obvious*. Inner Directions Publishing: London.

Hare, S. (2022). *Technology is not neutral: A short guide to technology ethics*. London Publishing Partnership: London.

Hargittai, E., & Sandvig, C. (2015). *Digital research confidential. The secrets of studying behaviour online*. MIT Press. London.

Hay, J. (2015). *Windows to the world*. United Kingdom Association Transactional Analysis Conference: Blackpool.

Haye, S., & Jeffries, S. (2015). Romantic terrorism. In *Romantic terrorism: An auto-ethnography of domestic violence, victimization and survival*. Palgrave Pivot: London.

Hebb, D. (1966). *The organization of behavior: A neuropsychological theory*. Wiley and Sons: New York.

Hibberd, G. H. (2022). *The Art of Cybersecurity. A practical guide to winning the war on cybercrime*. IT Governance Publishing: Cambridge.

Hirrons, P. (2020). *Viewers horrified at erect penis onscreen*. www.entertainmentdaily.co.uk/tv/viewers-horrified-at-unacceptable-channel-4-documentary-that-showed-erect-penises-onscreen/.

Horton, D., & Wohl, R. R. (1956). Mass communication and para-social interaction. *Psychiatry: Journal for the Study of Interpersonal Processes*, 19, 215–229.

Hughes, D. (2011). *Attachment-focused family therapy workbook*. W. W. Norton & Co: London.

Huxley, A. (1932, printed 1994). *Brave new world*. Vintage: London.

Information Commissioners Office. (2020). *The children's code of practice*. https://ico.org.uk/about-the-ico/media-centre/news-and-blogs/2020/01/ico-publishes-code-of-practice-to-protect-children-s-privacy-online/.

The Internet Watch Foundation. (2018). *Once upon a year*, annual report. www.iwf.org.uk/media/tthh3woi/once-upon-a-year-iwf-annual-report-2018.pdf.

Jaegle, A., Mehrpour, V., & Rust, N. (2019). Visual novelty, curiosity, and intrinsic reward in machine learning and the brain. *Current Opinion in Neurobiology*, 58, 167–174.

James E. (2012). *Fifty Shades of Grey*. Penguin House. Cornerstone Publishing: London.

Joyce, H. (2021). *Trans. When ideology meets reality*. Oneworld: London.

Kahneman, D. (2012). *Thinking fast and slow*. Penguin: London.

Kain, K., & Terrel, S. (2018). *Nurturing resilience. Helping clients move forward from developmental trauma. AN integrative somatic approach*. North Atlantic Books: Berkely.

Kandel, E., Scwartz, J., Jessel, T., Seigelbaum, S., & Hudspeth, A. (2013). *Principles of neuroscience* (5th ed.). McGraw Hill Medical: New York.

Karpman, S. B. (1968). Drama triangle script drama analysis. *Transactional Analysis Bulletin*, 7(26), 39–43.

Kaufman, S. B. (2013). *Ungifted. The truth about talent, practice, creativity, and many paths to greatness*. Basic Books: New York.

Kaufman, S. B. (2020). *Transcend. The new science of self-actualization*. Tarcherperigree: New York.

Kaufman, S. B., & Gregoire, C. (2016). *Wired to create. Unravelling the mysteries of the creative mind*. Tarcher Perigree: New York.

Kaur, P., Dhir, A., Tandon, A., Alzeiby, E., & Abohassan, A. (2021). A systematic literature review on cyberstalking. An analysis of past achievements and future promises. *Technological Forecasting and Social Change*, 163.

Kaye, L. (2017). *What your emoji says about you*. TEDx Vienna. www.ted.com/talks/linda_kaye_what_your_emoji_says_about_you.

Kaye, L. (2022). *Issues and debates in cyberpsychology*. Oxford University Press: Oxford.

Kerig, P., Ludlow, A., & Wenar, C. (2012). *Developmental psychopathology. From infancy through to adolescence* (6th ed.). McGraw-Hill Education: Berkshire.

Kidd, C., & Hayden, B. (2015, November 4). The psychology and neuroscience of curiosity. *Neuron*, 88(3), 449–460.

Kimmel, S. B., & Mahalik, J. R. (2004). Measuring masculine body ideal distress: Development of a measure. *International Journal of Men's Health*, 3(1).

Kirby, J. (2022). *Choose Compassion. Why it matters and how it works*. University of Queensland Press: Queensland.

Knibbs, C. (2012). *Sex, lies and social networking*. Workshop for UKCP CYP Conference, London.

Knibbs, C. (2016). *Cybertrauma; The darker side of the internet*. Self-published and available on Amazon Kindle and Blurb Books.

Knibbs, C. (2018). *Presenters, media and conferences. Cybertrauma by the experts*. https://childrenandtech.co.uk/2021/05/21/presenters-media-and-conferences-cybertrauma-by-experts-the-shock-factor/.

Knibbs, C. (2019a). *Fit, fat or frumpy? The effects of social media (writ large)*, BACP Private Practitioners Conference, 28 September, BACP, London.

Knibbs, C. (2019b). *The human algorithm*. https://childrenandtech.co.uk/2021/05/21/the-human-algorithm-that-schools-and-parents-feed-through-fear-concerning-social-media-trends/.

Knibbs, C. (2022). *Children, technology and healthy development*. Routledge: Abingdon.

Knibbs, C., Goss, S., & Anthony, K. (2017). Counsellors' phenomenological experiences of working with children or young people who have been cyberbullied: Using thematic analysis of semi structured interviews. *International Journal of Technoethics*, 8, 68–86.

Kohlberg, L., & Turiel, E. (1971). Moral development and moral education. In L. Kohlberg (Ed.), *Collected papers on moral development and moral education* (pp. 410–465). Scott, Foresman & Company: Glenview, IL.

Kotler, S. (2014). *The rise of superman: Decoding the science of ultimate human performance*. Quercus Publishing: London.

Kowert, R. (2021). *Jargon Schmargon: Parasocial Relationships*. Psychgeist Channel on YouTube. www.youtube.com/watch?v=Zjl2BFv0Z74.

Kuhn, K. (2022). The constant mirror: Self-view and attitudes to virtual meetings. *Computer Human Behavior*, 128, 1–7.

Kurzweil, R. (2005). *The singularity is near. When humans transcend biology*. Viking: New York.

Lamb, S., & Gilbert, J. (2019). *The Cambridge handbook of sexual development. Childhood and adolescence*. Cambridge University Press: Cambridge.

Lanier, J. (2010). *You are not a gadget*. Alfred A Knopf: New York.

Lanier, J. (2013). *Who owns the future?* Penguin: London.

Lanier, J. (2017). *Dawn of the new everything. A journey through virtual reality*. Bodley Head: London.

Lanier, J. (2018). *Ten arguments for deleting your social media accounts right now*. Bodley Head: London.

Le Doux, J. (2015). *Anxious. The modern mind in the age of anxiety*. Oneworld: London.

Lembke, A. (2021). *Dopamine nation: Finding balance in the age of indulgence*. Headline: London.

Levine, P. (2005, 2008). *Healing trauma: Restoring the wisdom of your body*. Sounds True: Boulder.

Lieberman, D., & Long, M. (2019). *The molecule of more. How a single chemical in your brain drives, love sex, creativity, and will determine the fate of the human race*. Benbella Books: Dallas.

Livingstone, M. (2002). *Vision and art. The biology of seeing*. Harry N Abrahams Inc: New York.

Longo, V. (2018). *The longevity diet. Discover the new science to slow aging fight disease and manage your weight*. Penguin Press: London.

Lukianoff, G., & Haidt, J. (2018). *The coddling of the American mind. Howe good intentions and bad ideas are setting up a generation for failure*. Penguin: London.

Maslow, A. H. (1943). A theory of human motivation. *Psychological Review*, 50(4), 370–396.

Maslow, A. H. (1962). *Toward a psychology of being*. Princeton: D. Van Nostrand Company.

Matos, N., & Winsley, R. J. (2007). The trainability of young athletes and overtraining. *Journal of Sports Science & Medicine*, 6(3), 353.

McGilchrist, I. (2019). *The master and his emissary. The divided brain and the making of the western world*. Yale University Press: London.

McGilchrist, I. (2021). *The matter with things. Our brains, our delusions and the unmaking of the world*. Perspectiva Press: London.

Mchugh, M. (2011). *Take this lollipop makes Facebook stalking personal – and horrifying*. www.digitaltrends.com/social-media/take-this-lollipop-makes-facebook-stalking-personal-and-horrifying/.

Megele, C. (2018). *Safeguarding children and young people online. A guide for practitioners*. Policy Press: Bristol.

Merleau-Ponty, M. (2002). *Husserl at the limits of Phenomenology*. Including texts by Edmund Husserl. North Western University Press: Evanston, IL.

Merzenich, M. (2013). *Soft-Wired. How the new science of brain plasticity can change your life*. Parnassus Publishing: San Francisco.

Miller, G. (1956). The magical number seven, plus or minus two: Some limits on our capacity for processing information. *Psychological Review* (63), 81–89.

Moss, M. (2013). *Salt sugar, fat. How the food giants hooked us*. Random House: Croydon.

Music, G. (2017). *Nurturing natures. Attachment and children's emotional, sociocultural and brain development* (2nd ed.). Routledge: Abingdon.

Music, G. (2022). *Respark. Igniting hope and joy after trauma and depression*. Mind Nurturing Books: London.

Nagasoki, E. (2015, revised 2021). *Come as you are. The surprising new science that will transform your sex life*. Scribe: London.

Naidoo, U. (2020). *This is your brain on food. An indispensable guide to the surprising foods that fights depression, PTSD, anxiety, OCD and more*. Little Brown Spark: Boston.

National Health Service (NHS). *Long-term plans for obesity*. www.longtermplan.nhs.uk/online-version/chapter-2-more-nhs-action-on-prevention-and-health-inequalities/obesity/.

National Heart Lung and Blood Institute (NHLBI). *Metabolic syndrome*. www.nhlbi.nih.gov/health/metabolic-syndrome.

Nelson, R., & Kriegsfeld, L. (2023). *An introduction to behavioural endocrinology* (6th ed.). Oxford University Press: Oxford.

Neufeld, G., & Mate, G. (2019). *Hold onto your kids. Why parents need to matter more than peers*. Vermillion: London.

New York Times. (2022). *A dad took photos of his naked toddler for the doctor*. Google Flagged Him as a Criminal. www.nytimes.com/2022/08/21/technology/google-surveillance-toddler-photo.html.

Nielsen Hibbing, A., & Rankin-Erickson, J. (2003). A picture is worth a thousand words: Using Visual images to improve comprehension for middle school struggling readers. *The Reading Teacher*, 56(8), 758–770.

Nissenbaum, H. (2004). Hackers and the contested ontology of cyberspace. *New Media & Society*, 6(2), 195–217.

Ofcom. (2022). *Life online podcast: The genuine article: Tackling misinformation*. South West Grid for Learning. Accessed August 23, 2022.

Office for National Statistics (ONS). (2022). www.ons.gov.uk/peoplepopulationandcommunity/crimeandjustice/datasets/stalkingfindingsfromthecrimesurveyforenglandandwales.

Ogas, O., & Gaddam, S. (2012). *A billion wicked thoughts. What the internet tells us about sexual relationships*. Plume: London.

Orcha Health. https://orchahealth.com/.

Orwell, G. (1949, republished 2008). *1984. Penguin in association with Martin Secker and Warburg*. Penguin: London.

Owens, L., Shute, R., & Slee, P. (2000). "Guess what I just heard!": Indirect aggression among teenage girls in Australia. *Aggressive Behavior: Official Journal of the International Society for Research on Aggression*, 26(1), 67–83.

Panksepp, J. (2004). *Affective neuroscience. The foundations of human and animal emotions*. Oxford University Press: Oxford.

Panksepp J., & Biven L. (2012). *The Archeology of Mind. Neuroevolutionary Origins of Human Emotion*. WW Norton and Co: New York.

Paulhus, D., & Williams, K. (2002). The dark triad of personality: Narcissism, Machiavellianism, and psychopathy. *Journal of Research in Personality*, 36(6), 556–563.

Pearce, J. (2019). *Child sexual exploitation: Why theory matters*. Policy Press: Bristol.

Peper, E., & Harvey, R. (2020). *Tech stress. How technology is hijacking our lives, strategies for coping and pragmatic ergonomics*. North Atlantic Press: Berkley, CA.

Pernecky, T. (2016). *Epistemology and metaphysics for qualitative research*. Sage: London.

Piaget, J. (1926). Cited in (2002), Piaget, J. *The language and thought of the child*. Routledge: London.

Piaget, J. (1969). *The psychology of the child*. Preseses Universitaire de France: Paris, Translated to English; Persues Books: New York.

Pierre, J. (2022). Mistrust and the possibility of civil war. *Psychology Today*. www.psychology today.com/us/blog/psych-unseen/202209/mistrust-misinformation-and-the-possibility-civil-war-in-america.

Pink News. (2018). *Literotica: 5 websites to quench your online erotica thirst*. www.pinknews. co.uk/2018/09/25/literotica-online-erotica-websites/.

Pinker, S. (2012). *Better angels of our nature. The history of violence and humanity*. Penguin: London.

Plomin, R. (2018). *Blueprint. How DNA makes us who we are*. MIT Press: London.

Plomin, R., DeFries, J., & Fulker, D. (1988). *Nature and nurture during infancy and early childhood*. Cambridge University Press: Cambridge.

Porges, S. (2011a). *The polyvagal theory*. W. W. Norton & Co: London.

Porges, S. (2011b). *The polyvagal theory. Neurophysiological foundations of emotions, attachment, communication and self-regulation*. W. W. Norton & Co: New York.

Porges, S. (2017). *Polyvagal theory in practice. 2-day seminar*. Breath of Life Conference: London.

Porges, S. (2021). *Polyvagal safety. Attachment, communication, self-regulation*. W. W. Norton & CO: London.

Pratchett, T. (2000). *The truth*. (25th Discworld Novel). Doubleday: London.

Pritchard, W. (2022). *YouTube is working with met police to take down rap and drill videos*. Accessed March 02, 2022. https://www.vice.com/en/article/bvnp8v/met-police-youtube-drill-music-removal.

Przybylski, A., & Nash, V. (2018). Internet filtering and adolescent exposure to online sexual material. *Original Articles*, 21(7).

Rettenmund, M. (2012). *Playgirl magazine history*. www.esquire.com/entertainment/a55592/playgirl-magazine-history/.

Ripped Body.Com https://rippedbody.com/body-fat-guide/

Robertson, A. (2021). *Taming gaming: Guide your child to healthy video game habits*. Unbound: London.

Roper, C. (2022). *Sex dolls, Roberts and women hating. The case for resistance*. Spinifiex: QLD Australia.

Rosen, L. (2012). *I Disorder. Understanding our obsession with technology and overcoming its hold on us*. Palgrave Macmillan: New York.

Rothschild, B. (2003). *The Body Remembers. Casebook. Unifying methods and models in the treatment of trauma and PTSD*. WW Norton and Co: New York.

Rudolph, J., Zimmer-Gembeck, M., & Walsh, K. (2022). Recall of sexual abuse prevention education at school and home: Associations with sexual abuse experience, disclosure, protective parenting, and knowledge. *Child Abuse and Neglect*, 129.

Rushkoff, D. (2019). *Team human*. W. W. Norton & Co: London.

Science and Media Museum. (2020). *A brief history of cinema*. www.scienceandmediamuseum. org.uk/objects-and-stories/very-short-history-of-cinema.

Shanahan, C. (2008). *Deep nutrition. Why your genes need traditional food*. Flatiron Books: New York.

Short, E., Guppy, A., Hart, A., & Barnes, J. (2015). The impact of cyberstalking. *Studies in Media and Communication*, 3(2).

Siegel, D. (2010). *The mindful therapist. A clinician's guide to mindsight and neural integration*. W. W. Norton & Co: New York.

Siegel, D. (2014). *Brainstorm. The power and purpose of the teenage brain*. Jeremy P Tarcher: New York.

Siegel, D. (2016). *Mind: A journey to the heart of being human (Norton series on interpersonal neurobiology)*. W. W. Norton & Co: New York.

Siegel, D. (1999, 2020). *The developing mind* (3rd ed.). The Guildford Press: London.

South West Grid for Learning. (2015). *Revenge porn and non-consensual intimate image abuse*. https://swgfl.org.uk/helplines/revenge-porn-helpline/.

Staminov, M., & Gallese, V. (2002). *Mirror neurons and the evolution of brains and language*. John Benjamins Publishing Company: Amsterdam.

Steiner-Adair, C. (2013). *The big disconnect. Protecting childhood and family relationships in the digital age*. Haprter Collins: New York.

Steinmetz, K. F. (2015). Becoming a hacker: Demographic characteristics and developmental factors. *Journal of Qualitative Criminal Justice & Criminology*, 3(1), 31–60.

Stephens-Davidowitz. (2017). *Everybody lies. What the internet can tell us about who we really are*. Bloomsbury: London.

Stilman, R. (2022). Attached to technology: Exploring identity and human relating in a virtual and corporeal world. *Transactional Analysis Journal*, 52(2), 93–105.

Strassman, R. (2022). *The psychedelic handbook. A practical guide to psylocibin, LDS, ketamine, MDMA And DMT/Ayahuasca*. Ulysses Press: Berkeley.

Sugarman, S. (2016). Beyond the pleasure principle: Beyond the Pleasure Principle (1920). *In What Freud Really Meant: A Chronological Reconstruction of his Theory of the Mind* (pp. 87–104). Cambridge University Press: Cambridge.

Taffel, R. (2020). The myth of micro-aggression. *Contemporary Psychoanalysis*, 56(2–3), 375–393.

Tancer, B. (2009). *Click. What we do online and why it matters*. Harper Collins: New York.

Tester, K. (1994). *Media, Culture and Morality*. Routledge: London.

Tester, K. (2001). *Compassion, morality and the media*. Open University Press: Buckingham.

Tovee, M. (2008). *Physiology of vision and the visual system* (2nd ed.). MIT Press: London.

Turkle, S. (2015). *Reclaiming conversation. The power of talk in a digital age*. Penguin: London.

UK Parliament. (2022). *Online harms and disinformation*. House of Commons: London. https:// committees.parliament.uk/committee/438/digital-culture-media-and-sport-subcommittee-on-online-harms-and-disinformation/.

United Kingdom programme of VAWG (2013- to date). www.gov.uk/government/publications/ what-works-in-preventing-violence-against-women-and-girls-review-of-the-evidence-from-the-programme.

United Nations Convention on the Rights of Children. (1989). www.unicef.org/child-rights-convention.

United Nations Convention on the Rights of Children. (1989). *Comment 25.* www.unicef.org.au/united-nations-convention-on-the-rights-of-the-child.

Van der Kolk, B. (1994). The body keeps the score: Memory and the evolving psychobiology of post-traumatic stress. *Harvard Review of Psychiatry*, 1(5), 253–265.

Venuto, T. (2012, 2021). https://www.muscleandstrength.com/articles/body-fat-level-see-abs.

Vervaeke, J., Mastropietro, C., & Miscevic, F. (2017). *Zombies in western culture. A twenty-first century crisis.* Openbook Publishers: Cambridge.

Vygotsky, L. (1933). *Play and its role in the mental development of the child.* IN: Vygotsky, L. S. (1967). Play and its role in the mental development of the child. *Soviet Psychology*, 5(3), 6–18.

Walker, M. (2017). *Why we sleep. The new since of sleep and dreams.* Penguin: London.

Wall, H., Kaye, L., & Malone, S. (2016). An exploration of psychological factors on emoticon usage and implications for judgement accuracy. *Computers in Human Behaviour* (62), 70–78.

Walsh, W. (2012). *Nutrient power. Heal your biochemistry and heal your brain.* Skyhorse Publishing: New York.

Wang, H., Tao, X., Huang, S., Wu, L., Tang, H., Song, Y., Zhang, G., & Zhang, Y. (2016). Chronic stress is associated with pain precipitation and elevation in delta fosb expression. *Frontiers in Pharmocology*, 7(138).

Weiner, N. (1988). *The human use of human beings: Cybernetics and society.* De Capo Press: Boston.

Wheal, J. (2021). *Recapture the rapture. Rethinking god, sex, and death in a world that's lost its mind.* Harper Collins: New York.

Wiener, N. (1954). *The human use of human beings.* De Capo: Boston.

Wilber, K. (2000). *Integral psychology: Consciousness, spirit, psychology, therapy.* Shambala: London.

Wilson, E. O. (1975). *Sociobiology: The new synthesis.* Cambridge, MA: Belknap Press of Harvard University Press.

Wilson, G. (2014). *Your brain on porn. Internet pornography and the emerging science of addiction.* Commonwealth Publishing: London.

Wilson, R. A. (1990). *Quantum psychology. How brain software programs you and your world.* Hilaritas Press: Grand Junction, CO.

Williamson, C. (2022). Modern wisdom podcast. #444 – *Mary Harrington – Modern Society Is Failing Men & Women.* https://modernwisdom.libsyn.com/episode-444.

Winnicott, D. (1971, republished 2005). *Playing and reality. Routledge classics.* Routledge: London.

Winsley, R., & Matos, N. (2011). Overtraining and elite young athletes. *The Elite Young Athlete*, 56, 97–105.

Wiseman, R. (2004). *Did you spot the gorilla? How to recognise hidden opportunities.* Penguin: London.

Women's Aid. (2020). Why don't women leave? Femicide Census (2020) *The Femicide Census: 2018 findings. Annual Report on UK Femicides 2018.* www.womensaid.org.uk/information-support/what-is-domestic-abuse/women-leave/.

World Health Organisation (WHO). (2019). *International classification of diseases and related health problems* (11th ed.). https://icd.who.int/.

World Health Organisation (WHO). *Definition of health.* www.who.int/about/governance/constitution.

Wu, T. (2010). *The master switch. The rise and fall of information empires.* Alfred A Knopf: New York.

Wu, T. (2016). *The attention merchants. The epic struggle to get inside our heads.* Atlantic Books: London.

Yasko, A. (2017). *Nutrigenomics. Your roadmap to health.* Neurological Research Institute: Bethel.

Yunkaporta, T. (2019). *Sand talk. How Indigenous Thinking can save the world.* Text Publishing: Melbourne.

Zuboff, S. (2019). *The age of surveillance capitalism. The fight for a new human future at the new frontier of power.* Profile Books: London.

People and organisations

Aitkin, M. (2015). *Cyberpsychologist.* www.maryaitkin.com.

British Psychological Society Cyberpsychology Section. www.bps.org.uk/member-networks/cyberpsychology-section.

Centre for Humane Technology. www.humanetech.com/. www.digitaltrends.com/social-media/take-this-lollipop-makes-facebook-stalking-personal-and-horrifying/.

Daniel Schmachtenberger. https://civilizationemerging.com/articles/personal-blog-posts/. https://swgfl.org.uk/magazine/digital-ghost-stories/. www.theguardian.com/uk-news/2022/jun/03/met-police-project-alpha-profiling-children-documents-show.

The Intellectual Darkweb. www.nytimes.com/2018/05/08/opinion/intellectual-dark-web.html.

John Vervaeke. http://johnvervaeke.com/. www.vice.com/en/article/bvnp8v/met-police-youtube-drill-music-removal. www.vox.com/the-big-idea/2018/5/10/17338290/intellectual-dark-web-rogan-peterson-harris-times-weiss.

Jonathan Pageu. https://thesymbolicworld.com/.

Rebel Wisdom. https://rebelwisdom.co.uk/. www.samaritans.org/about-samaritans/media-guidelines/.

Video links

American Pie. (1999). *3rd Base feels like apple pie.* www.youtube.com/watch?v=Ik1NKkN0ysI.

Game Changers. (2019). https://gamechangersmovie.com/.

Newhart, B. (2010). *Stop it.* www.youtube.com/watch?v=Ow0lr63y4Mw.

Wiseman video of gorilla. www.youtube.com/watch?v=y6qgoM89ekM.

Newspaper

Boffey, P. (1987). Infants' sense of pain is recognized, finally. *The New York Times.* https://www.nytimes.com/1987/11/24/science/infants-sense-of-pain-is-recognized-finally.html.

New York Times. (2022). *A dad took photos of his naked toddler for the doctor.* Google Flagged Him as a Criminal. www.nytimes.com/2022/08/21/technology/google-surveillance-toddler-photo.html.

Resource

Knibbs, C. (2020). *Safeguarding children online: A guide for practitioners.* https://childrenandtech.co.uk/product/practitioners-guide-to-safeguarding-when-working-online-remotely/.

Index

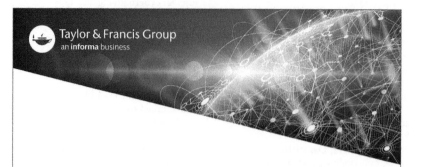

Ingram Content Group UK Ltd.
Milton Keynes UK
UKHW022124090623
423218UK00013B/123

9 781032 266428